THE LIFE OF
EDWARD E. AYER

By

FRANK C. LOCKWOOD

UNIVERSITY OF ARIZONA

* *
*

Chicago

A. C. McCLURG & COMPANY

1929

EDWARD EVERETT AYER
AT THE AGE OF SEVENTY-FOUR

PREFACE

SAYS Carlyle, "Biography is the only true history." We must accept this dictum; for history is simply the record of what man has thought and experienced and achieved, and to know history fully we should have to read the story of every man's life. To himself, every individual must seem exceptional, and in reality, no one is insignificant or uninteresting to his fellows if only his life story be well and truthfully told.

However, it is about extraordinary lives that we like best to hear. Well did the ancient scribe express himself when he wrote:

Let us now praise famous men and our fathers that begat us. The Lord manifested in them great glory, even his mighty power from the beginning. Such as did bear rule in their kingdoms, and were men renowned for their power, giving counsel by their understanding . . .: rich men furnished with ability, living peaceably in their habitations; all these were honored in their generations, and were a glory in their days. There be of them that have left a name behind them, to declare of their praises.

It is because Edward Everett Ayer belongs in the company of famous men—wise and glorious in his time—that we here record his deeds.

The author is sure, too, that the incidents in the life of Mr. Ayer have more than private and local interest. His activities continually throw light upon crucial and dramatic events in our developing national life. He had a part in the epic westward movement across the Plains; he played an honorable rôle in the central tragedy of the nineteenth century, the Civil War. He was an active force during the pic-

turesque and strenuous period of railroad expansion in the
West that followed the Civil War; he was an enthusiastic
and generous supporter of culture and the fine arts in America; he exerted himself in philanthropic and constructive ways
for the betterment of the American Indian; he threw his
energies, along with other gifted leaders, into the project
of making Chicago the finest city in the world to live in; and
he had a main hand in the movement to preserve the Redwoods of California. Indeed, his term of life was so long and
he retained such vitality of interest in all good things that his
influence has been deeply felt far into the twentieth century.
The world would be poorer if his works and ways and words
were not preserved. The record of such a life cannot fail to
advance culture and stimulate succeeding generations to good
deeds and genial living.

To a great extent I have written down the incidents in Mr.
Ayer's life in his own language. No words at my command
would be so graphic and so truly a part of the scenes and
events that enter into this narrative as those that dropped
readily and eagerly from his own lips, to be caught by the
alert stenographer. He grew up amid simple surroundings;
he had little schooling; and books were almost unknown in
the forties and fifties in the region where his boyhood was
spent. But he became an adept in the vernacular of the West.
At the time when most boys are completing high school or
entering college he became a United States trooper, and we
can scarcely doubt that his vocabulary increased in pungency
and color as a result. After the War, for years he was thrown
with teamsters, lumbermen, rough and ready workers in camp,
forest, and city; and there is every indication that he found
words to make his meaning clear in whatever company he
chanced to be. In his familiar conversation he modified somewhat, but rarely emasculated, the vigorous and colorful
speech of the times and places that he talked about.

But there was another side to Mr. Ayer's skill in the use of the English language. In middle and later life he became as much at home with scholars, and savants, and specialists in various fields that he entered as a collector, as he was and continued to be with men in the rough places of life, and business associates, often direct and crude in speech. He became the intimate friend and valued companion of historians, priests, statesmen, artists, archaeologists, directors of museums, and experts in every field of learning; and as a consequence he had at his tongue's end a learned vocabulary that was the envy of many a college man. He would speak of portolan charts, incunabula, libation cups, Mayan hieroglyphics, Mexican codices, and Etruscan sarcophagi with an ease and intimacy that amazed the ordinary writer or scholar. In view of all this, therefore, wherever possible, the vigor and charm and picturesqueness of Mr. Ayer's speech is set down with all its native flavor.

It has been the author's attempt to supplement Mr. Ayer's own vivid accounts of significant experiences in his life by statements and quotations drawn from the men who were in immediate association with him. Fortunately it has been possible to interview many of his closest and dearest friends—not a few of them his exact contemporaries. Ordinarily acknowledgment should be made in a preface to men and women who contributed to the making of a book in such large measure as have numerous relatives, friends, and associates of Mr. Ayer in the writing of this biography; but so generous and willing have been the responses from every quarter, and so completely are these various contributions a part of the story, that it would seem inappropriate to make specific mention here of those to whom the author is under obligation, great as he feels that obligation to be.

Two names, however, may not be omitted from this preface—those of Mr. George B. Utley, Librarian of the New-

berry Library, and Miss Clara A. Smith, Custodian of its
Edward E. Ayer Collection on the North American Indian.
From them and other members of the staff the author has
received many courtesies. Mr. Utley read the entire manuscript with sympathetic interest and critical alertness, and,
as a result, the stamp of his fine taste and scholarly accuracy
is more than once in evidence. Miss Smith, by her long association with Mr. Ayer's library, both before and after it became a part of the Newberry Library, is a ready source of
intimate and accurate knowledge concerning its early history
and development, as well as its chief literary treasures; and
of all this information she gave the author fully and gladly.

The faults of the book the author claims as his own. He
feels that his chief fitness for the writing of this biography
lies in the fact that he could from beginning to end enter into
fresh and ardent sympathy with the personality and experiences of the subject. The work, therefore, has not been a
task but a continual source of delight. Apart from the keen
enjoyment that has come from personal interviews with Mr.
Ayer and from prolonged absorption in his world of action,
beauty, and aspiration, there has come to the writer, also, an
enlargement of spirit and a growth in liberal culture. It was
almost an accident that the author discovered in Mr. Ayer a
congenial subject for an extended biography. It came about
through a common interest in Arizona, where Mr. Ayer received the prime impulse that shaped his unique career and
where the author lives in a state of abiding contentment and
enthusiasm. As acquaintance ripened, it became apparent that,
though they had at first passed each other only "as ships in the
night," they had in reality sailed many seas and traversed
many lands in common—lands and seas, for the most part,
not charted in any geography—realms, rather, of feeling and
imagination—of romance and high adventure.

FRANK C. LOCKWOOD

TABLE OF CONTENTS

LIST OF ILLUSTRATIONS

CHAPTER I

Ancestry and Parentage

EDWARD EVERETT AYER was fortunate in his ancestry. "Blood will tell"; and he was the sterling man he was because his heritage was good. Says Dr. Frederick F. Shannon:

The ancestral hills whence flowed the waters of his being had a certain majesty—an individual loftiness which distinguishes them among their human ranges. As one star differs in glory from all the countless stars to which it is related, so do races, nations, families, individuals differ from each other. Thus these high hills of life named the Ayer country carry a distinction entirely their own. After all, the child is a commentary, good or bad, on its parents. Therefore, we conclude that this dear man, who was once a little child and who never, happily, got over the wonder and simplicity of childhood, was blessed with goodly parents. So, like a spring, he had his clean beginnings among ancestral hills whose streams flowed forth pure and undefiled.

In his remote ancestors Mr. Ayer seems to have taken little interest, with one exception: It was a matter of pride to him that he was descended from Captain Samuel Ayer who was killed August 29, 1708, while defending the town of Haverhill, Massachusetts against an attack by the French and Indians. Edward Ayer lived for his own generation and for posterity, and sought no borrowed glamour from the past. However, from earliest boyhood to the end of his life, he was marked for the ardor of his devotion to his own parents. He took boundless pride in their character and their achievements, and lost no opportunity to do them honor, and to keep their memory alive in the hearts of succeeding generations. Yet it is worthy of note that in all the long line of Ayers, his own name was the most distinguished.

On both his father's side and his mother's, he came from ancient and sturdy American stock. John Ayer, born about 1590 in Wiltshire, England, was Edward Everett Ayer's first American progenitor. He came to New England and settled on the Merrimac near the present site of Newburyport, Massachusetts, in 1636.

The immediate ancestors of the subject of this biography were Elbridge Gerry Ayer and Mary Dean Titcomb, both descendants of early New England families. This couple were united in marriage in 1835 in Haverhill, Massachusetts.

During the Black Hawk War soldier correspondents wrote to various papers, both in the East and in the West, accounts of the wild, rich country in which they were campaigning. This undeveloped region seemed very fertile and attractive to these young men who had grown up in the East, and they had sent enthusiastic reports to their papers. During the War, and just after it, books and pamphlets had been published containing very highly colored descriptions of this new land and its resources; and these accounts had been eagerly read by Eastern people. As a natural result, a western wave of immigration had set in; and by 1835 shoals of eager pioneers were pushing into northern Illinois and southwestern Wisconsin in the hope of bettering their fortunes. In the spring of 1836 Elbridge Ayer and his young wife joined this migratory movement, determined to establish their home in the new land of promise.

Almost the entire journey was made by water. The main line of travel was from Albany to Buffalo by the Erie Canal, and then by way of Lake Michigan. The Ayers landed at Southport, Wisconsin, later to be known as Kenosha. They put off from the ship in a yawl; and family tradition has it that they raised a lusty song of rejoicing as they neared the shore.

They landed in Wisconsin the very year it was organized into a territory. In the autumn of the same year, 1836, a daughter was born to them, Mary Ayer—the first white child born in the town.

The young pioneers were, of course, in humble circumstances. When they reached their destination they had no money left. They had their own fortune to make, and right sturdily they went to work. Elbridge Ayer's father owned a little woolen mill in Lawrence, Massachusetts, and the young man had learned the wool-stapler's trade, and had become somewhat expert in it. Since Southport was a new town in an undeveloped country, it was impossible, of course, for him to find employment in his own trade. He, therefore, took any work he could find. Wherever opportunity offered, he bore a hand in the building up of the growing town. By 1846 Southport had become a somewhat important trading point. One of the military roads provided for by Congress in Territorial days ran from Southport (now Kenosha) by way of Geneva, to Beloit. During these ten years four more children had been born to the Ayers: Anna Maria; Edward Everett, born November 16, 1841; Julia Ann; and Henry Clay.

In 1846, Mr. Ayer took up two hundred acres of land at Big Foot Prairie, some thirty miles due west of Kenosha, and opened a little general store there. Being enterprising as well as energetic, he engaged a blacksmith, and ran a blacksmith shop in conjunction with the store. For some time before leaving Kenosha, he had found employment in one of the grain elevators there; and now he saw an opportunity to put his knowledge of grain-buying to use by purchasing wheat from the neighboring settlers and hauling it to town. Hard work and foresight brought increasing prosperity. Early in the '50's the Illinois and Wisconsin, afterwards the Chicago and Northwestern Railroad, began pushing westward from Chicago, and Mr. Ayer watched its progress with interest. By

1855, the trains were coming as far as Cary—thirty-eight miles from Chicago. He knew there was going to be a station about five miles to the south of Big Foot Prairie; so he sold his store and bought four hundred acres of farm land there. In 1856, with two or three of the railroad men, he laid out the town of Harvard, Illinois. A little later he took a contract to build a certain portion of the Northwestern Railroad in that section; and soon after the railroad came through Harvard, he got possession of the hotel that had been built by the company only about a hundred feet from the station, and for years ran this as a railroad hotel.

For decades this hotel was a landmark in that part of the country. It was not long before a junction was established at Harvard—the new line diverging to the north toward Fond du Lac and Green Bay. As time went on Mr. Ayer became a familiar and honored figure in the eyes of the numerous railroad men and the increasing streams of travelers who came and went through Harvard. In his prime he was stalwart and robust—of unusual weight and strength. Some of his old neighbors who still survive, and the members of his own family who are old enough to remember him, like to picture him (as he was always to be seen when trains drew into the station)—sitting in a particularly ample chair on the long veranda that faced the track.

"Judge" Ayer, as he was called (and not inappropriately), was easily the leading man in Harvard. He was respected and loved for his kindly and generous ways. A popular quality, too, was his abounding sense of humor. His neighbors came to him with their heated disputes, both those of a personal character and those having to do with some point of law; and Mr. Ayer was usually able to allay the wrath of the contending parties and settle those stormy controversies. Often the disputants went away reconciled, to become excellent friends once more. In politics "Judge" Ayer was an old line Whig;

ELBRIDGE GERRY AYER
FATHER OF EDWARD E. AYER
PICTURE TAKEN YEAR OF HIS GOLDEN WEDDING

and of course, in common with all northern Whigs, he later became a Republican. "Father was of a very jovial disposition, and very fond of his children," said Edward Everett Ayer. "He would play with us and enter into the little things we wanted to do—little plans, jokes, and so forth—more than Mother. Father and Mother both were interested in helping everybody that needed help, and there wasn't a birth or a death that Mother wasn't always helping, and Father, of course, backing her up with the necessary means and things that he could spare; and he was very generous and patriotic."

The mother, Mary Dean Ayer, was of early New England stock. She was one of a typical New England family of eleven children. Needless to say she was no less devoted to her children than was the father; and her personality was as strong as his. There was in her character a certain Puritan austerity and moral earnestness. As has been said, her hand was always directed to deeds of charity and good works. No matter how stormy or wintry the day or night, if a call for help came from a neighbor who was sick or in want, she would hurry off with needed supplies, dropping whatever she was engaged in at the time, whether important or not. She was a constant reader of the Bible and a ready, vigorous defender of the Faith as she understood it. There was great intemperance at that time, and she was a staunch tee-totaler. She objected even to the "hot toddies," "mild tonics," and "mugs of fine old cider" that her husband now and then indulged in; and sometimes she expressed the fear that they would bring him to "a bad end." Nor could she always appreciate the "Judge's" jokes. However, his hearty laugh usually served to clear the atmosphere and drive away the clouds of anxiety. Mrs. Ayer was an advocate of "Woman's Rights," too, in the day when that cause was very young. She wrote poetry occasionally concerning the reforms she was interested in, and her verses were published in the local papers. If she had had books and leisure, no doubt she would have developed considerable literary talent.

Mrs. Ayer was gifted with a fine soprano voice, and Mr. Ayer had a powerful bass voice, so one of the most enjoyable home and neighborhood recreations was to hear them sing duets, either in the family circle or at some church entertainment. They were church-going people. Both of them had been brought up in the Unitarian faith, and Edward grew up in this tradition, and always remained a liberal in his religious views. But as there was no church of their own choice in that section of the country, they gave their support to the Baptist Church, and the children attended the Baptist Sunday School.

The Ayer family had always been noted for its patriotism; and the time came when Elbridge Gerry Ayer and his wife, owners and managers of the railroad house at Harvard Junction, grew famous for their generous and untiring devotion to the thousands of sick and wounded Union soldiers who passed that way during the Civil War. By the time the War broke out the Northwestern Railroad had gone on up to Fond du Lac and Green Bay, and had also established connecting lines with the St. Paul Railroad to the Mississippi River and the state of Minnesota; consequently, the soldiers from all that wide region, as soon as they struck the railroad, came down through Harvard. During the whole period of the War, Mr. Ayer never charged a sick or wounded soldier a penny for meals or for any other comfort it was within his power to provide. He fed from a dozen to two hundred soldiers a day during the four years of the War. Whenever a troop-train stopped at the Junction with wounded or convalescent troops, hot coffee and appetizing food were waiting on the platform to be passed out to them. Both Mr. and Mrs. Ayer fairly devoted their lives to the welfare of these Wisconsin boys during those terrible years.

At the close of the War, under date of July 12, 1865, Gov-

MARY DEAN AYER
MOTHER OF EDWARD E. AYER
PICTURE TAKEN THE YEAR OF HER GOLDEN WEDDING

ernor James T. Lewis, of Wisconsin, addressed the following letter to Mr. Ayer:

Dear Sir: I am informed that on several occasions sick and wounded soldiers have been unavoidably detained at your place, and that you have at all times treated them with great kindness, furnishing them with food when they needed it, and otherwise ministering to their necessities, and that you have done this without pay, or expectation of reward, and that you still decline to receive any pay for the many meals furnished this class of persons, or for your services in their behalf.

Few as marked cases of disinterested benevolence and goodness of heart have come within my observation and I could not allow it to pass without assuring you of my appreciation of your service to these sick and wounded heroes. Permit me, Sir, in behalf of these noble men whom you have comforted and served, and in behalf of the people of Wisconsin, to tender you their sincere thanks and to assure you that your kindness to Wisconsin soldiers will not soon be forgotten.

In 1885, when Mr. and Mrs. Elbridge Gerry Ayer were about to celebrate their Golden Wedding, a circular was issued to all the posts of the Grand Army of the Republic in Wisconsin by the Commander of the Grand Army in that state, requesting that all veterans who remembered having received courtesies at the hands of "Judge" and Mrs. Ayer during the Civil War contribute twenty-five cents each (it was made clear that a larger amount would not be acceptable) to be used in the purchase of a suitable gift. Twelve hundred dollars came in from soldiers who still survived and still remembered. This amount was spent for a gold goblet. The Grand Army Commander of the state and a committee consisting of one member from each of fifteen different Grand Army Posts came to the celebration, without giving previous notice of their intention, and presented the cup. After the death of his parents, by a family understanding, this cup descended to Edward Everett Ayer. He took it to the State Capitol at Madison, where a fine case was made for it; and

there, in the State Historical Society of Wisconsin, together
with the original copy of Governor Lewis's letter, and a photograph of these worthy American pioneers, it reposes perpetually—a golden reminder of golden deeds.

The old soldiers never tired of showing their regard for
Elbridge Ayer. On one occasion, when the annual Grand
Army Reunion was held at Milwaukee, he was invited to be
present as an honored guest; and throughout the proceedings
of the week he was showered with attentions and courtesies.
One time in the early '80's Edward Ayer took his father with
him on one of his frequent business trips into the Southwest—
to the farthest point then reached by the Santa Fe Railroad.
The journey was to continue still farther through the desert
and wilderness; and with characteristic forethought, the son
had provided an escort and ambulance to transport the old
man in safety and comfort through the wilds to their final
destination. These plans, however, were all frustrated; for
the officer in command of the United States troops in that region, probably by direction of Robert T. Lincoln, then Secretary of War, a friend of Edward Ayer, met the old pioneer—
the soldiers' friend—at the train with a detail of fourteen
soldiers, told him he was under arrest, and placed him in an
ambulance. From that day until he was brought back and put
on the train for the East, he was fed on the fat of the land,
shown everything there was to be seen, and treated everywhere with military honors.

When Mr. Ayer died, in 1887, Edward Ayer and his
mother erected a monument on the family lot in Harvard
Cemetery. It is twelve feet square at the base, and rises to a
height of thirty-six feet, tapering gradually toward the top.
It was constructed of Quincy granite, for the reason that, as
far back as the son could remember, whenever there was any
discussion concerning the quality of building stone in the
presence of the old New Englander he would say:

"Yes, of course that is all right; but Quincy granite is so much better!"

Later, after the mother, too, had passed away, the devoted son had carved on the base of the noble monument:

ELBRIDGE GERRY AYER

AND

MARY DEAN AYER HIS WIFE

PIONEERS OF WISCONSIN

AND

FOUNDERS OF HARVARD

On the eve of the first Decoration Day after the monument was set up in the Harvard Cemetery, General Lucius Fairchild, Commander-in-Chief of the Grand Army of the Republic at that time, came down to Harvard, and, calling on Mrs. Ayer, said to her:

"Mrs. Ayer, I did not want this Decoration Day to go by without being here under the shadow of your husband's monument. I have refused a hundred invitations to speak elsewhere, just to be here."

The next day he marched at the head of the little Harvard Grand Army Post, and made the address of the day.

CHAPTER II

Boyhood

OR the most part, Edward Ayer's boyhood days were happy ones. He grew up in a large family bound together strongly by ties of affection; and he was the apple of his father's eye. A gun, a girl, school pranks and home tasks, memories of wild life and a first glimpse of city life, a growing eagerness to see the world and make his own way in it—such are the milestones in this chapter.

The child was father of the man, in that the boy very early took to barter; but it must be said that his very first independent pecuniary venture gave little promise of the extraordinary shrewdness that he later developed as a business man. Mr. Ayer always kept two or three cows and a pig or two, and it was his custom to let one of the children take care of the pig that was being raised for home consumption, the understanding being, of course, that the animal belonged to the child who was looking after it. When Edward's turn came he was proud of his fat porker. It was a very fine pig. It weighed two hundred and fifty pounds. Mr. Ayer was almost ready to butcher it, when one day a neighbor boy, Hyatt Maxon, somewhat older than Edward, came along with a little two-fifty shotgun, as they were called, and offered to trade it for the Ayer pig. The barrel was bent, and the lock had been broken, but the weapon quite took the eye of the future collector and contractor; so the swap was made without delay. The pig was turned out, and Edward helped the new owner to drive it two miles to Hyatt's home. Said Mr. Edward Ayer when he told me this story:

"Father laughed, and said, 'Dead game!' He never said a word more about that pig."

"What is the brightest spot in your boyhood memory?" I asked.

"I will give you a little account of it," he said. "Three miles south of us lived Maria Gardner, one of the prettiest girls in all the country. All the boys were in love with her, I among the rest. I was six years old and she was nine, and I knew I didn't have much of a chance. But there was going to be a party at the home of Hod Smith, one of the neighbor boys, and I knew Maria would be there. I had somehow got hold of five cents, and I sent this with one of Father's teamsters who was driving to Kenosha and had him buy me five sticks of candy—they were about six inches long. I broke them all up into pieces about an inch long, and of course Maria got her full share. It made me solid for that night and I was in Elysium."

There is a sequel to this childhood romance that Mr. Ayer never grew tired of telling. Maria married Hod Smith, and in the spring of 1860 the young couple set out across the plains for California. A few days later Ed. Ayer, now eighteen years old, also joined a wagon train and set out to conquer fortune in the Far West. Some fifty miles beyond Salt Lake City, Utah, young Ayer overtook his old friends, Hod and Maria, and together they pursued their westward journey over the hard trail. They were as good to him as anybody on earth could be; and though, after the three parted, more than half a century passed before they met again, he never ceased to cherish their memory.

When, at last, while on a visit to California in his old age, Mr. Ayer heard that Hod and Maria were living on the Pacific Coast, he telegraphed to his sister in Harvard requesting that she find out where they were living. Word came back that their home was in Hollywood. Said Mr. Ayer: "I drove

over there and went to the door, and this dear, sweet little old
lady presented herself, and it seemed as if I should have
known her anywhere, at any time, and I said:

" 'Maria Gardner, I have been looking for you thirty-five
years—I think it's awful for you to hide yourself this way!'

"She said: 'Well, well, who are you?'

"And I said, 'I am Ed. Ayer.'

"Of course I was received with every indication of joy. I
asked where Hod was, and she said he was in the back yard.
She called him, and a gray-headed man of seventy-seven came,
and I said:

" 'For God's sake! I wouldn't be as old as you are for a
million dollars.'

" 'Well, well, who are you, anyway?'

" 'Well,' I said, 'I am Ed. Ayer,' and you can imagine the
joy of the meeting."

From that day, as long as they were all alive, Mr. Ayer on
his frequent trips to California never failed to visit these old
friends whom he had loved so much in his boyhood and
adventurous youth.

School privileges in Wisconsin about 1850 were scant; and,
such as they were, the mischievous boy laid them under slight
tribute. He cared little for books and for the dreary interior
of the old cobble-stone schoolhouse at Big Foot Prairie. It
was the era of "the three R's" and the liberal use of the birch
or hickory rod.

"In the cobble-stone School," said Mr. Ayer, "the rules on
whispering and everything else were as rigid as the Rock of
Gibraltar. At the head of the school as a teacher, was a man
named Robert Southmead. At that time, if children talked in
school, the teacher would flog them. Our teacher never lost an
opportunity. If there was possible mischief to be in, I was in it.
Sometimes I would be feruled twice a day for a week; if I got
off with one a day I considered myself lucky. My sister, Julia,

was quite as much given to pranks as I was. So she got feruled a good many times. About two weeks before the close of school Father said to us:

" 'If you two children will not get whipped until the end of the term, I will give you each a dollar.'

"We knew we would miss some fun, but we must get that dollar, anyway—it was an enormous fortune! We talked it over and decided we would behave ourselves. The last day of school arrived, and Mother was on hand, and five or six other women, to see the closing exercises. A fat little fellow, Brookings Plummer, sat on the front seat, just ahead of me. The seats were rudely made of rough lumber. Between the back and the seat proper was a space of three or four inches. As luck would have it, about twenty minutes before school was out I dropped my pencil on the floor. As I looked for it, I could see a tempting portion of Brookings' little anatomy sticking out of the crack. I weighed the whole situation and took my chance. I felt sure Mr. Southmead would not thrash me before Mother on the very last day of school. At any rate the temptation was too great; so I bent up a pin, put it between my toes, felt around carefully, gave a slight push—harder than I intended—and with a whoop Brookings bounded into the middle of the floor. And that old curmudgeon took me out and gave me a thrashing—within ten minutes of the last hour of school!

"That night at supper Father took out a dollar—it looked to me as big as the full moon just rising above the autumn horizon—and went and gave it to Jule. Then he said:

" 'Young man, I believe you got thrashed this afternoon.'

" 'Yes. I didn't think Mr. Southmead would lick me the last minute of school. And besides I didn't intend to stick that pin into Brookings quite so hard; and you ought to give me fifty cents, anyway.'

" 'Ha! Ha! No compromise!' he replied; and he wouldn't

give me a cent. I always thought that Jule felt as bad as I did."

The boy went to school about three months each year until he was eleven or twelve years old; but it was an irksome business for him. He said he cared nothing about any subjects except geography and studies that had to do with nature. He abhorred grammar, and could do nothing with it. Said he: "I believe I could kill the man who invented it because of the agony it caused me at that time. I am good at figures now, but I wasn't then—I was a dead failure."

"But how about spelling?" I asked. "Didn't you have spelling matches?"

The response was a half-aggressive, half-disgusted movement, a humorous twinkle, and an indignant explosion:

"Yes, we had spelling matches all the time! But I wasn't in it—they didn't choose me until they got way down to the end of the list, and then I would generally go down about the third word."

Whatever his standing in school, he was a bright and sturdy lad; and he took responsibility very early. From the time he was ten years old his father would take him on business errands. He would say to him:

"That man owes me ten dollars; you go and get it for me."

The first piano that came to Kenosha was a Boardman and Gray, which Mr. Ayer bought.

"He went to Kenosha in the buggy to get it," his son said, in relating some of his boyhood experiences to me; "and he left his buggy in town and hired a *Democrat* wagon to bring the piano home in. When he was ready to send the wagon back, he loaded it up with paper and rags, and put me on top, with instructions to drive to Kenosha and bring the buggy back. It was in the fall and quite cold. There were taverns all along the road every half mile or so; and about sixteen miles out from Kenosha there was one run by a Dutchman named

P——. The afternoon was foggy, cold, and rainy; and I got to this tavern about four o'clock. My horse had cast a shoe in a little Dutch town about a half a mile back. I decided to stay over night at this tavern and have my horse's shoe replaced. As the dreary night settled down old P—— began to get drunk. About six o'clock in came a pack-peddler. He and I were the only ones in that inn; and the proprietor was drunk. At the first opportunity I went and found Mrs. P—— and said:

"'I find I must go on, and if your little girl will come and hold the lantern while I get out my horse, I can get away now.'

"'Why, boy, it will never do for you to go now,' she replied.

"But I said, 'I have to go.' So I went out into that dark rainy night alone; for I was bound I would not stay there. I got off the road into the mud, and traveled along as best I could until ten o'clock. Then I reached a place run by Beldens, and seeing a light, I yelled out to bring them to the door. I looked like a drowned rat; was wet through and almost frozen—a boy only ten years old. They, good people, took me in, washed me with warm water, put me to bed, and did everything they could for me. I cannot understand to this day how at that age I could make and carry out the decision to leave the drunken Dutchman's place."

While Mr. Ayer owned the store, he had teams hauling wheat to Kenosha all the time. The distance to Kenosha was about forty-eight miles, and there were taverns all along the way. In the summer after the wheat had been harvested and threshed, Mr. Ayer would load up two wagons at a time, and putting Hyatt Maxon on one and Edward on the other would start the boys off for Kenosha with the grain. If the roads were good, they would make two trips a week. They were both so small that they could not handle the bags. If a bag came untied they had to get someone to help them re-tie it, and they always had to hire a man to unload for them. There were three elevators in Kenosha, but the train of wagons bringing grain to town was so long that sometimes it would be strung out for a quarter of a mile waiting to unload. The boys would take just three days for the round trip—averaging a little more than thirty miles a day. They would drive about thirty miles the first day and stop at some tavern; then drive on into town and back to the same tavern for the second night. The necessary money to pay their bills was supplied them; but the grain was placed to Mr. Ayer's account.

Life was sometimes hard for the active, eager boy, but never dull. There was the swimming-hole down at the creek. In the winter there was skating and boisterous sleigh-rides to some neighboring village or county rendezvous. Deer had long since disappeared from that part of the country, but quail and prairie chickens were plentiful. The boy had a gun reasonably early—with lock, stock, and barrel intact, and he was always fond of shooting. Pigeons were abundant every season, as they migrated from the north in the autumn and from the south in the spring. On both migratory flights they would hesitate or linger for awhile in the woods about Big Foot Prairie. For three or four weeks during the fall there came sounds from the woods like the whir and throb of threshing machines. Speaking of those days, Mr. Edward Ayer said:

"They would string along, and I knew their call very well. In fact, I could go alone in the woods at night, get under a dead tree, and by making that call bring them about me. I never saw but one real flight. One beautiful Sunday morning when we were about a half mile's distance from a wood on the east, and about three and a half from one on the west, we heard a fluttering—a sort of premonition of what was about to happen—and looking up we saw blocks of pigeons extending for at least five miles, and massed twenty rods deep—just a cloud of them. And a mile or two behind, came another bunch, and another, and another, and another—four or five of those great clouds went over that morning, in a great flight to the north. It was the only big flight I ever saw; but all the years I can remember from the time I came to Big Foot Prairie at six years of age, up to the time I was twelve or fourteen years old there were always plenty of pigeons."

The boy made his first trip to Chicago in 1853, when he was twelve years old. He had seen an engine at Marengo before this time; but until now he had never ridden on a train. The Illinois and Wisconsin by this time had built twenty-seven miles of track from Chicago—the terminus then being Deer Grove. Mr. Ayer had sold his store sometime before to a Mr. Hunt and was making a trip to Chicago with him. A little box was put into the back of the buggy for the lad to sit on; and the first forty miles of the journey was made by the budding world-traveler in this humble fashion. At Deer Grove he got onto a train for the first time.

Three impressions of this trip fixed themselves indelibly in the mind of the youth. First, the town of Chicago, which at that time had a population of forty or fifty thousand, was being raised eight or nine feet (in the early days Chicago was periodically elevated in this manner); so the youngster remembered going down and up, and then down and up again over the rickety board sidewalks on his way to the Sherman House.

The second thing he recalled with particularity concerning this trip was a pretty little girl of his own age who was playing around the halls of this Chicago tavern. He got acquainted with her and joined her in her play. Her name was Adelina Patti. She was at that time making a concert tour with Ole Bull. That night Edward attended the concert with his father; and he said there was never a minute in all the years that followed, whenever he recalled that incident in his life, that he could not hear that wonderful little voice trilling away up amid the waves of enchanting melody that surrounded him.

The third memorable incident of the journey was a material loss that he suffered on the return trip. Frequently in later life, in the great railroad tie industry that he built up, in a single night a fire or a freshet destroyed tens of thousands of dollars worth of property. But such losses he was accustomed to laugh over. They were nothing compared with the agony occasioned by the loss of the snappiest and handsomest blue cap that was ever donned by a boy. He had come to Chicago wearing his serviceable regulation country cap—with long ear-laps tied over the top of his head. His father had bought him a new cap, a blue cap, with a visor, and with every other mark and insignia known to boyhood aristocracy. He had reveled in the thought of appearing before the boys of Big Foot Prairie with this adornment on his head; but suddently the dreams of his triumph were dissipated.

It was a fine warm day when the train started from Chicago, and the car window was open. When he was about a mile out of town he stuck his head out of the window to get a better view of the wonders about him—and off blew his cap; it was gone forever. To the end of his days, he never ceased to regret the loss of that cap. He told the boys at home about it, but he was confident that they did not believe a word of what he said.

Edward was early instructed by his father in the fine art of carving at the table. "Judge" Ayer and his wife were famous for their hospitality to the well-to-do as well as to the poorer people. Says one who often sat at the Ayer board two generations ago:

"There was always an abundance of good food in their larder. Especially was the "Judge"—coming from New England near the coast—fond of sea foods. It was a picture to see the old man, with a carving knife in his hand, seated before a finely done and well-trimmed roast pig, with an apple between its jaws, and the odor of rich stuffing of onion and sage filling the air, and all the "Judge's" family, and often poorer neighbors, too, around the board."

Ways of living in the earlier days on the prairie were of course somewhat primitive, and social enjoyments rather crude and infrequent. Dances, singing classes, and spelling contests were favorite amusements in both village and country.

The Fourth of July was the big event of the year. It was celebrated with abundant noise and color. Mr. Ayer said that one Fourth of July when he was about ten years old his father put him on one of the work horses with its clumsy bridle, tied a bag across its back (there was no saddle on the place), gave him fifty cents, and sent him to Delavan, a neighboring town, to have a good time. Two friends were also celebrating the Fourth in town. They must have been used to town ways and big celebrations. One of the boys came up to a ginger ale stand, and throwing down a dollar said:

"Give me a bottle of ginger ale."

"I never was so astounded in my life," said Mr. Ayer, as he spoke of the incident. "I thought, my Lord, what a lot of money! If ever I got able to do a thing like that, I'd be the happiest fellow in the world."

However, he enjoyed the day to the extent of his cash and his capacity; and after listening to the music, and watching the dancing, he started for home, and got there at three o'clock in the morning.

The boy and his father were very fond and proud of each other; and now and then they matched their wits against each other. About all Edward had to do in the way of chores was to milk a couple of cows. When he was about nine years old he said one day to his father:

"I don't like to milk these cows, and I guess I'll skip."

"All right; skip," was the reply.

When the youth was about sixteen, his father some way, in a trade, got hold of a hunting-case gold watch, with a long gold chain that went over his neck. He would wear it on rare occasions when he went to Chicago, and sometimes he would let his son wear it when he went to the city. When Edward got home from one of these trips he found his father engaged in conversation with two or three gentlemen.

"I pulled out the watch and snapped it open so he could see engraved on the case: *Edward E. Ayer, from his Father.*

"Father laughed, 'Ha! ha! ha! you rascal!' "

In 1859 the boy was growing restless, and was eager to see something of the world, and enjoy some adventure on his own account. A large portion of the population of America was bent upon seeing Pike's Peak about this time. "Prairie Schooners" were forever on the move toward the gold fields; and every now and then one of these vehicles would appear bearing some such inscription as *Pike's Peak or Bust!* When he was seventeen years old, Edward said very longingly to his father one day:

"I want to go to Pike's Peak."

"You couldn't do it," the father replied.

"Yes I can. I know I can earn my own living."

Mr. Ayer, with an image in his mind of ten cords of wood that he had piled in the back yard said:

"You go saw that wood up and split it, and if you do that all right I will let you go."

The boy got about half through, in spite of the fact that his father had encouraged some of the other lads to sit on the fence and "guy" him. But before he was able to complete the task he became sick, and for a week was under the doctor's care. When he got up, he again went pluckily to work at the wood pile.

When the job was finally finished he went promptly to his father and said:

"Now may I go to Pike's Peak?"

"That trade's off," was the reply. "I knew you couldn't do it. You got sick under that job. I told you you would, too."

"So he got his wood sawed all right," were Edward Ayer's concluding words as he told this story.

CHAPTER III

Facing West

EDWARD AYER'S determination to strike out for himself was sudden and decisive. One April morning he went out to find a cow that had strayed away. As he was returning with the animal about ten o'clock, he met Horace Smith and the beautiful Maria Gardner, now husband and wife, starting out to make a home for themselves in far-off California. He said good-bye to them, and went on his way much excited. When he reached home he went straight to his father and said:

"I want to go to California."

Mr. Ayer treated the request lightly at first; but he was a wise as well as a fond father and he soon saw that this time he must yield. He perceived at once that the enterprising, independent youth had come to the crossroads of life, and that, if he was not given freedom to choose for himself, he would either rebel or remain at home in bitter discontentment; so Mr. Ayer gave his consent. The die was cast; and on the last day of April, 1860, when he was nearer eighteen than nineteen years of age, Edward Ayer set out to carve for himself the romantic career that is to be set down in these pages.

Since up to this time there had been hardly a break in the family circle, there was a general heartache when the time came for the boy to depart. Fortunately a wagon train *en route* for California came through Harvard from Kenosha a few days after young Ayer's decision to go West. Horace Hartwell and his family, good friends of the Ayers, were to join the train at Harvard. Edward threw in his lot with this company. Adolph Hutchinson, his dearest chum, rode along with the train eight or ten miles on horseback before he could bring himself to say good-bye to his comrade. That night the party slept at Belvidere, Illinois; but for many weeks after that their bed was the ground and their canopy the sky. They crossed the Mississippi River at Fulton. Then for two or three weeks the route lay through the rich but sparsely settled Iowa country. The first main objective was Council Bluffs, on the Missouri River. Between Des Moines and Council Bluffs there were almost no houses, but now and then a stage station gave evidence that they were within touch of civilization.

As it was the first time the youth had been away from his family for any considerable length of time, he was of course growing pretty lonely; and when at Council Bluffs, the company received the first mail they had since leaving home, Edward, not daring to trust himself to open and read his letters in the face of the whole crowd, sought the seclusion of a big sunflower patch on the banks of the Missouri, and at leisure read the home letters, meantime indulging in copious tears as he thought of the dear ones back in Harvard—including his best girl, Nancy Root—from whom he was to be so long and so widely separated. Not many days elapsed after the journey was begun before young Edward had to pay the penalty for his over fealty to all the opinions, words, and ways of his good and wise parents. Whenever any question came up among the young men of the train as to matter of fact, or the proper way to do this thing or that, Edward would quote as final authority the opinion of his father or his mother, or would tell how they did that particular thing. About the sixth day out from Harvard one of the boys ahead called back:

"Ed., come on up here, I want to find out how your father or mother did this!"

The cure was instantaneous and permanent.

For a quarter of a century, Council Bluffs had been the great supply station and point of departure for the ever-growing stream of traders, pioneers, and emigrants who were wheeling their weary way across the Great Plains and over the mountains to the Oregon Country, and Great Salt Lake. Early in the century, the hunters and trappers—almost as wild as the animals they hunted, as savage as the red men against whom they matched their craft and their strength—had traveled the remotest places of the West and the Northwest. They knew the whole region between the Missouri River and the Pacific—every mountain stream, every peak and pass of the Rockies. As early as 1836, Dr. Marcus Whitman with his bride took a wagon across the Rocky Mountains, and established a missionary station near the junction of the Snake and Columbia Rivers. From that time on, increasingly, wagon trains followed the Oregon Trail. It was over this route that the Mormons, led by the astute and indomitable Brigham Young, after their expulsion from Nauvoo, and their terrible winter near Council Bluffs, made their trek to the new Land of Promise in the Great Salt Lake Valley. The Oregon Trail followed the Platte River all the way up to its source in the Rocky Mountains. The route was from Council Bluffs to Grand Island; then to Julesburg, where the river forks; then up the North Platte by Laramie, and on to South Pass; thence across the Green River; and finally to the Pacific slope by the Snake River, or to Great Salt Lake, Nevada, and San Francisco by Fort Bridger, and so over the Salt Lake rim.

From Council Bluffs the party with which Edward Ayer was traveling crossed over to Omaha, and there spent two or three days laying in supplies, purchasing ammunition, and making all the final arrangements for the great adventure. For the first one hundred miles there were little towns, such as Fremont and Columbus, far from each other, and now and then a rude house on the prairie. At the Loop Ford River they followed the north edge of the Platte Valley. Few exciting incidents enlivened the way, as there was little danger from

Indians at that time. However, there was still enough glamour and romance in an overland trip to the Golden Gate to stir the heart of any young adventurer; and if anything unusual was going on Edward Ayer was in the midst of it.

At one time a band of Pawnee Indians appeared, their ponies heavily laden with buffalo meat. This unusual sight so alarmed all the horses of the emigrants, except the few that were picketed, that they ran away. Edward and another boy mounted two of the horses that had been so well secured that they could not get away, and without saddle or horse blanket followed the runaways twenty miles on the back track before they were able to recover them. When the boys returned with the animals about four o'clock in the afternoon, Ayer said there was some skin left on his legs, but very little. Two or three days after this, some children of the party were playing on the banks of the Platte, when one of the smallest of them, Mr. Hartwell's boy, fell into the swift muddy river. The other children, in terror, sounded the alarm. Almost instantly "Big Hank," a Kenosha man, and Ed. Ayer waded into the stream a few rods below the point where the boy had disappeared, and just in the nick of time a little hand came into sight above the surface. Hank seized it, and returned the youngster unharmed to its agonized mother. All mail for the party had been sent to Fort Kearney on the south side of the river. The stream was high and full of sand bars; but Ayer volunteered to take a horse and go across for the mail. His animal was swept into a deep channel, and both horse and rider narrowly escaped drowning in the swift-flowing water, heavy with sediment. But the coveted bundle of letters was secured, and cavalier and steed returned safely to camp.

The fact that the emigrants were able to communicate with their families and get replies to their letters though on the march and moving ever to the westward, farther and farther from friends and centers of population, deserves comment. As the tide of population set steadily to the west, and as mining camps, farming settlements, and towns continued to spring up in remote places, across wide unsettled stretches infested by savage Indians, it became a task of the greatest urgency for the Government to see to it that the mail pouch and the wagon road should follow the Flag. For the most part these wild regions were Federal, not state territory; so the problem was one that Congress had to solve. Americans of that day were not very different from Americans of this day. They wanted their mail, and they wanted their express and freight, as much as the city-dweller of today demands his paper the moment he arises in the morning, and his daily delivery of milk, cool from the ice. The task was a gigantic one, but American enterprise met and conquered it.

Few aspects of the conquest of the West are more dramatic than the establishing of the Overland Mail Routes. In 1857 a contract was awarded to John Butterfield to carry the mail overland in coaches from Tipton, Missouri—then the westernmost point reached by the railroad—to San Francisco, 2,795 miles away. Butterfield was given a year to make the necessary preparation for this epic enterprise. He obligated himself to make the trip in twenty-five days, and to maintain a semi-weekly service. The Government was to pay him six hundred thousand dollars a year, and the contract was to hold for three years. Beginning September 15, 1858, the first trip was made within the required limit of days. No work of fiction is more fascinating than the story of this achievement, but to go into details concerning that great enterprise would be inappropriate here. An equally fascinating story, though, and one pertinent to this narrative, is that of the Pony Express.

The Pony Express was initiated in the spring of 1860, the very year that our pilgrims were toiling westward; and the riders traversed the Platte Trail. The demand for an expedited mail service had grown more and more urgent. So by the courage and enterprise of Alexander Majors the Pony Express was instituted, with the promise of a ten-day schedule between Atchison, Kansas, and Sacramento, California. Relay stations were provided ten or fifteen miles apart; mettlesome horses were secured; and light-weight men or boys were hired, whose duty it was to ride at full speed day and night through savage as well as civilized country, unarmed, and with the lightest possible accoutrement. On April 3, 1860, at the same hour, riders set out from Atchison and from Sacramento. The mail from the East passed the mail from the West in the heart of the continent. On this first run, previous mail schedules were cut down by two weeks; that is, the mail was transmitted from point to point in a little more than ten days. On a later trip, Lincoln's inaugural address was carried from Atchison to Sacramento in seven days and seventeen hours. It cost five dollars to send a letter written on the lightest paper, yet the Pony Express did not pay expenses. It went out of business in October, 1861, as at that time telegraphic communication was opened between New York and San Francisco.

Brief as was the day of the Pony Express, it was just Ayer's luck to see it in glorious operation. From the time that his train had reached a point three hundred miles west of Omaha, day after day, he saw the express riders dash by on the wings of the wind. These couriers were the bravest of the brave. The men that Ayer saw were mounted on wild bronchos. At various places along the route the Indians were bad. The Pony Express riders had to depend upon speed alone for safety; and often they were fired upon, and not a few of them were killed. In his *Reminiscences** Mr. Ayer has the following note:

---

*A typewritten journal of the principal events in Mr. Ayer's life which he prepared at the request of his family and friends.

About six or seven years ago I attended a reception and dinner given by all the diplomats of Paris to Buffalo Bill. I said it wasn't necessary to introduce me to Bill Cody; that I crossed the Plains in 1860, and that he was riding by our train about a month, and would give us news in a loud voice as he rushed by, so that we all became much attached to him. At the reception Bill wouldn't let me get out of his sight, and insisted that I should sit at his side, thereby disarranging the seating plan at the banquet.

Some of the way points that particularly impressed young Ayer and his company were Independence Rock, South Pass, Green River, Fort Bridger, and Salt Lake City. Independence Rock, some twenty acres in extent, rises in the center of a great valley to a height of one hundred feet. The party made camp here, and the hero of this story spent the best part of a morning carving on the rock with the aid of a hammer and cold chisel: *Ed. E. Ayer, Harvard, Illinois.* After going through South Pass, the emigrants emerged on the Pacific Slope. There was still ice and snow at this high altitude. Wherever the ground was free from snow the flowers were growing profusely. To the north, the great Wind River Range of mountains was in sight. The road now led to the southwest, down the Pacific Creek, along Sandy Fork, across the Green River, and on to Fort Bridger.

Young Ayer left the only coat he had to his back on the bank of the Green River, and did not discover his loss until he had gone six miles further on his way. His worldly fortunes at this time were at low ebb. It is a common saying among his friends that he had a million dollar disposition; but at that time he had little else—a shotgun with a broken stock, which he sold for ten dollars a few weeks later; a hickory shirt; a pair of blue jean overalls, with light pants underneath; a pair of very heavy, high-topped boots, out at the toes and very red for want of greasing; a black hat, crownless and all but rimless; an extra shirt; two handkerchiefs; and the coat before mentioned. Of course he had to return for this most important garment. He found it on the back of an Indian, but was able to secure its release by the exchange of a red bandana handkerchief.

It was no easy task to overtake and locate his own company. His pony was almost tired out, and he himself was far from fresh, when just before dark he picked up in the road the bleached jawbone of a horse that had perished there. On this white skull he wrote the doleful inscription: "Ed. E. Ayer, 3,000 miles from home, without a cent." A week later the Carey family, old neighbors at Harvard, passed that way; and Carrie Carey, a girl he had been very fond of back home, walking along behind the wagon, saw the bone, picked it up, and knew from this record on the sands of time that Ed. Ayer was also plodding westward. A month later, after a hard day's work, the youth rode thirty miles on horseback to spend a few hours in her company.

Fort Bridger, founded by James Bridger, one of the most famous of all the early mountain men, was an important outpost of civilization in 1860. In 1842, as Bridger was on his way to St. Louis in charge of a fur caravan, he met Frémont and a party of emigrants in the far Northwest. He perceived at once that the day of the trapper was about over, and that the day of the emigrant was at hand. The Indians were on the war path, and would continue to be. Yet the emigrants were coming, and would continue to come; and more than anything else, they would need protection and supplies here in the heart of the hostile Indian country. So Bridger determined to establish a fort—not merely a saloon and trading-station for trappers, but a haven where the weary and hard-beset emigrant could break his journey, recruit his animals, and find provender and supplies for man and beast. He knew that the emigrant trail would cross Green River Valley near the Black Fork, so there in the extreme southwestern corner

of Wyoming he built Fort Bridger, and occupied it early in
August, 1843. In December of the same year he wrote to a
friend in St. Louis:

I have established a small fort, with a blacksmith shop and
a supply of iron, in the road of the emigrants on Black Fork
of Green River, which promises fairly. In coming out they are
generally well supplied with money, but by the time they get
here they are in need of all kinds of supplies, horses, provisions, smith-work, etc. They bring ready cash from the
states, and should I receive the goods ordered, will have considerable business.

At beautiful Salt Lake City, then only a small town, the
party stayed about a week to rest and get ready for the most
trying experience of the whole journey—the long waterless
drag across the sandy desert west of Great Salt Lake. Salt
Lake City and the surrounding valley had become a paradise,
thanks to the supervising genius of Brigham Young. Already
the village was a lovely place, with stately avenues lined with
poplar trees, and streams of pure, cold mountain water running down each side of the main streets. The Mormons at this
time were busy with ox-teams, hauling stones from the quar-
ries, with which to lay the foundations of the splendid Salt
Lake City Temple.

The emigrant train proceeded by way of the south end of
the lake. In the foothills beyond, where the grass was good, a
halt of ten days was made to recruit the stock before undertaking the terrible desert stretches. Many other emigrants
had parked their wagons in the same region; and here Ed.
Ayer found his dear friends Horace and Maria Smith. As the
Indians were bad ahead of them, the two parties now kept
together for greater security nearly all the way to Carson
City. When the travelers approached the famous chain of
mines—Silver City, Gold Hill, Virginia City—Ayer having
decided to leave the wagon train and find work in the mines,
started on foot to make the ten-mile walk to the nearest mine.

He marched boldly up to the manager of the quartz mill at Devil's Gate and asked:

"Do you want to hire a hand?"

"What can you do, young man?" was the response.

"Anything."

"Do you think you would make a good shoveler?"

"I don't think anything about it, I know I would."

"All right," said the manager, "I will give you a job shoveling quartz at this mill, commencing at twelve, midnight. Your shift will be from midnight till noon, with an hour off for breakfast. Your wages will be four dollars a day."

The youth found that he could get board at the toll house, not far away, at fourteen dollars a week. He bought a pair of blankets with the ten dollars he had received for his shotgun; made a bunk in the corner of the mill, spreading one blanket on the boards and the other one over him and using his coat for a pillow; and there he remained as long as he held the job. However, the place was so rough, and the conditions under which he had to work so bad, that he remained only long enough to earn the necessary money to take him to San Francisco.

The trip across the mountains and down to San Francisco was a delightful experience, after the hardships and toil and disgusting surroundings he had been compelled to endure. He paid for his passage in a fruit wagon to the town of Fulsom, across the mountains. If he had been touring in the Alps, he could not have enjoyed himself more; for his route was over the Sierra Nevadas, up over the Carson Canyon, then within sight of Lake Tahoe, Strawberry Valley, Hangtown, and so on to Fulsom. From Fulsom to Sacramento—about thirty miles below—there was a railroad. From Sacramento to San Francisco he traveled by steamboat. So his means of transportation were as agreeable and diversified as the scenery was varied and picturesque. He landed in the Coast metropolis five months after he left home—with twenty-five cents in his pocket.

Fortune was good to him from the first. In 1859, Wesley Diggins and his wife Eliza, with a fine family of four children, had crossed the plains, and they were now fairly well settled in San Francisco. This family and the Ayers had been intimate friends in the East; so naturally the young man looked them up at once. They were all working hard, and among other things were running a wood, coal, and coke yard. It is a fact worth noting that Edward Everett Ayer, who was to become one of America's famous lumbermen, and who was later to be a chief factor in the movement for the preservation of the Redwood forests, began his career on the Pacific Slope in Wesley Diggins' woodyard, sawing wood with a bucksaw. So far as the wood and lumber business is concerned, it could certainly be said of him that he worked his way up from the bottom.

Nothing was more characteristic of Edward Ayer than his loyalty to old friendships; and throughout life it was his habit to give warm and unstinted praise to all the friends who had been kind to him in his days of loneliness and hardship. As for Wesley Diggins and his wife, "Aunt Eliza," he could scarcely find language ardent enough to tell of their good deeds; and the memory of their kindness to him glowed as brightly when he was eighty-five years old as it did when he was twenty-five. He writes in his *Reminiscences:*

They took me into their home. . . . Better people never lived on earth. The service that they were to me during the year I was in San Francisco, the friendship and hospitality extended, were something that never could be forgotten. At the end of the first week, I asked Uncle Wesley:
"What is my bill for board?"
"Oh, you must ask Aunt Eliza," he replied.
I had previously found out that the boarding houses were getting five dollars a week. I went to Aunt Eliza and said:

"I want to pay my board."

She commenced to cry, and said, "Oh, Edward, we cannot charge you board."

"That's very sweet of you, Aunt Eliza," I replied, "but while I love all of you dearly, and always will visit you with the greatest pleasure whenever I have an opportunity, unless you take at least as much as it would cost at a common boarding house I shall have to leave."

So we settled it on that basis, and I boarded with them as long as I stayed in San Francisco—bless them! I cannot dismiss the life in California without paying a special tribute to Aunt Eliza. She was one of the sweetest and best women that ever lived. Many a time I would get up in the morning with a hole in my trousers mended. The dear creature would come into my room during the night while I was asleep and take my clothes out and put them in order.

During these days in California, young Ayer came under the spell of two eminent and charming Americans—one an actor, the other a preacher—Joe Jefferson, and Thomas Starr King. During the winter of '60-'61, Joe Jefferson was playing *Rip Van Winkle,* and *Lend Me Five Shillings* in San Francisco. Edward and the Diggins boys were so fascinated by him that they went down town to hear him ten nights in succession, sitting in the pit with Chinamen, Negroes, and Islanders. They never tired of him. Here, again, was an instance of the pure good luck that always stepped up at just the right moment to slap the youth on the back, and pour for him his usual cup of undiluted joy. Twenty-five years later, Mr. Ayer met Joe Jefferson in Chicago and became well acquainted with him. When he told the actor of that winter in California, Mr. Jefferson said:

"Oh, Mr. Ayer, how I do wish I had known you people at that time and what you were doing!"

There was a strong pro-slavery sentiment in San Francisco during the autumn of 1860, and, indeed, for a considerable time after the outbreak of the War; and there were bold

expressions of disloyalty to the Union. There was doubt on
the part of the public press, and on the part of many influential public men whether it was worth while for California to
take any part in the great struggle, since it was so isolated
that anything it might do would be of little consequence one
way or the other. Edward and his associates heard the matter
discussed *pro* and *con;* and the air was electric with partisan
heat. Union men, partly to test the sentiment of the community and partly to stimulate a feeling of loyalty to the
Government, called a mass meeting on Washington's Birthday, 1861. The day was fine; there was stirring music; flags
were flying everywhere; and fourteen thousand people assembled to give emphasis to the fact that California was for
the Union.

On the other hand, many eminent Californians were half-
hearted or worse in their support of the Union. There was
even a conspiracy to sever California's connection with the
Federal Government. One fashionable and influential Presbyterian clergyman, in his public prayers asked God's blessing
on "the Presidents of these American States." Later, this same
minister, Doctor Scott, when resolutions expressing loyalty to
the Union were presented at a meeting in the city by fellow
clergymen, voted against them. This incident was reported
in the newspapers, and the next Sunday morning a United
States flag floated above Calvary Church, and the lamp-posts
all about were decorated with the Union colors. That morning Doctor Scott did not pray for "American Presidents";
yet after the service it was only with difficulty that he was
able to reach his carriage through the jostling, elbowing
crowd. He resigned his pulpit and sailed for Europe.

The most convincing voice raised for the Union during
these exciting months in San Francisco was that of the Rev.
Thomas Starr King, a Unitarian minister. He had spoken
with thrilling effect at the mass meeting on February 22. He

was not only an ardent patriot, and a preacher whose tongue was tipped with fire, he was a man of large intelligence and lofty personality. Edward Ayer attended his services and heard his lectures that winter; and no doubt his character and his decisions were much influenced by this great and good man. Bancroft, in his *History of California,* has the following to say of this eminent preacher:

Small of stature, delicate in health, with a soft and luminous brown eye, betokening his gentleness of disposition, he was yet, when aroused, able to sway multitudes. All through the most doubtful and trying period of the Civil War his voice encouraged the people whom his eloquence fascinated.

At the end of three months, as Edward Ayer felt that the sawbuck had done all that could be expected of such a lowly instrument by way of training in the rudiments of the lumber business, he began looking about for higher things. A friend from Harvard had opened a planing mill in San Francisco, and he was able to get work there. He continued this occupation until the outbreak of the Civil War. Sir Philip Sidney once said in his early youth, "If there are any good wars I shall attend them." Very likely Edward Everett Ayer had never heard of this remark by the *beau ideal* of all Knightly Spirits, yet something within him akin to the chivalric ardor that animated the immortal Englishman told him that this was a good war, and that it was his war. So, suddenly a new chapter opened in this eventful life.

CHAPTER IV

In Army Uniform

As SOON as the call to arms came, young Ayer, and two or three young men who were working with him in the planing mill, went down and enlisted in a cavalry company. Four days after they signed the roll, a boy came to the plant to tell them that they were to report at the Presidio at ten o'clock that morning to be sworn into the service. Ayer was running a few pieces through the surfacer, and as soon as he had finished this work, he ran off the belt and went around to talk to the other boys. They stopped the mill; and the rest, whose ardor for war seemed much abated, gathered about Edward to persuade him that it was not worth while to go, as they were so far away from the center of activity that no good would come of their enlisting.

But there was some far-off call in his blood that sounded the note of war. He told his companions there were several reasons why he must go. For one thing, he believed that it would be a long struggle and that it was his duty to participate in it to the utmost. Besides, he said, it would be hard for him to maintain his self-respect during the years after the War, if he did not take part; and, most important of all, he declared that he would not dare to return home and face his father and mother if he had neglected to offer his service to the Government at the first opportunity. So August 14, 1861, off he walked to the Presidio to be sworn in for military service. It so happened that his company—Company E—was the first one to be examined; and as the list was arranged alphabetically, and as his name began with the first letter of the alphabet, he was the first man mustered in on the Pacific coast.

36

He was always proud of this fact. Yet in speaking of it he never failed to point out that he was not entitled to any more credit than thousands of others, since it merely happened that way.

After the recruit had spent one night in camp, his captain asked:

"Do you know anything about military matters?"

"Nothing whatever," was the reply of Private Ayer.

"Did you ever see men drilling?"

"Yes, I saw the Ellsworth Zouaves drilling in Chicago, but I know nothing about military drill myself."

"I will make you first corporal," said the captain.

"What in the devil is that?" asked young Ayer.

"I will teach you," the captain replied.

So at the very start the youthful patriot became a corporal in Company E. For a month his company went into camp at Alameda, across the Bay. At the end of that period his outfit was brought back across the Bay to take ship for Wilmington, a port eighteen miles below Los Angeles. The Diggins family all came down to the dock to see him off. As he was not permitted to go ashore, Byron, the youngest boy, called out:

"Ed., is there something I can do for you?"

"Yes," the Corporal replied, pointing to a large table on the dock that was covered with pies for the sailors. "Do buy me one of those pies."

The boy did as he was requested, and this was the last pie that the young soldier tasted for two years—and to him, it was a pie in name only.

Mr. Ayer's own account of his soldier days in California is so graphic that I shall quote from it freely.

We had a rough passage down the coast to Wilmington, and landed there in a drizzling rain, the rainy season having commenced. We went into camp on that adobe soil with mud everywhere, and pulled out the next morning to a place selected for a permanent camp, called Camp Carlton, after General Carlton, who had charge of our outfit. It was one of the muddiest marches I ever made. Adobe soil would load us up until it seemed each foot weighed about a ton; but we finally arrived all right, and went into camp ten miles from Los Angeles—just where the Soldiers' Home is today, between Santa Monica and Los Angeles. Los Angeles at that time had about two thousand five hundred, I think. Two thousand four hundred of these residents were Spaniards, and the other one hundred white men; at least ninety percent of these were gamblers, and two or three, perhaps, were judges and lawyers. There were only about one or two two-story houses; and practically all the ranches and homes there were in the hands of the original Spanish owners and the Americans who had married into their families.

The young man had chosen to serve in a cavalry company. After a month at Camp Carlton, Company E and two other cavalry companies were ordered to San Bernardino. As the men had not yet been provided with horses, the march was made on foot. From boyhood Edward Ayer had a weak ankle; and the march caused him such distress that the last day he had to ask permission to fall out and rest under a mesquite tree. However, he was able to limp on into camp in time to roll in for the night.

There were only sixty or seventy people in San Bernardino at that time—all Mormons. The troops had been ordered to this point because a majority of the men in that region were Southern sympathizers. Most of those who were openly rebellious had already departed by way of Northern Mexico to join the Confederate army. The Union officers feared that there might be an invasion of the Territories of the Southwest from Texas, so it seemed desirable to have a force at San Bernardino, where it could be used to hold Arizona and New Mexico for the Federal Government.

After the cavalry volunteers had been in San Bernardino about four weeks, they were supplied with horses. The para-

phernalia of a trooper at that time was clumsy and made up
of many items; and the men were, as yet, untrained and awk-
ward in the handling of their mounts. As a natural result
there were some very funny mishaps at first. Corporal Ayer
described with glee the first attempt made by the commanding officer at mounted inspection.

The command was drawn up in one line facing the colonel,
and the order was given: "Two, Three, and Four to the
front," the object being to secure space for each man to mount
his horse. "There were about three hundred men in that condition—four lines of horses about ten feet apart, a man to each
horse, with a carbine, muzzle up, slung over his shoulder."

When all were ready the command was given, "Prepare to
mount." At that command a trooper seized the reins in his
left hand, placed his left foot in the stirrup, and grasped the
mane of his horse with his right hand. Of course there was
considerable commotion before the officers were able to get
the men in this position. When the word "Mount" rang out,
three hundred men raised themselves in their stirrups, intend-
ing to throw the right foot over the back of the saddle and
settle into it. But at least one hundred horses in the outfit
began bucking violently and running into each other. The
whole thing was one of the most awful and comical mix-ups
imaginable. When the thing cleared up there were at least a
hundred of the horses running on the prairie, nosebags all in
the air, and everything in turmoil. It was an hour before we
could get our animals together again. This was the last effort
made by our commanding officer for mounted inspection.

A short time after this, while the horses were out grazing
twelve or fourteen of them got away from the orderly, and it
was just the kind of a night we couldn't follow them. The next
morning I was detailed as a corporal with six or seven men to
hunt them up. Of course, the first thing I ordered was to make
a circle of the camp to find the tracks made by the horses the
day before. We found that the tracks led north. This was a
certain Wednesday morning in the winter of '61-'62. We followed those tracks that day fifty miles, and became convinced
that these horses had formerly come from the San José Ranch,
located about fifteen miles south-east of San Gabriel, as is my

recollection. It commenced to rain about three o'clock, and we got to a stage station called Mud Springs or Chapman, about six miles from San Gabriel.

At 5 :00 P.M., it was still raining hard, and it rained all that night. The next day we started out in the rain and found four or five of the horses. It rained solid and hard every minute of the time from about three o'clock Wednesday until the next Monday morning, with apparently hundreds of water-spouts coming down in tremendous torrents from the mountains. It absolutely tore Southern California to pieces. The streams coming out of each valley in those mountains were inundating the plains, and were something terrific. Geologists assert that there never was a rain like that for the last five hundred or a thousand years at least.

In going back to San Bernardino we found the whole country transformed, almost. In particular, the Cocomongo Desert, between the Cocomongo Desert and San Bernardino, was washed out in almost every direction; and there were great crevasses and water courses a mile wide where water had never before been known to run. We camped between San Bernardino and the Santa Ana River, now running in wash-outs in the desert fifteen feet deep and twenty rods wide. There were in the bottom of this new river bed cottonwood trees three feet in diameter that grew on the banks of the stream, and that had been uprooted by the freshet. The river was nearly three miles wide and everything was washed out clear to the ocean. Places where the water had never run, hundreds of tons of sand had been washed out. We were the first party that had come from the north, and the commanding officer wanted to send a quick express to the colonel in command at Camp Carlton, a hundred miles away. I was detailed to carry it, and was given two horses to ride alternately, so I made the trip in about sixteen hours. I was held at Camp Carlton for orders.

From Camp Carlton I was detailed to take an express down to Wilmington, and ordered to be back to Los Angeles at seven o'clock the next morning. There was a drizzling rain that afternoon, and I had taken a short cut to get across to the Wilmington Road. The consequence was that it was long, long after dark before I got to the road at all, the horse being nearly up to his belly in the mud, and I walking and leading him along. It was very dark, but I knew I would know the road by lack of grass, when I finally found it. I also remembered that when I marched over this route there had been a big hollow between Wilmington and Los Angeles that had to be crossed, and that was full of water. I struck that water about ten o'clock at night. I could see about sixty or seventy feet across it, and it was water, water everywhere! I put my horse into it and it seemed ages before I struck bottom. I again proceeded, and had been an hour or two more on the road when I saw I was in a hilly country, so I knew I had taken the wrong road and was off in the San Pedro hills north of Wilmington.

About three o'clock in the morning, I found a corral on the road made of rails and logs, with the water seven or eight inches deep all around it. I was very tired of course, and it was the first place I had found where I could hitch my horse. I tied him; took off his saddle; put it on a pile of rails I had taken off the corral; laid down on the rails with my saddle for a pillow; and the first thing I knew I was aroused by reveille at sunrise down at Wilmington, about four or five miles off to the south. It took me from sunrise until eleven o'clock in the morning to reach camp. I immediately reported to the commanding officer, and he sent another man to Los Angeles with dispatches to follow General West who had already set out for San Bernardino and Yuma.

While we had been away on these various duties, a new officer had come to take command, Major Ferguson, a very talented and fine chap. He had married General Vallejo's daughter—the General, to my recollection, being an accomplished Spanish gentleman. The day we returned, the last day of March, was cold, with a northern rain. When we rode into San Bernardino every man was wet to the skin and very cold. Our officers felt very sorry for the men and made arrangements with a Jew to give each of them a drink of barley whiskey, which was very strong. They gave large drinks to each of the men—there were only three of us that didn't drink, Sergeant Fairchild, myself, and a man named Warner. By the time we got to the bank of the Santa Ana River, which we had to cross, there were ninety-seven men, including the captain and two lieutenants, who were more or less under the influence of the liquor; and the officers commenced to dispute among themselves about the proper way to cross, the men joining in and taking sides with the officers they liked best. We finally got across, after pulling three or four fellows out of the river. It was ludicrous in the extreme!

The camp was then about two miles away. When we were within a quarter of a mile all the command, including Major Ferguson, came out to inspect us; so the captain made up his mind that he would show off before the new major. Thereupon, he put his company into a trot and the men were all reeling around in their saddles. Next, he put the command into a gallop. All this time we had been marching by fours; but when we were about fifteen rods from the camp, the order came: "Front into line—March." When this command had been executed, and we all came up into line, we were about a hundred feet from the two hundred men who had come out to greet and inspect us. When the word "Halt" was given, of course every horse stopped as if he were shot; but not so the troopers—at least sixty of them went straight over their horses' heads.

You can imagine our reception. Major Ferguson didn't let our company come into the lines, but made us go off about two miles and a half and camp by ourselves. Of course we straightened out by morning, and were led into camp. But the Major was disgusted with our company; and when the command was ordered south, into Arizona, he sent half of our outfit forward with one of the other companies, and took the other half north with him to Wilmington, by way of Los Angeles. The men resented very much the attitude of the Major, as they knew that their intoxication had been a mere accident.

Major Ferguson himself stopped at Los Angeles, but he told the captain to march out three miles and go into camp. This made the men madder than ever, as they desired to stay in Los Angeles, and really ought to have been permitted to do so. I was called on guard that night. We had only one post. The captain said:

"Corporal, do not let any man go out."

I said: "Well, Captain, how can I prevent it? This guard can't watch all these men."

He replied, "Well I guess they won't go." And that ended it.

But about ten o'clock that night there was nobody left in the camp but one sick man, the guards, and the captain—and he was asleep. About midnight Major Ferguson rode into camp.

"Who goes there?" I challenged.

"Wake up the captain, Corporal," was the reply.

Captain Mead got up, and Ferguson said to him:

"Where are your men?"

"They are sound asleep in the grass," he answered.

"No they aren't," said Ferguson, "they are all in Los Angeles, drunk."

I had orders to put them all under arrest, when they returned, including the orderly sergeant. This I proceeded to do. They began coming in about one or two in the morning, and they were the worst looking lot of fellows I ever saw. When we got ready to pull out in the morning—and the arms were in the wagons, and the men under arrest, all lined up, dirty, muddy, and in awful condition—Ferguson said to Captain Mead:

"Fine lot of men you have here." Then he had brains enough to recognize the conditions, and he continued: "Men, I have made up my mind I am making a mistake with you. Now you men have got to be with me for several months, at least, and I am going to turn over a new leaf and trust you implicitly. As soon as I get down to Wilmington I am going to send for each one of the three or four saloon-keepers there and tell them to sell my cavalrymen all the liquor they want and that they can pay for; and I feel quite sure that there isn't one of you men who will go back on me under those conditions. Captain Mead, give the men their arms, and release them from arrest."

From that time on for many months, he retained this company under his command; and there never was a man intoxicated, and he was absolutely devoted to us and we to him.

On an April morning in 1862, young Edward Ayer, in patriot uniform, having escaped at last from the cold and mud of an "unusual" California winter, crossed the Colorado

River into dazzling Arizona. As the Corporal now rode into the blazing Arizona desert he was not so brilliantly armed and accoutred as were Sir Walter Scott's chevaliers when they fared forth on their adventures; but it may be doubted whether any knight errant in fiction ever rode more bravely and blithely to meet danger and the future. He was a soldier not for gain or glory but because he was passionately devoted to his country and his flag. Patriotism had been bred into his bones by his parents; and they in turn had inherited it through generations of liberty-loving ancestors.

Ayer rode one of the Oregon-bred American horses that had been turned over to the volunteers by the regular army in California. He was armed with a Sharp's carbine, then the regulation army rifle, a revolver, and a sword—a useless weapon for an Arizona soldier. His accoutrement consisted of everything on earth: one blanket, in addition to a saddle blanket, an overcoat, a picket rope, hobbles, saddle-bags in which were all his personal effects, and a bag in which were carried all the personal effects of his charger—currycomb, currybrush, and nose bag. His company rode into Tucson on a May day, after many thirsty marches across the desert. The Corporal was quartered in an adobe house, though most of his comrades were assigned to tents. The rations consisted of the regular army issue—but worse. On the march the men had been supplied with cans of pemmican (the tin can tradition in the Southwest is very old) put up at San Pedro. The bacon was of the Missouri variety—the slices four inches thick and all fat. Later, some California beeves were driven in; but these creatures must have been akin to the seven lean kine that Pharaoh saw in his dream. They were so thin and weak that it was necessary to brace them up against a wall before they could be shot. There was scarcely a shred of flesh to be found on their bones.

Company E of the First California Cavalry was the only

mounted company in Tucson at this time. Corporal Ayer was
assigned to duty in the corral. All cavalry detachments arriving or departing reported to him. He had to receive and
dispatch the express riders, also, as they came and went east
and west with reports and orders. Not many weeks after he
arrived in Tucson, the young vedette (he was not yet twenty)
was sent with a detail of five or six men to escort an ox-train
to the neighborhood of old Fort Buchanan to get some ash
logs, which were to be whip-sawed and used for mending army
wagons in Tucson. The march was a dangerous one through
the desolated, Apache-infested valleys of the Santa Cruz and
Sonoita rivers. Johnny Ward, an Irishman about sixty-five
years old—a pioneer ranchman of Southern Arizona—was
sent along as a guide. He was a curious old fellow, and like
all the mountaineers and frontiersmen of that day, was a crack
shot. He offered to bet any young trooper in the escort a dollar
a shot that he could stretch a horsehair between two stakes
and cut it with a bullet fifteen feet farther than any of them
could see it. It was a safe challenge, as no man in the detail
had a dollar to his name. However, they persuaded the old
scout to do it for fun, and he succeeded in doing it. The teamsters secured their logs, and to the surprise of everyone, the
expedition returned to Tucson without accident, or attack
from the Indians.

About this time an incident occurred that was to shape
Edward Ayer's entire future. It had to do with books rather
than arms; yet it came about in the regular discharge of duty.
Colonel Lalley, a retired army engineer, who was then in
charge of the Cerro Colorado mine near the Mexican border,
came to Tucson to visit his old friend and classmate, Colonel
West, then in command of the Union troops. When Colonel
Lalley returned to the mine, as there were hostile Indians all
about, Corporal Ayer, with a detail of eight men, was sent
along to conduct and guard him on his way. When Ayer was

about to set out on his return trip to Tucson, Colonel Lalley
handed him a letter and said:

"Corporal, deliver that to Colonel West, in person."

"Very well, Colonel, I will do so."

When he got back to Tucson, he reported at Colonel
West's headquarters, saluted, and said:

"Colonel West here's a letter that Colonel Lalley asked me
to deliver to you in person."

The Colonel read the letter, then turning to Ayer asked:

"Do you know anything about the subject matter of this
letter?"

"No, sir," the Corporal replied.

"Did you do anything out of the ordinary in escorting
Colonel Lalley to the mine?"

"No, sir."

"This is a very remarkable request that Colonel Lalley has
made. He wants me to send a detachment of fifteen soldiers
down to the mine to guard it while he comes up and goes to
the Rio Grande for two or three months; and he requests that
I send you in command of the detachment."

"Colonel West, you certainly cannot be more astounded
at that than I am," was Ayer's reply.

"I am going to send you," said the Colonel.

A day or two later an order came from Colonel West to
the officer in command of Company E to detail Corporal Ayer
with fourteen men for duty at the Cerro Colorado mine. As
this was something like a second lieutenant's command, everyone was surprised that a corporal had been designated; and
the sergeants all felt that they had been ignored. So Ayer's
orderly sergeant picked out fourteen of the most unruly men
in the company. Ayer protested, asking that he might take his
own squad, who were well-behaved men and fond of him, as
he was of them. His request was refused. He took his complaint to the captain of the company. The officer said:

CERRO COLORADO (OR HEINTZELMAN MINE)

Courtesy of Harper & Brothers

"I have just resigned and can do nothing for you."

Ayer then marched to headquarters and asked to see Colonel West. "Colonel," he said, "my orderly sergeant has picked out for my detail fourteen of the most unmanageable men in the company; and I do not want to take them down there. I respectfully request that my own squad be detailed for this duty."

The Colonel immediately wrote this note to the company commander:

"Corporal Ayer will select his own men for the Cerro Colorado expedition."

Much pleased, young Ayer took his own men. With a supply of money, and a wagon to send down to a near-by Mexican settlement each week for grain for the horses, the detachment set out on the sixty mile ride to Arivaca. And now it was that the young soldier had the adventure that was to give color and direction to his whole life. Colonel Samuel Colt, inventor of the Colt revolver, and at this time chief owner of the Cerro Colorado (or Heintzelman) mine, had sent a few books out to the mine for the use of the employees during their hours of loneliness and leisure. Rummaging through this little library, Edward Ayer came upon *The Conquest of Mexico,* in three volumes, by W. H. Prescott. Here was a perfect illustration of George MacDonald's statement that: "As you grow ready for it, somewhere or other you will find what is needful for you in a book." Up to this time Ayer had never read a book. There were no books in the Wisconsin and Illinois wilderness in the '40's and '50's when he was a boy. He had been to school a little in the old cobble-stone schoolhouse; but the magic and the meaning of books he knew nothing about. He picked out these three volumes by Prescott because he was near the Mexican border, so naturally anything about Mexico aroused his interest. The books were read through with astonishment. Concerning this experience, he said to me: "I read those three volumes of Prescott's through twice while I was at the mine. They seemed to open up an absolutely new world to me."

I must here interrupt the present thread of my story to complete this little "Drama of the Books." Young Ayer returned to his home at Harvard, July 1, 1864, after completing his war service. Early in August he went to Chicago on business. As he was walking along Lake Street, he glanced across the way toward the old Tremont House and saw the sign "Cobb and Pritchard's Bookstore." Since his adventure with the Prescott volumes two years previous, he had read no books. This was the first bookstore that had ever attracted his attention. At once the thought struck him, I wonder if they have Prescott's *Conquest of Mexico*. He rushed across the street and into the store, and asked,

"Have you got Prescott's *Conquest of Mexico?*"

"Yes," the salesman replied, and forthwith he handed down Lippincott's edition of 1864, bound in black cloth, consisting of five volumes, the two on Peru, as well as the three on Mexico.

"How much are they?" the young man inquired eagerly.

"Seventeen dollars and fifty cents," was the reply.

"What!" said Ayer, almost paralyzed.

"Seventeen dollars and fifty cents," was again the reply.

"I'm so disappointed! I didn't think they could be worth more than fifty cents a volume."

"They are three-fifty a volume," said the dealer.

The young man was in a dilemma. He had never before wanted anything so badly in his life as he wanted these books. But it was out of the question to buy them, as he did not have enough money. Finally he said to the salesman, who proved to be one of the proprietors:

"My name is Edward Ayer. I have been four and a half years on the Plains, and in the war three years. I just got back

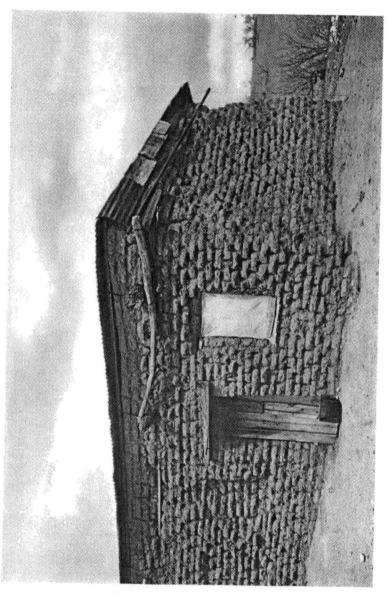

THE ADOBE HOUSE AT THE CERRO COLORADO MINE, WHERE CORPORAL AYER WAS STATIONED. HERE HE FIRST READ PRESCOTT'S "CONQUEST OF MEXICO"

a month ago after four years among the Indians. My father
has given me a thousand-dollar interest in his store at Harvard Junction. I want that first volume on Mexico awfully
bad, and if you will let me have it, I will pledge myself as a
gentleman to economize and save three dollars and fifty cents
a month, and in five months I will have paid for the rest."

The bookseller looked at Ayer a moment and replied:
"Young man, you can take that whole set right home with
you. Give me three-fifty now, and three-fifty each month until
they are paid for."

Edward Ayer, at eighty-five years of age, after having
drunk deep of life's joys—sitting in his parlor at the Huntington Hotel in Pasadena, and looking over the lovely California
prospect that lay spread out before us—Edward Everett
Ayer, the patron of the arts, and one of the chief book
collectors of the world, said:

I have blessed him ever since. I feel that that day, taking
those books home, was, perhaps, the happiest day of my life
up to that time; and going home I only touched the earth in
high places. And I want to reiterate that the finding of Prescott's *Conquest of Mexico* in that mine in Arizona in '62, has
been responsible and is to be credited as the principal force
that has given me a vast amount of enjoyment in this world,
and is absolutely responsible for the "Ayer Collection" in the
Newberry Library, Chicago.

To complete this episode and digression: About twenty-two
years ago Mr. Ayer took the three volumes of Prescott's
Conquest of Mexico to London with him, and carrying them
to Zaehnsdorf, his favorite bookbinder, he said:

"Zaehnsdorf, I have brought you over three of the most
valuable books in the world to bind. I will select morocco:
and, as you know, I have adopted the Grolier as my pattern
for binding histories. So use that design. I don't want you to
allow any sacrilegious hand to touch these volumes. I want

your best people right through; and you do the best job you ever did in your life, and send me the bill."

"What are your books, Mr. Ayer?" Zaehnsdorf inquired.

"Prescott's *Conquest of Mexico*."

"Fudge!" said the famous binder, "I can go anywhere and buy them for two or three dollars."

Mr. Ayer related the story of these books as I have given it here, and then asked:

"Zaehnsdorf, if you had these books and they had done as much for you as they have done for me, would you sell them for fifty thousand dollars?"

He replied, "Mr. Ayer, I wouldn't sell them for one hundred thousand dollars!"

"Neither would I," was the final rejoinder.

And so the books were bound, and they came forth in raiment more sumptuous than the apparel of a king.

But we must return to the young corporal on the Mexican border.

During the summer of 1862, the Mexican Government had agreed to give our Government a free port of entry at Libertad, on the Gulf of California, if we would open a port there. If supplies for Arizona could be received at Libertad, or at some point near there, the Americans would reduce the long desert haul to Tucson by about two hundred miles. One morning while Ayer was still at the mine, Major Ferguson arrived from Tucson with a lieutenant and fourteen infantrymen on his way to the Gulf to determine whether it would be feasible to open a port of entry at some convenient point. Ayer and his cavalrymen were relieved from duty at the mine and ordered to accompany Major Ferguson, the infantrymen taking their place.

The expedition went by way of Altar and Pitiquito; and then, by a thirty-three hour waterless march across the desert, to the neighborhood of a mountain spring. The wagons were left on the plain, and the suffering mules and horses were taken nine miles up into the mountains to the spring. Range cattle from far and wide came here to drink. As the soldiers were out of meat, a guard was stationed at the water hole, and that night two beeves were shot. This was a legitimate act if the person who killed an animal cut off the branded ear and surrendered it to the magistrate in the first town visited, together with two dollars for each steer killed. As soon as the detachment reached the Gulf, a well was dug, and warm fresh water was found at a depth of twenty feet. This, when drawn in the evening, and cooled during the night, proved excellent for use. In order that soundings might be made, the materials for a boat had been brought along. While the craft was being put together, the soldiers enjoyed themselves swimming and gathering the fresh, beautiful shells that covered the sand everywhere.

The second day, when Ayer was in swimming, Major Ferguson called to him requesting that he go out about one hundred feet and dive for bottom, to see how deep the water was. He did so, and when he was about half way back to shore, he noticed that the boys were all yelling and throwing shells into the water beyond him. As soon as he could touch bottom, he turned around and saw three or four sharks swimming about a hundred feet away. Said Ayer:

"I hadn't lost any shark, so I simply waded ashore."

After soundings had been made, and the party had returned to Pitiquito, Corporal Ayer was ordered to take three wagons and eight men and go to an out of the way ranch to purchase barley. About noon on a very hot day he came upon a rich plot of ground two or three acres in extent, covered with the most luscious watermelons one can imagine. The custodian of the field was a dirty, ragged, and very ancient Mexican. "Of course," said Mr. Ayer, "if we had been in our own country we would have taken what melons we wanted for use without a question. But we were in Mexico; and it was of prime importance that Major Ferguson do only the right thing. So I said to the men:

" 'Has anybody got any money?'

" 'No, nothing,' was the unanimous chorus.

"I had been supplied with three twenty-dollar gold pieces to pay for the barley we were to get. I looked at the melons longingly and said to the men:

" 'Do you suppose that old Mexican can change a twenty-dollar gold piece?'

" 'No, of course he can't,' came the chorus.

"So I asked the old man: 'How many melons will you give me for a dollar?'

" 'Twelve,' he replied.

" 'Bring them on,' I said, feeling that I should be held blameless if the Mexican could not make the change after I had offered to pay for them.

"We ate our melons as if we were millionaires. Then I took out a twenty-dollar gold piece and slipped it to the old man. To the consternation of the whole squad, he went down into his rags and pulled out nineteen silver dollars in change! When we had gone about half a mile, I stopped the outfit and said:

" 'Here, now, there must be some money among you eight men, and I've got to have it.'

"They were all dead honest, and among them they raked up eighty-seven cents, and turned it over to me. When we got to the place where I was to buy the barley, I told the man how we happened to be thirteen cents short. Much to our delight, he laughed and said:

" 'Distribute the money back to the men. I will give you sixty dollars worth of barley for fifty-nine.' "

Ayer and his men returned to Tucson early in October, and a few days later the paymaster—the first one they had ever seen from the States—arrived from the Rio Grande and paid them off in greenbacks. While Ayer had been in the south, Company E had been ordered to the Rio Grande and was now stationed at Mesilla. Thither Ayer's detachment proceeded as an escort to the paymaster on his return trip. Soon Ayer was detailed to conduct a wagon train to Fort Craig, about a hundred and twenty-five miles north of Mesilla. On this march the troopers went ninety miles without water—the route being over Jornada de la Muerte. The nights were so cold that the soldiers, to keep from freezing while they slept, had to make holes in the ground, and in them burn grass and any other dry stuff at hand so that a warm bed of ashes might be provided on which to spread their blankets.

The men had had no vegetables for a year or more. When Ayer went to draw rations at Fort Craig to supply his detachment on the return trip to Mesilla, he saw a pile of onions in the commissary department. He said to the sergeant:

"Please give me three or four of those onions."

The sergeant did so, and the corporal put them in his haversack when he started back to Mesilla next morning. That night when the time came to prepare supper he gave the boys all his onions except one. As he was peeling his own onion, a large, tall man about sixty years old, covered with dust and grime, stopped before him and said:

"By George, young man, I wish you would give me a piece of that onion!"

Ayer looked up and answered: "All right, my friend," and, cutting it in two, gave him half of it.

"Young man, where are you from?" asked the stranger.

"From Harvard, Illinois."

"What is your name?"

"Ed. Ayer." replied the youth.

"Good Heavens!" the man exclaimed, "I know your father

well. My name is Murray. I live up at Clinton Junction, and have a big farm there."

Of course these old-time neighbors stuck close together on the journey back to Mesilla, and revived happy memories of home and mutual friends.

About this time, General Carlton organized a new cavalry company, called "The Carlton Escort." Ayer was made a sergeant in this company. With the other members of the company he marched from Mesilla to Santa Fe with General Carlton, who had now become Commander of the Department. The boys expected to have an easy time at Santa Fe, but their hopes were blighted in the bud. There was hard, solid work all the time. The Indians in the Department were all hostile, except the dwellers in pueblos. No train could move, no dispatch could be sent, without an escort. Ayer was in the saddle most of the time. Once or twice these escort trips required six or eight hundred mile rides. On these occasions he would remain only one night when he reached his objective; and next morning, on a fresh mount, would set out on a new expedition. The troopers never had tents, but slept on the ground in sleet and snow. In summer it was intensely hot, and in winter—especially at night—very cold.

One experience in New Mexico Mr. Ayer recalled very vividly. About July 1, 1863, Lieutenant Wardell, in command of Ayer's escort, took him and about twenty men to Fort Union, to meet there a big provision train and conduct it to El Paso. On July 3, the train pulled into the little town of Las Vegas, seventy-five miles east of Santa Fe. Most of Ayer's company were in Sante Fe, and the young sergeant was eager to spend the Fourth of July there with them. When camp had been made and supper eaten, Ayer went to Lieutenant Wardell and asked:

"Are there no dispatches you would like to send into Santa Fe tonight?"

The officer replied, "No, Sergeant; what is the matter with you?"

Ayer, knowing that he was engaged to the daughter of Judge Watt of Santa Fe, answered: 'Well, I know of a mighty nice girl in Santa Fe who would like to get a letter from you on the Fourth of July."

"Do you really want to go to Santa Fe tonight?" he inquired.

"Yes, sir."

"Well, you are likely to run into hostile Indians, anywhere. You must not start until after dark or you might get killed before you get out five miles."

"I understand that," said Ayer. "I won't start until after dark, and you can set your mind at rest because I will leave the road in the morning at daylight and take to the foothills, which will be comparatively safe. I know I can make it all right."

The Lieutenant replied: "Very well, you can go."

At eight o'clock, Sergeant Ayer was handed a package for the young lady, and off he went. He reached Santa Fe at nine o'clock the next morning, and duly delivered the letter to Miss Watt. Between 7:00 A.M. of July 3, and 9:00 A.M. of the 4th, he had ridden one hundred and five miles. His recollection was, as he related this incident, that he got little sleep during the next twenty-four hours.

In the autumn of 1863, a regiment of volunteers was recruited, called "The First New Mexican Infantry." Ayer accepted a second lieutenancy in Company I of this regiment. He spent about a month visiting the various pueblos in the recruiting service. He remembered with particular delight his visit to the village of San Ildefonso. Here he witnessed a remarkable Indian dance of about four hundred Indians, arrayed in peculiar symbolical costumes. Fifteen or twenty children, with fawn skins drawn over them, represented young fawns. Some of the men appeared with the bodies of turkeys on their heads. Others wore buffalo robes that reached the ground; and many other animals were represented. These costumes (none of which are now in existence) had been used in this festival from time out of mind.

Ayer's duties were diversified for the remainder of the time he was in the service. For a while he was acting-adjutant of the regiment. He was next ordered to the Navajo Reservation on the Pecos River to sit as a member of a court-martial, presided over by General Kit Carson. A short time after this Company I was ordered to Arizona; but Ayer had stipulated when he accepted his commission that he desired to be released in the event that his company should be ordered to Arizona, since his period of enlistment had almost expired. He accordingly forwarded his resignation to General Carlton at Santa Fe, with the request that it be accepted as soon as he reached Fort Craig, whither his company was about to march on its way back to Arizona.

Ayer's letter of release awaited him at Fort Craig; and at last he was free to set his face homeward. From El Paso to Santa Fe the journey was made by stage; and, again, at Santa Fe he took a similar conveyance for Kansas City. The stage broke down about twenty-five miles out of Santa Fe, and the journey as far as Fort Union was made in a lumber wagon. At that point the nine men who composed the party expected to get another coach. This proving impossible, four horses were hitched to a narrow, three-seated ambulance, meant to carry six people—two in a seat. A day and night, and another day, the passengers rode in this painfully cramped condition. At Old Fort Bent the travelers lay down on the floor and got some rest—the first they had enjoyed since leaving Santa Fe. Their next stopping place was at Fort Lyon, twenty-five miles farther east.

At the very close of his long experience as a soldier, the

young veteran of the Plains was to get his first real baptism of fire. The Indians had never permitted the erection of a stage station anywhere between Fort Lyon and Fort Larned, two hundred and forty-four miles away. In consequence the stage company was compelled to make this great distance without change of animals. It was the custom to send an extra coach on this long lap with supplies, blankets, and feed for the mules. So it was on this trip. There were rumors that the Indians had grown hostile, and the homeward bound party knew they would be in luck if they got through without a fight. Provided with an escort of soldiers, the expedition set out, hoping for the best. A certain Captain Hardie, who was on his way back to the States, was in command of the detachment of soldiers.

All went well until they were within about fifteen miles of Fort Larned. Captain Hardie, as his horse was fresher than the other animals of the escort, decided to ride ahead into Fort Larned. The soldiers were lagging along far behind their commander. The story of the fight that now opened I must leave to Lieutenant Ayer's own graphic narration.

About four o'clock in the afternoon, the driver yelled, "Indians!" We looked off to the north of a low bluff on the right, and about a quarter of a mile away, and there came the Indians, riding in full war paraphernalia. I swung myself around toward the driver and ordered him to stop. It was evident that if we undertook to go towards the Captain we would lose some of the men behind, and if we undertook to go back to the men we would lose the Captain. I gave an Indian war whoop which was heard by both the officer and the troopers, and there was a race for life in the direction of the coach. The Indians approached to within a half a mile of us, and then divided; one bunch attempting to keep the Captain from reaching the coach, the other trying to cut off the men. As fast as the soldiers caught up, we hitched their horses to our coach; and as soon as the Indians came within rifle range we began firing; and succeeded, thus, in driving them off so that everybody reached the stage in safety.

Before this, all the way along, two men had monopolized the rear coach, riding on the blankets. They had an easy time of it. As soon as their coach stopped, they rushed to ours and were getting in before the Indians were anywhere near. In our party at this time was a woman with her child. We put them in the bottom of the coach and packed blankets and cushions around them so that the arrows and bullets couldn't touch them, and held the Indians off until we got entirely loaded up. Then we started on the run to Larned.

I got into the rear coach. It was the softest thing I ever had in my life, there being twenty rolls of blankets to ride on. I immediately cut the curtains off about sixteen inches so I could look behind and on each side, and could lie down and load my revolver. I was practically the rear guard. As we would run, the Indians would run up very close, so that the arrows would come pretty thick. They had some guns, also, and we were in more or less danger from that source; but nothing happened, except that the Captain had a part of one ear shot off, and one of the horses was wounded. We made five runs, driving the Indians off each time. Of course we didn't know whether we killed any, but we did disable some of their horses. At the last run there were only about half of the Indians in pursuit, and, finally, they dropped off altogether. At last we got to Fort Larned; and there we were given another escort, so we finished the trip in safety.

Eastern Kansas was overrun with General Price's soldiers; and Lieutenant Ayer felt some uneasiness lest he should fall into the hands of these bushwhackers; for he had his commission and his discharge with him, and he knew that if he should be stopped and searched these evidences that he had been a Union soldier would very likely result in his death. As soon as he reached Council Grove he sent these papers home by mail. However, no further trouble was encountered. At Kansas City, with a population at that time of three or four thousand, he took a steamboat to Leavenworth. From there he went to St. Joe over a little branch railroad. On all the principal bridges he noticed that there were blockhouses where soldiers were stationed on guard. After he had crossed the Mississippi at Quincy, Ayer put his six-shooter into his satchel. During the fight with the Indians five or six arrows had lodged in the coach he was riding in. He selected one of these as a souvenir; and, after breaking off the shaft, he put the remnant on the outside of his satchel. But it was stolen while he was en route for home on the Burlington Railroad.

Ayer had supposed that the money he had saved while he was a lieutenant would be enough to pay the expense of his trip home. But the fare from Fort Craig to Chicago was four hundred dollars; he had had unexpected delays after he reached Kansas City; and he had bought a suit of clothes in that metropolis. As the outcome of all this, he had only a dollar and eighty cents left when he reached Chicago. But at the station he was so fortunate as to meet Arthur Hobart, a good friend of his who had been a conductor on the Northwestern when the young adventurer left home. Hobart was now a superintendent; and, as the Ayer family, by virtue of the fact that they operated the railway house at Harvard, were entitled to free transportation, this friend gave him a pass to Harvard. At eleven o'clock the night of July 1, 1864, four years and two months after he left the paternal roof, he entered the door once more—amid a tumult of rejoicing.

CHAPTER V

Getting Under Way

WHEN Edward Ayer returned to his home town after an absence of four years and two months, he was a young man of mark. Not yet twenty-three years of age, he had traveled far and had seen much. On foot, on horseback, in wagon and stage, by railway and sea he had compassed the whole circuit of the mountains and plains of the great West and Southwest. He had tales to tell

"Of moving accidents by flood and field."

He was a veteran soldier, and he had won the right to be addressed as *Lieutenant*. He had secured little schooling but much education. He possessed neither silver nor gold nor real estate; but what a wealth of adventure, romance, and solid achievement he had to his credit!

What the gallant son lacked in worldly goods the generous father at once supplied by turning over to him a third interest in the little store at Harvard. It was a sudden transition from the tented field and the wide, wild, active West to the humdrum trivialities of trade in a small town; but Ayer was no longer a boy; he was an energetic, ambitious young man; and he threw himself heart and soul into his business. From the very first he showed himself to be a man of vision and daring, as well as of force and indefatigable industry. The management of the store was not enough to engage fully his mind and energy. He was not one to be "cabin'd, cribb'd, confin'd" within the four walls of a country store; and, as a natural consequence, he very soon began to branch out into other larger activities.

At that time the railroads were burning nothing but wood in their engines. Ayer began to buy up woodlands, and to chop the timber into cordwood, which he sold to the Chicago and Northwestern Railway Company. By the time he had been home two years, he was doing an extensive business and was working very hard. About seven miles from his home he had a wood lot where he was employing sixty or seventy choppers. This wood was delivered at the railroad several miles distant. Ayer had to be down at this timber tract early of a winter morning, no matter how cold the weather. The supervision of this work and the management of the store at the same time were over-taxing his strength.

One of the teamsters who was drawing wood for him at this time was Lot Smith, a strapping young fellow, eighteen years of age, six feet and one inch in height, and two hundred pounds in weight. Lot's sister had crossed the Plains with Ayer and had been exceedingly kind to him; and it was his way to return benefits to those who befriended him and to all who were bound to them by the bonds of consanguinity, even unto the third and fourth generation. He was, therefore, deeply interested in Lot—particularly as the boy's father was dead, and he was a strong, somewhat turbulent, undisciplined youth. Of course at that time nearly every one drank more or less, and as the town was near, with its barrooms and taverns, Lot sometimes got into trouble with the rough fellows he met in these drinking places. Priding himself on his athletic prowess and fistic skill, he never tried to avoid a fight. As a result of all this, Mr. Ayer was much concerned about him at times, and anxious to do something for the young fellow that would put him in the way of a career worthy of his great ability.

The young contractor determined to give Lot a big chance. Meeting him one day while he was teaming, Mr. Ayer asked,

"Lot, how much are you making?"

The young fellow replied, "Thirty dollars a month."

"Well," said Ayer, "I would like to do something for you, and I think I will give you a trial. I need some one here to keep the time of these men, see that they do their work right, and that the wood is properly piled. You send your team home and let a boy take care of it. I will give you thirty dollars a month and board. It will be your duty to take charge of these men, keep their time, measure their wood for them, and give them orders."

Lot said, "I'd like the job, Mr. Ayer, but I don't think I could do that."

Ayer replied, "I know you can do it, Lot, and I will take you into my employ under one condition, and that is, that you promise me you will never touch another drop of intoxicating liquor until I tell you you can. And if you will do your best, Lot, I am quite satisfied I can make a good, strong, business man out of you."

He replied, "Mr. Ayer, if you will do that for me, I can't tell you what I will do for you—I will be your slave."

"No, I don't want anything of that kind, but we'll start in right now."

Lot agreed and sent his team home.

Mr. Ayer started the young fellow at thirty dollars a month and all expenses. He developed very fast. He had a fine mind, overpowering energy, strict integrity, and, indeed, every quality that goes to make up a first class business man. Within a few years Mr. Ayer trusted everything to him. He went away when he chose and knew that his affairs would not suffer. All the railroad men loved Lot. Presidents and managers respected him as Ayer's representative; and for many years, indeed, until Lot died in the prime of his manhood, the relationship between the two men was most agreeable and satisfactory. He became one of the leading business men of the region; and later, for fifteen years, he had entire charge of the tie business that Mr. Ayer had built up during the '70's and '80's.

The relation between employer and manager with respect to salary was a strange one. Nothing was ever said about salary from the time that Mr. Ayer started Lot at thirty dollars a month in 1866, until 1886. At the end of each year Lot would simply ask:

"What shall I credit up to myself?"

The year 1886 had been a big one in the tie business, and Mr. Ayer had made much money. One evening about the close of the year as the two men were driving home together, Mr. Ayer said as he stopped at Lot's house to let him out:

"Lot, we have had a fine year."

"Yes," the other man responded.

"But for the next five years we are going to have hard times," Ayer continued. "Lot, you are getting twelve thousand dollars a year, and you have your house and your horses and are spending six or seven thousand a year. Whatever the times are like, I want you to feel perfectly free to go right on living as you have been. No matter how hard the times are, you will get ten thousand; and if they improve, your salary will be advanced accordingly."

"No," said Lot, "I won't have it."

For a moment Mr. Ayer was somewhat staggered.

"Well, why not?" he asked.

"See here, Old Man (he always called Mr. Ayer "Old Man"), I have been with you now for twenty years, and I'm going to stay with you all my life, and nothing can stop it. I would never think of leaving you. It is true that I am spending six or seven thousand dollars a year, and it seems necessary for me to do that. But it is just as necessary for you to spend fifty thousand a year as it is for me to spend seven thousand. Do you suppose, if we have hard times (and I know we will), that I want you to put your hand into the money you have

saved to pay me? Not much! If we have bad times, I will take
an economical living out of your business; and, if the times
are good, I'll get all of your money that I deserve and more
besides.   Don't let you and me ever talk about this salary
question again."

But we have outrun the thread of our narrative. For a
young man to get under way requires something more than
industry and business success. Now came love and marriage.
Emma Burbank enters the story. She was a stranger in this
western world. Born in Lowell, Massachusetts, also bred and
educated in the East, she had spent much of her childhood
amid scenes of New England rural beauty. It was this girlhood environment which gave her that great love of nature
that filled her after life with so much joy as she traveled the
wide world over with her husband. Though her father was in
modest circumstances, she had been tenderly reared. Mr.
Burbank moved to Rochester, New York when his daughter
was in her early girlhood. Here she attended a select school
for young ladies, and later entered the Benedict and Satterlee
Collegiate Institute of Rochester. She stood at the head of
her class in Latin, and discovered she had a bent for foreign
languages. This bent she was to develop later, and put to good
use in connection with her wide foreign travel and in the
translation of certain rare books in French and Spanish that
her husband added to the collections he made in the years they
were together.

She was a shy and solitary girl, and had few playmates;
and being born late in the life of her parents, grew up in intimate companionship with elderly people, taking little part in
the ordinary gayeties of young people. When Abner Burbank
—called by a son who had married a sister of Edward Ayer—
moved to Harvard, the home town of the Ayers, his daughter
was just entering young womanhood.

Harvard seemed dull and dreary; studious and ambitious Emma Burbank desired to go on with her music and the languages. But as there were no classes to attend, she took up her reading again, as she had always been an ardent reader of all the books she could acquire—good, indifferent perhaps, never bad, thanks to her training. So she had experiences varied in their kind, and ideals as alluring as those that perpetually accompanied the footsteps of the adventurous Edward Ayer.

Her reading gave her much to dream about, though little about heroes. She found an old copy of Washington Irving's *Tales of the Alhambra* which she read and re-read with the greatest delight, and she decided that life would never be complete or hold any joy for her until she could travel in those enchanted countries across the water (especially Spain) and wander by moonlight, alone—she did not picture a hero; heroes rarely had a part in her dreams—and hear the splashing of the water into the basin of the Fountain in the Court of the Lions at the Alhambra. Of course she knew this could never, never come to pass. Strange to say, it did happen, as many another dream had its fulfillment in her after life; and she walked by moonlight, not alone, but with a greater hero than any she had ever read about—through the enchanting halls of *The Alhambra!*

It was about the time the Burbanks came to Harvard that Edward Ayer returned from his adventurous life in the Far West. But not until Emma Burbank had been in Harvard some weeks did she meet the vivid and dominant lieutenant. Naturally she had wished to see this young hero of Indian-fighting on the Plains. When the opportunity came, she was disappointed. He did not look at all as she imagined a hero should. The days went by, and she had forgotten all about Mr. Ayer, when one day in the early spring of 1865 he came to call on her father. After this he called rather often, and while he talked with the parents he *looked* at the daughter!

One day after the young man had left, Miss Burbank said to her father: "People talk about that Mr. Ayer so much. I don't see anything so wonderful in him! He is ordinary looking, and is so brown! And he is so careless in his dress. His clothes are very ill-fitting."

"Silly child!" the father chided, rather sternly, "don't judge Edward Ayer by his clothes. He is just home from army life in the West. He has been a long time on the Plains, and fought with the Indians on his way home. Have you looked at his eyes? They are honest and bright. He looks one in the face when one is talking to him. He has nothing to conceal! They show he has intelligence and great force of character, and he is going to make his mark in the world, I can tell you!"

Edward Ayer kept on calling, and Emma Burbank ceased to wonder. The inevitable occurred, for the young man was in love now; and though there were obstacles, obstacles always fared badly when they got into the pathway of Edward Everett Ayer. The young lady's reluctance was finally overcome, and in September, 1865, there was a happy marriage in the Burbank home. In temper, training, and natural bent there were striking differences between these two strong, highly endowed personalities; but there were also deep ties of affection and understanding that throughout life drew them together in a rare comradeship of purpose, interest, and achievement. And so, for nearly sixty-two years, they found joy in each other's companionship, and pursued ardently like aims and like enjoyments.

Ayer's business was constantly expanding. One day in 1866 he was in Chicago in connection with his business of supplying cordwood to the Northwestern Railroad. In the course of conversation Mr. Brewer, the purchasing agent of the road, told Ayer he was going to Iowa to let some tie contracts for the Iowa division. Ayer said to him:

"Brewer, if you don't find anyone who meets your terms, I

will take that contract and get out the ties on terms that will be satisfactory to you."

Sometime later Brewer recalled him to Chicago and told him that the road wanted sixty thousand ties delivered at Clinton, Iowa, during the coming year. He offered to pay sixty cents apiece for these ties, naming, of course, the different kinds of wood that he was willing to accept. He expected them to come from the Wisconsin River or from other tributaries of the Mississippi. Ayer at once went up on the St. Paul Railroad, west of Madison, along the Mississippi, and made contracts for the desired material with people who were used to handling ties on the Wisconsin River, and running them down the Mississippi in rafts. He did not have enough money to finance the whole deal, so, as soon as the ties were piled on the banks of the river ready to be rafted, the Northwestern advanced about the amount of money needed to pay for this part of the undertaking. Ayer made occasional trips over the ground with the company inspector, inspecting the ties. His venture turned out well, and, upon delivering the material the following summer, he made a fair profit. This was his first tie contract. It was entered into in 1867, and was renewed at various times for more than a generation.

Mr. Ayer was very proud of his long and honorable record of business dealing with the Northwestern Railroad, and he had a copy of his contract framed and hung on the wall in the main office of the Ayer and Lord Tie Company. The document hangs there to this day, with an interesting annotation in Mr. Ayer's handwriting under date of July 1, 1903.

CHICAGO & NORTH-WESTERN RAILWAY Co.
TIE CONTRACT
THIS ARTICLE OF AGREEMENT, entered into this twenty fifth day of October, 1869, BETWEEN Edward E. Ayer, of Harvard, Illinois, party of the first part, and the Chicago & North-Western Railway Company, by R. W.

Hamer, General Fuel Agent, party of the second part, WIT-NESSETH, That said party of the first part hereby agrees to sell and deliver the party of the second part, subject to directions from the General Fuel Agent, on the line of the Chicago & North-Western Railway Company, on the Iowa Division of same between Clinton and Council Bluffs by the first day of June, 1870, fifty thousand hewn Rail Road Cross Ties; said Ties to be of good quality of White and Burr Oak, Red Elm, Rock Elm, Black Walnut & Butternut in the following proportions viz. the whole number of Butternut and Black Walnut not to exceed ten (10) thousand in all, and the balance to be of oak and elm as specified, all to be cut out of sound, straight, thrifty timber, to be eight feet long, measuring half the kerf; to be six inches thick, and six inches face and upwards in the narrowest place, on either face side, between the bark, and to be truly lined in finishing so that the two opposite faces may be straight and parallel with each other, and to be piled on ground at or above the grade of the Railway Track. The said ties to be subject to the inspection and count of the above named General Fuel Agent, or any authorized Agent the party of the second part may designate. It is further agreed and understood that in case the ties delivered by the party of the first part do not fill the specifications, &c., as hereinbefore named, the party of the second part may at their option receive all or such portions of those which are delivered as they see fit; and the count and inspection thereof by the person or persons hereinbefore designated, shall be final and conclusive.

For and in Consideration of Which, the party of the second part hereby agrees to pay the party of first part ($.52½) fifty two and One half cents per tie, current funds, and in the following manner, viz: Monthly as delivered. It is hereby expressly stipulated that if the said party of the first part owing to competition by purchasers or other railway companies cannot buy the above ties along the line of said Iowa Division at fifty-one (51) cents each or under, he shall have the privilege of delivering said ties at Clinton, Iowa, via the Mississippi River at fifty-five (55) cents per tie in the water or fifty-seven (57) cents per tie delivered by side of the railroad track.

In Witness Whereof, we hereunto affix our hands and seals, the day and year first above written.

R. W. HAMER
General Fuel Agent   [SEAL]
EDWARD E. AYER   [SEAL]

The foregoing contract is hereby approved by me:

A. V. PIERCE, V.P.
C. & N.W.R'Y Co.

(*Notation in handwriting by Edward E. Ayer.*)

Third contract made by me with N.W.R'y—First one in 1867.

EDWARD E. AYER.
July 1, 1903.

Have had it ever since and had it through Ayer & Lord Tie Company until 1908.

Soon after he began selling ties to the Northwestern, he made a contract to deliver ties to the Union Pacific Railroad. In 1867, while looking over his business in Iowa with his superintendent, he went on west to Omaha just to see how this city looked now after six years, the time that had elapsed since he stopped at Omaha on his way across the Plains. By this time the Union Pacific had been completed to a point about three hundred and fifty miles west of Omaha. He saw a pile of ties as he was looking about, and he began to investigate, with an eye to business. Going to the superintendent's office, he introduced himself, and the result was that the company intimated that he might sell them about sixty thousand ties to be shipped to Chicago. He returned to Chicago, looked the situation over, and then went back to Omaha and made a bid for the contract. The bid was accepted, and the particular ties that he sold them at that time were used in the original construction of the Union Pacific out of Cheyenne.

Mr. Ayer's business now expanded rapidly. Almost from the beginning of his entrance into the tie-contracting business he had been so fortunate as to secure the friendship and finan-

cial backing of Mr. George Sturges, a leading Chicago banker
of forty years ago. Mr. Sturges had confidence in Mr. Ayer
from the first and took deep interest in him. As long as he
lived, he did everything in his power to aid him in any business undertaking he had at heart. Mr. Ayer declared that he
was under more obligation to Mr. Sturges for financial favors
than any other man in the world. The late John J. Mitchell
told the writer that Mr. Sturges had not only been the man
who had helped Ayer financially, but had also been his, Mitchell's staunch friend and backer in his early business career.

It was not by chance that the young contractor built up his
credit. The following characteristic incidents will show how it
was that he was able, early, to win the confidence and unquali-
fied support of bankers and other big business men with whom
he had dealings.

He relates that in the days when he gave much of his time
to shooting as a recreation, he received a telegram on one
occasion from Mr. Marvin Hughitt, President of the Northwestern Railroad, requesting him to come to Chicago. He
complied, and upon reaching Chicago was told that Mr.
Charles Osborne (a prominent stockbroker of New York,
and at that time one of the Executive Committee of the
Northwestern Railroad) was coming west with a couple of
friends. Mr. Hughitt said that, as far as possible, he wanted
these gentlemen to see the entire country that was tributary
to the Northwestern road. As they wanted to do some shooting, he asked Mr. Ayer to take his (Hughitt's) private car,
with a baggage car and engine, for a ten-day trip over the
Northwestern road, seeing to it that they should get not only
a good idea of the road and its supporting territory, but as
much good shooting as possible. After about a week the party
got up into Minnesota and saw the splendid expanse of unoc-
cupied territory extending from one hundred to two hundred
miles west of Winona. Osborne became very much interested.

He was surprised to see into what a rich and undeveloped country the road reached, and he began to make pools as he went along. He immediately determined to get large interests in this property, and two or three times a day he would telegraph to New York, buying, and making pools.

"He seemed fond of me," said Mr. Ayer. "We were giving him a good time." He said to me one day:

" 'Ayer, this stock will double in a year. You ought to buy a couple of thousand shares or more; it will make you a lot of money.'

" 'Mr. Osborne, I haven't the money.'

" 'Well, that's all right; if you want a couple of thousand shares, I will buy them for you and carry them at the regular interest.' "

Ayer replied: "Mr. Osborne, I am worth about forty thousand dollars; I am in the tie business on these railroads; it's going to be an enormous business; I'm going to get rich in it, and nothing on earth can prevent it. To do this, I must have the absolute confidence of my banker. He knows that I never speculate on anything outside of my business; and it wouldn't do for me at all, for if I should speculate even once, it would shake his confidence, and that I have got to have unshaken."

"Well, if you made a hundred thousand dollars on this trip, you wouldn't need your banker."

"Oh, Mr. Osborne," said Ayer, "I can this very day see myself borrowing in the future a million dollars at a time, and I shouldn't wonder if it might be twice that much. It wouldn't do at all. I am so firmly grounded in this idea, Mr. Osborne, that I will say to you that if you positively agreed to make one hundred thousand dollars for me on this trip between now and the time we get back to Chicago, I wouldn't make the investment."

"You're a curious chap," said Osborne.

"Well, I expect I am," Ayer replied.

About 1877 there was another experience, very similar
to the one just related, that shows how firmly Mr. Ayer was
fixed in his determination not to speculate outside of his own
line of business. Having some money to spare, he, with two
other men, had built a malt house in Harvard. The time came
when the concern wanted two hundred carloads of barley
from California. The rate on barley from California was one
dollar and seventy-five cents a hundredweight—so high as
almost to prohibit the shipping of grain from that quarter.
Mr. Ayer went to Mr. Wheeler of the freight department of
the Northwestern Railroad and told him that it was entirely
out of the question to pay the required rate, but that, if he
could secure a rate of a cent and a quarter a pound, he would
ship two hundred carloads. Mr. Wheeler said he would telegraph Stubbs (Traffic Manager of the Union Pacific) and
ask him what he would do.

Two or three days later he telegraphed Mr. Ayer at Harvard: "Stubbs wants to know if I recommend the rate. This
is virtually stating that he will grant it if the Northwestern
wants it. I am going to California day after tomorrow, and
I will take it up with him."

Mr. Ayer took a fifteen thousand dollar draft and started
for California on the same train with Mr. Wheeler. When
they were about one day out of San Francisco, they received a
copy of the *California Bulletin* and read that the railroad had
finally come to its senses and had reduced the rate of barley
fifty cents a hundred. This, of course, instantly put the price
of barley up fifty cents a hundred. When Mr. Ayer got to San
Francisco, he was talking the matter over with A. N. Towne,
General Superintendent of the Central Pacific:

"It was mean of you to put that rate up," he remarked.

"You ought to have bought the barley before you put in a
complaint about the rate," Towne replied. "How much
money have you got with you, Ayer?"

"Fifteen thousand dollars," was the reply.

Towne took a letter out of his pocket (it was from the superintendent of the great mines in Virginia City, Nevada), and showed it to him, after folding it so that the name of the writer could not be seen. The letter stated that a big body of ore had been found, and that he, the superintendent, was buying all the stock he could get. Said Mr. Towne to Mr. Ayer:

"I have bought several hundred shares today, and if you want a couple of thousand shares, you can get them."

Mr. Ayer replied: "No, Towne, I can't speculate, and I'm not going to. I am quite a borrower, and I must not speculate outside of my regular business."

"Well, that's all right," his friend answered, "but you would certainly make a lot of money on this."

"I know that, of course," was Mr. Ayer's rejoinder, "for no man ever had a solider tip than that; but, no, I can't do it."

Mr. Ayer stayed in California about a week. Mr. Towne had bought his stock at $57 a share. Before Mr. Ayer returned to Chicago, one half of it had been disposed of at $425 a share, and four weeks later the other half was sold at $700 a share. In commenting upon this incident, Mr. Ayer said:

"I never cared any more about that than I would to drop a three-quarter-smoked cigar."

By the time Mr. Ayer had reached the age of thirty, that is, by 1871, he was selling almost a million ties a year, and his business was constantly expanding. The decade between 1865 and 1875 was marked by tremendous activity on his part. He knew almost every great railroad officer in the West, and he was very much liked by everyone with whom he had dealings. During these years he was traveling almost incessantly. He averaged 180,000 miles a year on the railroad, and spent 150 nights of the 365 on Pullman sleepers. Up to about 1880 he had continued to live in Harvard and to carry on his enterprises from there; but as his business was increasing rapidly, and was centering more and more in Chicago, he now established an office near the river in the lumber district of that city.

At that time three concerns in the city were handling practically all the railroad ties supplied to the roads that operated through Chicago; and there was an arrangement among these three companies—in the nature of a pool—whereby they received equal shares of the business. As these concerns had been in business a good while and were well established, Mr. Ayer well knew that he would have to fight for a place in the game. Within two years he had gained entrance to the pool and was getting his full share of the tie business. Indeed, he was doing twice as much business as any other member of the combine. In consequence, by 1883, though there were only four dealers, the business was now apportioned in five parts, Mr. Ayer having two parts and each of the other concerns one part.

The story of Mr. Ayer's success as a business man must be interrupted at this point in order that we may trace the beginnings of his avocation—the fascinating and absorbing art of Collecting—a pursuit that was to yield him continued joy throughout his long life, and ever-increasing honor after death.

CHAPTER VI

Beginnings as a Collector

SURELY collectors, like poets, are born, not made. We have no record of Edward Ayer's boyhood exploits as a collector of bird's eggs and arrow heads, but can one doubt that the boy was father of the man? He was a country lad, familiar with woods and field; there was the site of an Indian village only five miles from his home; and many times he must have seen the tree in which, according to report, the son of Chief Big Foot had been buried. So we take it for granted that his pockets were not infrequently stuffed with specimens, and that somewhere in garret, shed or storeroom he had the beginnings of a museum or a menagerie.

At any rate Edward Everett Ayer became one of the great collectors of the world. His intimate friends, themselves travelers, scholars, and "museum men," one and all, declared that he was a natural born collector. Collecting was his chief recreation and delight. Art and antiquity excited his highest enthusiasm, and he had a keen scent for relics and articles of exceptional literary or historic value. In view of his limited educational opportunities in youth, it is surprising that he was able to find his way so unerringly into the hidden treasure houses of beauty and intellect. He rarely if ever, made a mistake. A sort of sixth sense seemed to direct him toward things rare and exceptional, and to guard him against impostors and spurious specimens. He knew whom to trust and was wise enough to accept the guidance of approved experts, and so to deepen and broaden his culture.

After he had become widely known as a collector, he said in explanation of his purposes and incentives:

"There is one thought that has always been uppermost in my mind since I began to prosper; namely, an intense thankfulness for such prosperity. As I always deeply regretted the lack of opportunities in youth for a liberal education, I determined, if my prosperity continued, to do something that would give the boy coming after me a better chance for an education than I had been able to get. That has been the prime moving thought in my work in the Newberry Library, the Field Museum of Natural History, and the little I have been able to do for the Art Institute, and the Thomas Orchestra, and other efforts—to show my gratitude to my Maker, my Country, and my fellow men."

Mr. Ayer was not merely a collector; he was besides, an eminent public-spirited citizen and practical man of affairs. The leading captains of industry of his day were his intimate friends. He was everywhere counted as one of them. Had he been interested solely or primarily in the accumulation of money, he would, no doubt, have ranked with the chief multimillionaires of the generation that has just passed. Mr. D. M. Riordan, now deceased, one of his close business associates, wrote thus glowingly of his place in the business world:

Edward E. Ayer stood high. Figuratively speaking, he was a tall man—a man sun-crowned, with head and heart and character above the fog. Wherever I happened to meet him, whether on the frontier, or in the heart of busiest cities, he loomed large. To me he partook of the majesty of that splendid peak in the San Francisco Mountains north of Flagstaff, Agassiz. He is to be named with such men as Henry C. Nutt, William B. Strong, and others of high import in the past generations in Boston; with such men as Lyman J. Gage, and Marshall Field, and others of Chicago; with A. A. Robinson of the Santa Fe and D. B. Robinson of the Atlantic and Pacific; with Arthur G. Wells, George Sturges, and Robert T. Lincoln. All of these men were men of high vision, great ability and rare personal worth in their respective lines

of effort; and they stood high in the communities in which
they lived. It was well known his contracts were always kept,
but he always managed, somehow, to do a little more than
he agreed to do, to put some finishing gracious touch to every
transaction. He has been an inspiration and an example, not
only to me, but to many, and his influence will continue long
after all of us now here are gathered to our fathers.

But, as has been said, it was not Mr. Ayer's ambition to
grow superlatively rich. He desired rather to endow coming
generations with the imperishable riches of art and learning;
and it was to that end that he directed his splendid energies.
In the process of inspired getting and generous giving he came
to be a widely educated man—a lover of the true, the beautiful, and the good. He kept in contact with "the best that has
been thought and said in the world"; he walked constantly in
the company of men of genius, specialists, thinkers, artists,
musicians, and poets; he visited art galleries, libraries, and
cathedrals; and, carrying with him unconsciously the flavor of
these refining associations, he came to be known everywhere
as a wise and cultivated man, a charming companion, a
fascinating raconteur.

He did not at first have the definite intention of becoming
an outstanding collector. But he found this avocation an absorbing one, and the more he gratified his desire, the wider
his fancy ranged, and the warmer waxed his enthusiasm.
Says Mr. J. Christian Bay, in an illuminating article on the
personality of Mr. Ayer: "There was in Mr. Ayer's admiration of the life of birds and other animals, in his explorations
of Indian relics, and of cultural monuments of the past, an
element of reverence. It was felt in his speech and glance, in
his estimate of the value of organized collections for educational purposes: the seriousness and awe of the marvels in
nature and history became infectious because of the youthful
intensity pervading his whole being." Side by side with this

comment on the mental attitude and genius of our great collector the following incident may appropriately be set down.
One day when Mr. Ayer was in conversation with two other
collectors "the question arose at what moment the collector
finds his greatest pleasure. The first said at the moment of
discovery; the second, the moment of acquisition; but to Mr.
Ayer, it was when the treasure is placed where the public may
have access to it."

During his trip across the Plains in 1860, and subsequently,
during his army service in Arizona and New Mexico, Edward
Ayer had seen much of the Indians and had become deeply
interested in everything that pertains to them. It followed
naturally that his first acquisitions were articles purchased
from the Indians. About 1871 he went to Denver for the first
time; and on his way out, in Omaha, and later in Denver, he
found large quantities of Indian paraphernalia for sale. In
those early days all the Prairie Indians, and indeed the Indians
throughout the West, had costumes of featherwork and beadwork in abundance; and they were now bringing these articles
into the stores to sell. Mr. Ayer bought a considerable amount
of such material on this trip—enough to fill two bushel bags.
It was chiefly Indian beadwork and garments made of buckskin beautifully ornamented with beads. At this time he
bought few weapons. Later he did secure many arrows,
spears, shields, and tomahawks—in fact everything that had
to do with the life of the North American Indian. From this
time on he became an eager and discriminating collector of
Indian relics and handiwork.

After a long absence he visited the Plains again in 1880,
and at that time was struck with the fact that everything pertaining to Indian life was much changed. The game had vanished, and the Indians dressed differently from what they did
in the old days. His observant eye saw that aboriginal life
in America would soon be a thing of the past, so he set dili-

gently to work collecting Indian material, wherever it could be found.

Just about this time he began to make frequent journeys into Mexico in connection with his business as a tie contractor. On horseback trips into out of the way places in Mexico, he found opportunities to acquire rare Indian relics, curios, and specimens of Indian handiwork. With mischievous glee he related how, on one occasion when he had been in Mexico accompanied by Mrs. Ayer, just as he was about to step aboard the train to return North, his friend D. B. Robinson, handed him the still moist scalp of a slaughtered Indian that he had got possession of in some way. This reeking trophy, with a bit of paper wrapped around it, he placed in his wife's handbag. Inured as she was to the strange ways of a collector, the discovery of this very unusual relic somewhat unnerved Mrs. Ayer; and then and there America's foremost collector of Indian remains was made aware that there should be temperance in all things. No doubt Mrs. Ayer's housewifely feelings were sometimes shocked by the exuberant ardor of her husband in the display of his trophies and his plunder. Here is her colorful account of one experience:

"He had been away one time longer than usual. After he had been at home some days, one morning a wagon came to the back door of our house, and the driver began to unload boxes, bundles, and bales. Mr. Ayer directed that these should be brought at once to our living room. All of these were thrown down there on the floor. Mr. Ayer quickly slipped off the cords and burst open the boxes to get at the treasures. There came to view all sorts of Indian work—belts, moccasins, red flannel bands decorated in gayly colored beads, deerskin garments, also embroidered and fringed feathered-headdresses, silver bracelets, necklaces of curious designs, wonderful baskets in all sizes, Navajo blankets in blue, crimson, and scarlets, and many other barbaric objects. Mr. Ayer rubbed his hands in glee over this collection, the largest he had yet acquired."

Said Mr. Ayer, "In 1887 I went to Alaska, sailing with old Captain Carroll, at that time the great navigator of the Northwest. It was the first trip that season for the old *Ancona,* so the Captain had to put in at every bay where there was any cannery, or fishery, or other establishment in need of supplies. He was good enough to get me out night or day at every Indian village; and I had good luck, for I had two cabins full of Indian stuff. It was fortunate that the boat was destroyed later, because after that trip it was impossible to get any passengers within two or three cabins of where my relics had been stowed."

Asked concerning personal experiences with the Indians on his various business and recreational expeditions, he said: "My personal experiences were always interesting. I very rarely purchased relics through chiefs, though; mostly through dealers. For instance, on our trip (to show how little these traders thought of those beautiful things at that time), there was a man named Carl Spoon, quite a character on the Northwest Coast, who was head of the land department of Killisnoo. He was on my ship, and he got interested when I was buying these costumes and relics, so he said,

" 'Lord, up in our loft we have any quantity of these things, and you can get all you want.'

"I went up and got all that three or four men could carry, expecting of course, to pay for it. When it came to paying he said,

" 'Nothing.'

"They would really be worth several thousand dollars now. He was a very fine chap."

Rather early the Ayers had established their beautiful summer home at Lake Geneva, and it was here that Mr. Ayer now began to display his wealth of Indian material to the

numerous friends who enjoyed the hospitality of this extraordinary country place. Close to the house he had built a
bowling alley. This was now turned into a museum. He was
continually augmenting his already remarkable collection. He
bought everything he could lay his hands on—blankets in
many colors and designs, baskets of beautiful and curious
weaves, and even three or four totem poles, which he piled up
against the barn. Later, after he began to travel in Egypt, he
cut off a portion of the bowling alley as a depository for the
rare Egyptian antiquities he brought back with him—ala-
baster canopic jars from tombs, ushabti figures, scarabs, etc.
Eventually, all of these objects both of Indian and Egyptian
origin were presented to the Field Museum, where they may
still be seen and enjoyed.

Mr. Ayer, about the same time that he began to buy Indian
paraphernalia, began collecting books. The more he saw of
the Indians, the more he wanted to know about their origin,
their prehistoric life, their primitive customs, and their first
contacts with white men. It was to satisfy this curiosity that he
now set about the purchase of books. It was probably just
about the time that he moved from Harvard to Chicago, in
1880, that he made definite choice of the North American
Indians as a prime subject of inquiry. He declares that his
whole career as a collector was based on the desire to know
who was the first white man in every five hundred square
miles of North America, how he treated the Indians he found
there, how they treated him, who followed in exploration, and
what became of the Indians. This basic aim he eventually
realized: the Ayer Collection in the Newberry Library
answers all the large questions posed above.

At first he had no idea that he would gather a great library
of American history such as now perpetuates his name in the
Newberry Library, Chicago. But, as has been said, this all
came about in the natural order, since, when he began to get

together his collection of Indian paraphernalia, he wanted at once to get books that told about the people. In 1887 when he built his house in Chicago, he included in his plans a basement library twenty by thirty feet in dimensions. This he called his Indian Library, and the shelves were soon filled with volumes on Indians and ornithology. The ordinary books were kept in cases in the hall upstairs.

The marvelous Prescott volumes, his first and most prized acquisition, inspired him while still a young man to provide himself with a personal, or reading library. At the beginning he was particularly attracted to the reading of European history. He read Gibbon's *The Decline and Fall of the Roman Empire* and found this much to his taste. When he got down to the time of Mohammed, he was deeply interested in the propagation of the Mohammedan religion by means of the sword. He next read *The Conquest of Granada*, and this introduced him to Ferdinand and Isabella, and Columbus. Luther and the Reformation next claimed his attention, nor was he satisfied until he had read several accounts of the Reformation and had familiarized himself with the mighty figure of Luther. Then he turned to accounts of Philip II and the Wars in the Netherlands, making the acquaintance for the first time of the Spanish generals Alva and Palma, and with William of Orange. Since England took an active interest in the Wars of the Netherlands, he now found himself face to face with Queen Elizabeth; and prompted by his newly aroused interest, he read several histories of England, closing this cycle of his early reading with the gigantic Allison's *History of England* in thirty-one volumes.

Other books that he read during these ambitious years—books that are included among the one thousand volumes that made up his private library—are Guizot's *History of France*, Lord's *Beacon Lights of History*, the *Iliad* and the *Odyssey*, Plutarch's *Lives*, Strickland's *Queens of England*, the works of Shakespeare, Burns, Byron, Sir Walter Scott, Thackeray, Dickens, Lever, Jane Austen, Charles Lamb, James Fenimore Cooper, J. G. Holland, Holmes, Mrs. Jameson's works on Art, and many other books of like character. These books, all acquired by 1880, he read for the most part on his travels during those early years when he was building up his business and spending just about half of his time on railroad trains.

While Mr. Ayer's original design had to do chiefly with Indian material, as the years went by the stream of his purpose —like the abounding Nile—quite overflowed its banks. Eventually he ransacked the world for treasures to his taste, adding to his stores of Indian baskets, beads, blankets, costumes, and weapons of every sort gathered in America, Korans and jewels from Africa, pewters, paintings, and porcelains from Europe, and books, arms, laces, tapestries, and manuscripts from everywhere. His purpose grew until he added to his collection of books about the aborigines of North America, matchless source material dealing with the discovery, settlement, and early history of America; and with the habits, manners, languages, and history of the native races of the Hawaiian and Philippine Islands. In the chapter on *The Field Museum* space will be given to Mr. Ayer's work as a collector of Egyptian and Roman antiques, but it seems appropriate here to relate the fascinating events in connection with the acquisition of his material dealing with the Philippine Islands.

When news of the Battle of Manila flashed around the world on May 1, 1898, Mr. Ayer was in Venice. The following day he went to Rome. No sooner was he settled in his hotel than he sat down and wrote letters to his numerous agents in Europe, South America, the United States, and other parts of North America requesting them to send him at Chicago lists of everything they had to sell concerning the Philippine Islands, whether printed or in manuscript. He stated in his letters that he would be back home within thirty days and that he would send them substantial orders. It took him two or three days to get all these letters off. He was frank enough to confess that if anyone had asked him two days before Dewey's victory where the Philippine Islands were, he would have answered, "In the Pacific Ocean." Up to May, 1898, so far as he knew, there had never been any particular demand for books on the Philippine Islands.

When he got back to Chicago, he found that a great many replies had come from his various agents. Indeed, there was on his desk a pile of letters almost a foot high. They came from Paris, London, Spain, and especially South America. With his librarian and his stenographer he set industriously about studying and sifting these lists of material. Within thirty days he had figured out what he wanted to buy. From the great number of titles that had been received, he drew up four lists, and these he sent off to four different agents or book-dealers in Europe and South America. Before many weeks had gone by, he was the possessor of the largest private collection of books on the Philippines to be found in North America.

Yet he was not quite satisfied, for in Chili there was a gentleman named Medina who had a remarkable collection on the Philippines. Mr. Ayer communicated with this man, and tried to buy his material. But he refused to sell. In the end, however, Mr. Ayer was triumphant. Two years after his first attempt to secure this South American collection, while in Paris, he was informed that Medina had brought his collection on the Philippines to Europe and had disposed of about half of the items to Mr. Ayer's agent in Paris and the other half to his agent in Madrid. He immediately went through the Paris material and bought every title that he did not already possess. This having been accomplished, within a day or two he went on to Madrid and bought everything there

that he did not already have. By this time it had become well
known wherever books on the Philippines were available that
Mr. Ayer was in the market for this material. The greatest
library on the Philippines at that time—more complete even
than Mr. Ayer's—was that which had been brought together
by the Barcelona Tobacco Company, in Barcelona. The members of this firm were dealing in Philippine tobacco, and in the
organization there were men of intelligence who had got together this notable library and had had it catalogued by
Retana. Concluding that the Philippine Islands were lost to
Spain for good, these tobacco merchants lost interest in the
Islands, and, as a matter of course, in the books and manuscripts they had been collecting. The result was that this rare
collection also came into the possession of the ever eager Chicago collector.

When Mr. J. A. Robertson, a distinguished scholar, and
Miss Emma Helen Blair of the Wisconsin Historical Society
decided to write an extended history of the Philippine Islands,
they used more than three hundred of Mr. Ayer's original
manuscripts. While their work in the preparation of this
monumental history was done mostly at Madison, in the Wisconsin Historical Society rooms, Mr. Robertson spent two
years in Spain, and during that time transcribed ten thousand
pages from the Spanish archives. Had he only known it, he
might have found his material much nearer home; for Mr.
Ayer had every book in the original that the author translated
for use in this great fifty-five volume history. It is, therefore,
manifest that the Ayer Collection is not only a notable one,
but a very useful one, to scholars and research workers. Even
to this day writers do not sufficiently realize the wealth of
source material that it contains.

From the time that Mr. Ayer began to collect material on
the Philippine Islands, he had sought the advice of Mr. Dean
Conant Worcester, a distinguished scholar, who went to the

Philippines as early as 1887 as a member of the Steere Scientific Expedition. He was one of the two men in the Menage Scientific Expedition to the Philippines in 1890. In 1899 he was appointed as a member of the United States Philippine Commission, and he later became Secretary of the Interior in the Philippine Insular Government. As a commissioner after the Spanish American War, he was concerned with the scientific and educational aspects of the work. He carried on various scientific experiments and came into contact with the wild peoples of the Islands. A good many years after the Philippines had come into our possession, Mr. Ayer visited the Islands and saw much of Mr. Worcester. One day the scientist was showing the collector his photographs of the primitive people. Mr. Ayer looked at one or two hundred of these pictures and then, naturally, grew tired.

"How many of these photographs have you?" he inquired.

Mr. Worcester had been there more than ten years by that time, and his reply was: "I have eight thousand photographs of the primitive peoples of the Philippines."

"How many linguistic groups do these pictures represent?" was the next question.

"Thirty-six," Mr. Worcester replied.

After a few minutes thought Mr. Ayer asked: "What will you charge to make me a copy of each one of your eight thousand photographs, say six inches square, with a little written sketch of each one of the linguistic groups beginning with the Tagalog Nation? I should want the account to cover six or seven typewritten pages descriptive of the various linguistic groups—their habitat, how they differ from the nomads, etc., etc. Then I should want you to take the first photograph you have of the Tagalogs and mark it "Number 1, Series 1, Tagalog" and describe it. The next oldest photograph would be "Number 2," and so on through all the photographs you have of the Tagalog Nation. What I should desire would be to have you indicate how each group differs from other linguistic groups, with a description of each race, and a long list of photographs to illustrate each group, by individual examples. What will you charge me to do that with eight thousand photographs?"

Mr. Worcester replied, "Four thousand dollars."

"All right! Commence right away, and finish the work as soon as you can."

Mr. Worcester did as he was requested. As soon as Mr. Ayer had received all the photographs, together with the accompanying scientific notes, he had each picture mounted on thin cardboard, the cards a little larger than the photographs, and these he placed in slip-cases in a box, two slip-cases to a box. It required forty-eight boxes to hold the collection. Said Mr. Ayer to the writer, after relating all these details:

"You can go into the Newberry Library today and take out any picture from the middle of one of those cases, and turn right to the catalogue and have it described in a minute. Or you can be reading in the catalogue of any one of the eight thousand photographs, and pull out the paper drawer and have the picture before you in an instant."

Mr. Ayer was president of the Field Museum at the time of the Spanish-American War, and soon after the Battle of Manila he sent two men to the Philippines as collectors for the Museum. As a consequence of his foresight, there was in the Field Museum, even before he secured his photographs, a fine collection of paraphernalia from the Islands. Just as rapidly as he received from Mr. Worcester the pictures with their accompanying descriptions, he sent them to the Museum and had them copied there; so now there is in the Field Museum one of the most complete and useful Philippine collections in the world.

In the Ayer Collection are two original diaries in the handwriting of José Rizal and eighteen letters written by him. In

view of this fact the Rizal Club of Chicago, in the autumn of
1927, made known to the Librarian its desire to present a
life-size bronze bust of Dr. Rizal to the Newberry Library.
The proffer was accepted by the Trustees; and at the annual
banquet of the Filipino Association of Chicago, at the La
Salle Hotel, on the evening of January 1, 1928, this gift was
presented by the President of the Rizal Club and was accepted by the Librarian, as the representative of the Trustees
of the Library. It is an excellent art production, executed by
Viuda é Hijos de Crispulo Zamora, Manila, upon the express
order of the Rizal Club of Chicago.

CHAPTER VII

Big Business

UP TO about 1878 all the railroad tie dealers and shippers considered Mr. Ayer a Northwestern man, for invariably he shipped his material over that road if it was possible to do so. As a result of his undeviating loyalty to the Northwestern he was not able to sell ties to the Southwestern roads. But late in the '70's Mr. Ayer's fast friend, Charles C. Wheeler, formerly with the Northwestern, was appointed general manager of the Santa Fe Railroad, and at once the whole situation changed. Mr. Ayer was given the opportunity to sell the Santa Fe all the material it wanted from Chicago. From this time on for many years he did an enormous business with the Santa Fe and, a little later, with the Mexican Central.

The construction of the Mexican Central was begun in 1881. The laying of the track was carried on simultaneously from El Paso on the north and the City of Mexico on the south. Mr. Ayer's first transaction with this road was a peculiar one. The company wanted ties shipped from Chicago for the part of the construction that was to start at El Paso. Mr. Ayer made a contract to supply the ties. The freight rate from Chicago to El Paso was so high that the ties could be secured only at great expense. Dry cedar ties were demanded —the driest that could be had. The best timber for this purpose was to be found in tracts through which the fires had run, for such timber was very dry and light, and would last a long time, even though the ties were placed on moist soil or buried in the earth. The purchasing agent bought seventy thousand ties from Mr. Ayer, to be delivered on the dock in Chicago.

The contract specified that the material must be of dead cedar and all dry. These ties did not look well, of course, but they were what the road bought and what it wanted. The ties were inspected in Chicago by an inspector selected by the railroad company, and each tie that was accepted as a good tie under this inspection Mr. Ayer paid for, to be shipped to the purchaser in El Paso.

The manager who was in charge of the building of the road was having some trouble with the chief owner of the property, Mr. Thomas Nickerson of Boston. So selecting three or four thousand of the worst of these ties, he piled them up to show to the Directors the first time they should come out as a sample of the sort of material Thomas Nickerson was sending him with which to build a railroad. The Directors went out to look over the road and were shown this pile of bad-looking railroad ties. Two of the Directors, Mr. L. G. Lighter and Mr. Calvin Fairbanks, were friends of Mr. Ayer, and he explained to them that he had nothing to do with the situation, that he had never seen the ties, that they had been delivered on the dock and inspected by the railroad's own inspectors, and that the company took only what it wanted. He explained, too, why this class of material had been purchased. Mr. Ayer later received a letter from Mr. Nickerson in which that gentleman stated that he was greatly disappointed with the material, and that he thought Mr. Ayer was responsible inasmuch as he (Mr. Ayer) should have given more personal attention to what was going on.

In his reply to the letter Mr. Ayer enclosed a copy of the contract, and a copy of the agreement with respect to the choice of an inspector. He stated, also, that he himself had paid for every tie that had been shipped. In conclusion he wrote: "If you feel, under the circumstances, that I am to blame in any way, make out a bill for what you think ought to be refunded on the contract. While you will see that there is no legal obligation on my part of any name or nature, and will realize that I was entirely blameless, still you may make a draft on me for anything you think fair." Mr. Nickerson made a draft on Mr. Ayer for nine hundred dollars, which was promptly paid. As a result of his manner of handling this deal, Mr. Ayer had the entire business of the Mexican Central during all the years they were building the road, and indeed, the business, also, in connection with the renewing of the ties, at least once. Moreover, from his Flagstaff mill, erected in 1882, he had the contract for the material required by the company for the building of its bridges, stations, and every thing of that sort. From first to last, he sold the Mexican Central, previous to the time that it began to secure ties in Mexico, six or seven million railroad ties.

"Wasn't that nine hundred dollars worth while?" Mr. Ayer asked with satisfaction as he concluded the narration of this characteristic incident.

Mr. Ayer always enjoyed doing business with the Mexican Central. He liked the leading officers of the road and was on excellent terms with them. The president of the company was Mr. Edward Jackson, and the general manager Mr. David McKenzie, a very witty Scotchman. Mr. Ayer enjoyed telling the following stories as examples of the good natured banter that was aimed at him by these gentlemen. There was nearly always a little dry rot in the center of a cedar tie, but if the affected part was small no attention was ever paid to it, since the tie never rotted from that point. Said General Manager McKenzie to President Jackson one day when Mr. Ayer was present:

"Mr. Jackson, of course Ayer is doing our business. No one seems able to get it away from him, and we don't want them to. I have thought of a scheme though, whereby I think Ayer can make twice the money on those ties that he is now earning without making the difference of a cent to us."

Jackson replied, "Well, Mr. McKenzie, we should like to have Mr. Ayer make more money if it doesn't cost us anything—what is this scheme?"

"Mr. Jackson, I have an idea that Mr. Ayer on his freight has a contract per tie. Don't you see, if we would let him put the little ties inside the big ones, that he could get two ties through for the same amount it costs for one, and we would lose nothing."

When the company decided to re-tie the road, Mr. Ayer went down to El Paso in a special car to meet Mr. McKenzie and go over the road with him. The trip to Mexico City required several days. All the way along they stopped now and then to examine the ties, trying to decide whether it would be better to re-lay the road with cedar ties, or to establish a treating plant at El Paso, and treat Texas pine for the purpose. The first day out from El Paso Mr. Ayer had bought a small Chihuahua dog. When they got to the City of Mexico after completing their examination of the road, Mr. Jackson asked McKenzie:

"Well, how did you find things, and what recommendation have you to make?"

McKenzie replied: "The inspection shows that we must re-tie with cedar, and I have fixed upon a new method of inspection with Ayer which I think will be beneficial to him and not hurt us at all."

"What is it, Mr. McKenzie, I shall be very glad to learn of that process?"

"Well, the first day out Ayer bought a little Chihuahua dog, and whenever there was any question as to whether the holes in the ties were too big, Ayer would put his little dog in, and if he had to back out Ayer would say the tie was all right, but if the dog came right through Ayer would admit that the tie was slightly defective."

Before 1880 Mr. Ayer had done a good deal of business

with the Santa Fe Railroad. An agreement was entered into in 1880 between the Santa Fe and the St. Louis and San Francisco to push the Atlantic and Pacific lines west into California. From his army experience in Arizona and New Mexico Mr. Ayer knew that in the neighborhood of the San Francisco Mountains, through which the road was to pass, there was a great amount of fine timber. In 1881 he proposed to the Santa Fe that he build a lumber mill in this extensive Arizona timber region and supply the material necessary for the projection of the road into California. Another reason why he considered it desirable to establish a mill near Flagstaff was the fact that he needed ties and telegraph poles for the Mexican Central Railroad. Accordingly the Santa Fe gave him an option on eighty-seven sections of their Government timber land, south and west of Flagstaff. He was to look it over and build the mill or not as he might decide.

So in 1881 he took a special car and went out to New Mexico. He had not been back into this territory since he was mustered out of the Army in 1864. The railroad by this time had reached Winslow, Arizona, where construction was being delayed until the long, high bridge across Canyon Diablo could be completed. As there was unrest among the Indians of Arizona, Mr. Ayer asked General Phil Sheridan, who was a friend of his, if he would send along an escort of soldiers from Fort Defiance. This request was readily granted, and with a detachment of eight or ten men, wagons for transporting supplies, and an ambulance for Mr. Ayer's party, the expedition set out for the Flagstaff region. Leaving the rest of the party about six miles south of Flagstaff to do some shooting, Mr. Ayer, with a sergeant and a couple of other soldiers, scouted about the country two or three days, sleeping on the ground at night and examining the quantity and quality of the timber. Finding that the prospect was all that he could desire, he decided to enter into the contract.

Up to this time there was not a mill in Arizona that would cut more than eight thousand feet of lumber a day; so in order to fulfill his contract, it became necessary for Mr. Ayer to build a large sawmill. This he did at a cost of two hundred thousand dollars. To the astonishment of the very few residents in that region to be astounded, this mill had a capacity of 150,000 feet of lumber a day.

But the capacity of the sawmill was not so wonderful as the energy and entérprise of the builder in overcoming the difficulties he had to meet in order to build it and put it in operation. What these obstacles were and how they were overcome is related in a letter to the writer under date of May 2, 1927, from Mr. Ayer's friend Mr. A. G. Wells, Vice-President of the Atchison, Topeka, and Santa Fe Railway System. "I first met Mr. Ayer at Albuquerque, New Mexico, in the summer of 1882. He was then a comparatively young man and was engaged among other activities in furnishing ties and bridge timbers for the Atlantic and Pacific Railroad which was being constructed west from Albuquerque across New Mexico and Arizona. . . . In the construction of the railroad an obstacle was encountered at Canyon Diablo, thirty-two miles east of Flagstaff. This canyon had to be crossed by an open truss bridge 541 feet long and 223 feet high. The erection of the steel comprising the structure delayed track-laying for over six months. This delay to his operations did not harmonize with Ed. Ayer's conception of the fitness of things. There was timber waiting to be cut, and the machinery for the sawmill that was to turn the trick was on cars at Canyon Diablo. With characteristic energy Mr. Ayer imported men, teams, wagons, and commissary, got his mill stuff across the canyon, and installed it, and put it in operation long before the first locomotive whistled into Flagstaff, and this through a country uninhabited and which did not afford a drop of water for men or mules. This accomplishment typifies the re-

THE SAWMILL, BUILT BY EDWARD E. AYER AT FLAGSTAFF, ARIZONA, IN 1882

sourcefulness and energy which have characterized the under-
takings of Mr. Ayer and made him a success."

The Mexican Central and Atlantic and Pacific railroads
needed only about one half of the output of the mill. So, in
order to dispose of his surplus lumber, Mr. Ayer established
a line of lumber yards from Albuquerque to Los Angeles, and
from El Paso to the City of Mexico. Previous to this time his
activities had been confined to the forests of Wisconsin,
Michigan, and Canada. He found that it was difficult to secure men from the North who could carry on this new enterprise successfully, for conditions in the Southwest differed
from anything they had met before. It was particularly hard
to find an efficient manager. Just about this time it so happened that Mr. Ayer wrote to the agent in charge of the
Navajo Indians inquiring whether the Navajo Indians could
be induced to weave blankets for the annual exposition in Chicago. The reply, penned by the agent, Mr. D. M. Riordan,
was such an excellent business letter that it made a decided
impression on Mr. Ayer. As the management of the Flagstaff venture continued to be unsatisfactory, some months
later, while he was in Washington, Mr. Ayer called on his
friend, the Secretary of the Interior and asked,

"What kind of a man is that Navajo agent?"

"He is very much the best Indian agent we have in the department," the secretary replied.

"What do you pay him a year?"

"Fifteen hundred dollars."

"Well, if he's as good as I think he is, and as what you
say about him, I think I can use him at a much better salary."

"I should hate to lose him, but I wouldn't want to stand in
the way of his getting a business engagement. He is here in
the East now with an Indian delegation."

When Mr. Ayer returned to Chicago, he had word from
his brother Henry, who was then serving as secretary of the

Flagstaff concern, that things were still going badly and that the management was as unsatisfactory as ever. A telegram was at once sent to the Bureau of Indian Affairs in Washington requesting that Mr. Riordan be asked to call at Mr. Ayer's office as he passed through Chicago on his way West. About a week later the contractor was sitting in his office at his desk, some fifty feet from the door which was in plain view, when he saw coming toward him one whom he at once recognized as being a very remarkable man. His whole appearance was striking; it could be seen that he was from the West—he hardly touched the ground when he walked.

"Your name is Matt Riordan," was the salutation the stranger received.

"Yes, sir, that is my name."

"Do you want to work for me?"

"What do you want me to do?"

"I want you either to go to Aguas Calientes and start a lumber yard there that I am contemplating, or to Flagstaff and take over the management of my sawmill."

"Why, Mr. Ayer," Riordan replied, "I don't know anything about the lumber business."

"Well, I'm blamed glad you don't. I've had all the experts I want," was the emphatic rejoinder.

Immediately Riordan asked, "What would be your terms?"

Mr. Ayer replied, "If you go to Flagstaff I will give you twenty-five hundred dollars a year, all expenses for your wife, children, and nurse, will furnish you a house, and pay your traveling expenses when you are away from home. And if you prove successful, I will advance you."

Said Riordan, "I accept!"

"Telegraph Joslyn that you resign."

While the telegram was being prepared Mr. Ayer penned these lines to his brother: "This note will be handed you by

D. M. Riordan whom I have made manager of the plant. See that he is put in charge immediately, with full authority."

When Mr. Riordan returned after sending his telegram to Washington, Mr. Ayer said, "Here is a letter to my brother who is in Flagstaff. The train starts at six. I hope you will be on it."

"I certainly shall," he replied.

Said Mr. Ayer to the writer, with a rare warmth of appreciation:

"He proved one of the very best managers that I ever had, and a most charming personality—one of the squarest, most honest, and efficient men that I ever knew."

After a few years, as the Mexican Central Railroad had now been completed, Mr. Ayer no longer desired to conduct a system of lumber yards so far from his home base in Chicago. He telegraphed to Mr. Riordan one day and asked him to come to Chicago. The manager arrived within two or three days, and Mr. Ayer said, without preliminaries:

"Matt, I sent for you to buy the plant at Flagstaff."

"Why, Mr. Ayer," the young man replied, "I have only six or eight thousand dollars that I have saved since I have been with you. I couldn't buy your plant."

"I haven't asked you for any money."

"What do you mean?"

"Matt, I want you to go back to Flagstaff and inventory my property at a fair valuation and send me your notes, due in one, two, and three years at six per cent." (The normal interest at that time was ten per cent.)

"But of course you will want a mortgage on the plant."

"No, Matt, I do not. You couldn't run the mill without more money. You will have to mortgage it to run it. It is insured, of course, and I shall not ask you for any security whatever—only the insurance if it burns."

Riordan returned to Flagstaff. The plant was old, so not

worth so much as when it was built. The new owner sent back his notes—three of them, one due each year—for a total amount of $145,000. They were met promptly as they came due.

Before leaving this western field of activity in Mr. Ayer's life there, we must give his account—(taken mostly from his Reminiscences) of his first, and second trip especially, to the Grand Canyon of the Colorado River.

It was while Mr. Ayer was visiting the saw mill that he had built at Flagstaff, Arizona, that he made some trips to the Grand Canyon, which was about eighty miles from Flagstaff.

The Grand Canyon was only beginning to be known then, as one of the greatest wonders of the world. We take from his Reminiscences, that he went to the Canyon the first time, about 1884, in February, when there was snow on the ground. He had a friend with him, with whom he was looking over the timber lands around Flagstaff. When Mr. Ayer saw "this stupendous abyss open before his feet, with its great depth, its width, its crags, its temples, its castles and cathedrals," he writes he was "tremendously impressed."

He decided then that he must bring his family the next year and camp on the brink of this indescribable canyon.

He writes in his Reminiscences, "The next year, 1884 (or '5), in May, I took Mrs. Ayer, my daughter and her friend, Miss Ethel Sturges (now Mrs. Frank Dummer), to Flagstaff with me. I organized a party and went over to the Grand Canyon again. We took two wagons, with six mules each, for supplies, a six mule wagon for water, and an ambulance for the ladies, several riding horses, and about twenty men.

"We made a camp on a point jutting out into the Canyon. Mrs. Ayer wanted to go to the bottom, but Bill Hull, the adventurous cowboy who had been down once, protested strongly against that. No white woman had ever climbed

Mrs. E. E. Ayer

GRAND CANYON OF THE COLORADO

SHOWS RIVER TO WHICH MR. AND MRS. AYER DESCENDED IN MAY, 1885, BEFORE THERE WAS ANY TRAIL. THEIR GUIDE WAS BILL HULL, AN ADVENTUROUS COWBOY OF THE VICINITY

down. Bill, with a comrade, had blazed the original trail later, but at this time there was none.

"I selected two of the strongest men I had in the party, and known to be good climbers, and they, Bill Hull, my brother Henry, Mrs. Ayer and I started to go down to the bottom of the canyon, 6000 feet.

"It was a remarkable climb down, and I know of no other white woman who ever went to the bottom of the Grand Canyon, until trails were made. We descended, or slid down, steep slopes of sand and broken rocks, crawled along narrow edges over precipices where many times, a mis-step would have sent us to death.

"After a time we arrived at a point where there was water, immediately under our camp above—from where they could see us with a glass. We were 3000 feet below them and looked like small ants (they said); at any rate not taller than an inch or two. Here we got our lunch. By the way, it consisted of a can of tomatoes, and of coffee, heated over a fire of twigs—and some broken up bread and crackers." Here— it may be inserted, all the provisions were carried in bags on the backs of the men, with the coffee pot slung above. Also on their backs they carried rifles and a small roll of blankets, for it was necessary that their hands should be free for the descent.

To resume: "Leaving some of our supplies we went on until that night, and camped in a deep canyon, probably two miles from the bottom. Here some twigs were scattered on a flat rock, one blanket thrown over it and one used for a cover, and we slept there.

"The next morning we went to the roaring, rushing, mud-colored water of the Colorado River, terribly impressive.

"We made some more climbs up the high crags to get a wonderful view of the Canyon chasm.

"We arrived at our camp on the rock that night, with sore

muscles and aching bones. The second night after we got to this place, we were still in sight and they were able to see a fire from the camp above, so we built a large one and shot off our rifles to attract their attention, and in a few minutes a fire started at a point near their camp. It looked almost as large as a half bushel basket.

"We climbed out the next afternoon and arrived about four o'clock, worn and battered, "looking ten years older" they said.

"It was one of the hardest trips we ever took for *fun*. We asked them when we got back why they did not build a big fire. They said they did. It was nearly twenty feet high and they burned nearly a cord of wood, but the fire being so far away, looked small.

"In this party, Alida Dunham, a cousin of mine, went with us, so that Mrs. Ayer, my daughter, Mrs. Dummer and Alida Dunham were the only women—except Indian women—who had ever seen the Canyon, up to that time; especially at that point and (as written before) Mrs. Ayer was the only white woman who ever went to the bottom, until trails were blazed. The descent was made at one of the very difficult places in the Canyon. A mountain in the Canyon (showing in the picture) was named Mount Ayer in recognition of her nerve and endurance. However, this was changed afterwards to Coronado." From Reminiscences of Edward E. Ayer.

Mr. Ayer's relations with the Santa Fe continued to be very friendly. He was doing a heavy business with this road as a result of the establishing of his Flagstaff mill, and he was shipping a million ties to Mexico each year over the Santa Fe. He estimated that for many years his annual freight bills over the Santa Fe averaged from seven hundred to nine hundred dollars a day. In 1886 the Santa Fe was preparing to build about two thousand miles of track. A. A. Robinson, formerly chief engineer of the Santa Fe, and at a later time president of the Mexican Central, was in charge of this tremendous construction program. He was one of the finest men in the railroad profession, and Mr. Ayer held him in very high esteem. For some reason, the road was late in making its purchases. In the spring of 1886 Mr. Robinson telegraphed Mr. Ayer that he and his purchasing agent would like to see him at the Grand Pacific Hotel in Chicago. Accordingly, taking his manager, Lot Smith, with him, Mr. Ayer went to the Grand Pacific at the appointed time to meet these gentlemen.

Mr. Robinson asked, "What are ties worth, Ayer, and what will you ask for 500,000?"

Mr. Ayer replied, "I have sold three and one-half million ties this year at thirty-eight cents, so far. You can have one-half million at the same price."

"I will take that many," said Robinson. "Will you give me the refusal for thirty days on 500,000 more?"

Mr. Ayer said, "Yes."

"I might want to consider the purchase of many more," continued Mr. Robinson. "Do you think you could arrange to get them for me?"

At this Mr. Ayer said: "Now, Robinson, hold on! I have laid my cards on the table, but you haven't laid down yours. I know what you want—pretty near. You are going to build about two thousand miles of railroad. You haven't bought your ties yet, except this million you just bought from me. Really, Robinson, I don't believe you could buy your ties for delivery at the time you want them unless you purchase the amount that I have ready for sale. I feel perfectly sure that I could have asked you forty-five cents for these ties, and that you would have been obliged to pay that price or suffer great delay—and that you couldn't afford to do. But for many years now I have dealt with you people, and our business has always been carried on with the utmost frankness, and I want no change in our good understanding. When you came here this morning, I had 3,500,000 ties for sale. You have bought a million; that leaves me 2,500,000 ties for sale. You may have any portion of what is left at thirty-eight cents."

Robinson drew a long breath and said, "Mr. Ayer, including the million I have just bought, I will take 2,600,000."

A few minutes after that he bought 40,000 telegraph poles and 2,000,000 fence posts.

As has been said in a previous chapter, the railroads that ran to Kansas City and had connections also with Omaha would not buy from Mr. Ayer, because he would not turn over to them a part of his freight from Chicago to Omaha. Up to about 1880 he had done no business with either the Wabash or the Burlington. In the '70's roads that paralleled each other saw the folly of attempting to enter into sharp competition with each other, so at that early day business was light. They were looking to the future rather than the present for profits. Under the circumstances the chief railroads centering in Omaha came to an amicable understanding known as "The Omaha Pool." It was agreed that after deducting enough to cover operating expenses, the various roads should share equally all receipts from the Chicago-Omaha business. The success of the scheme was dependent upon each road keeping faith. The plan worked very well for more than a decade.

In practice there was little necessity of dividing the receipts, as the eastern connections of the roads involved, adopted the method of handing over in turn all the business for a given week to a particular road. Not until 1882 was it necessary to draw up a written agreement and to provide definite means for the enforcement of this agreement. Later the problem grew more complex. New roads were constantly being projected, and other towns on the Missouri River were vying with Omaha as popular shipping points. So it became necessary to enter into some sort of arrangement for the harmonizing of rates to Missouri River points and thus prevent rival towns from entering into suicidal competition with each other. The solution was the organization of another pool, "The Southwestern Railway Rate Association." The roads concerned were to have their accounts balanced each month.

"It was expected that in practice the amount of traffic on each road would tend to become stabilized, as in the case of 'The Omaha Pool,' and practically do away with the necessity of monthly payments. No such happy consummation occurred, and the traffic varied greatly from month to month. In fact all the affairs of the pool proved a great deal more complex than were expected."

Mr. Ayer, as a heavy shipper, was vitally concerned with the pools and agreements entered into by these various roads. In the late '70's under the Gould regime, the Wabash became one of the most aggressive competitors for Kansas City business. About this time Mr. Ayer's personal friend, Mr. John Gault, left the Northwestern and became general manager of the Wabash. This road soon forced its way into the pool, and as a result a certain percentage of the business was assigned to it. Finding that Mr. Gault was far behind the share of the freight supposed to be allotted to him, Mr. Ayer, without saying anything to any of the other roads, transferred to the Wabash his entire shipping business to Kansas City. He gave Gault four hundred carloads the first week, and, as a result, within a month or two the Wabash was getting its allotment and more.

The first break had been made. At that time the Wabash and the Burlington were in deadly competition. One day Edward Ripley, freight agent of the Burlington, came into Mr. Ayer's office and asked,

"What is the reason that the Burlington can't get some of your freight?"

"The very good reason is," Mr. Ayer replied, "that the

Burlington doesn't furnish me any business—you don't do
business with me."

"What do you want for some of that Kansas City business?"

"I want you to buy 200,000 cedar ties of me at the present
market price."

Mr. Ripley left the office. In about half an hour Mr.
George Harris, purchasing agent for the Burlington Railroad
came into Mr. Ayer's office and asked,

"Have you any ties?"

"Yes, I have."

"What will be the price for 200,000 cedar ties?"

He was offered the ties at the current price; the offer was
accepted; and he took his leave. Having placed Mr. Gault in
an independent position, Mr. Ayer now transferred a due proportion of his freight business to the Burlington, and for
years he continued to ship a fair share of his material over
that road.

The 2,600,000 ties, 2,000,000 fence posts, and 40,000
telegraph poles contracted for by Mr. A. A. Robinson of the
Santa Fe in 1886 were, of course, sold for delivery on dock
in Chicago. Just previous to this large sale to the Santa Fe
Mr. Ayer had sold 1,000,000 ties to the Burlington and
1,000,000 to the Mexican Central. This enormous quantity
of material would all have to be shipped to the Southwest.
As the shortage of vessels on the Great Lakes made it impera-
tive that they should not be held in dock longer than was
necessary for the discharge of their cargoes, Mr. Ayer stipulated that the ties must be taken as rapidly as they were
discharged. He foresaw that, at the best, the Santa Fe would
be unlikely to receive the material fast enough, and that the
demurrage required by the boats would amount to a great
deal. He pointed out to Mr. Robinson that it might be as
much as $100,000, and would almost certainly amount to

$50,000. Hearing this, an idea instantly came into his mind. "Robinson," he asked, "what rate are you paying the railroads for freight to Kansas City?"

His friend replied, "Fifteen cents a hundred."

The million ties Mr. Ayer was selling to the Mexican Central he was shipping to Kansas City at about two-thirds of the rate indicated by Mr. Robinson.

"If you want to turn the business over to me on the basis of fifteen cents a hundred and take my delivery in Kansas City instead of in Chicago, I think I can save you a large part of the demurrage that you would have to pay."

"All right, Ayer," said Mr. Robinson, "that's a fine suggestion. We will note on the contract that you can deliver in Kansas City at a rate of fifteen cents a hundred any portion of this material that you choose."

Immediately Mr. Ayer instructed Lot Smith, his manager, to write to the Burlington, Rock Island, St. Paul, and Wabash roads asking them, respectively, what they would do to protect him against demurrage in case he turned over to them a certain portion of his shipments to the Southwest. A day or two after these letters had been dispatched, Mr. Ayer and Mr. Henry Stone, Manager of the Burlington Railroad, started in Mr. Stone's private car for a trip to Mexico. They had scarcely got beyond the city limits of Chicago before Mr. Ayer addressed this remark to his companion:

"Henry, if you were half big enough to fill your position properly, I would let your railroad make a half-million dollars off of me this year."

Mr. Stone replied, "I ought to be big enough to get that."

"I don't know about that," Mr. Ayer answered.

"What's your scheme?"

"I've got a million ties sold to the Burlington, and a million to the Mexican Central, and more than three million pieces to the Santa Fe—all going to Kansas City. The rate of that going to Mexico is ten cents a hundred, but the rate on all the rest is fifteen cents a hundred. I will give you the Mexican shipment and all the rest if your road will handle it and protect me from demurrage."

"Henry," Mr. Ayer continued, "you've got those two big slips up the river. If you will move all your other freight, and your general business, onto one of those docks and turn the other one over exclusively for this work, I believe you can handle it. You will want to take one of the brightest young men you have and put him in full charge. Lay as many additional tracks as necessary, and electrify the whole thing so that it will be as light by night as by day, and give your man *carte blanche* to hire men, take cars—anything he demands in order to clear the docks—and it can be done."

Naturally Mr. Stone inquired, "How many cargoes will you give me a day?"

"Most of these ships upon which I depend are sailing vessels. If the wind should blow from the south for three or four days and then turn to the east, west, or north, I would perhaps give you forty cargoes in twenty-four hours—cargoes of from 2,500 to 7,000 on the cars."

"Suppose we have strikes?"

"That you must prevent in a big undertaking like this, just as far as possible."

"Suppose there should be a shortage of cars?"

"You should load every cattle car going west over your line with this material—and if you don't get the cars you don't get the business."

"What will it cost to pile this material up again?"

"About five dollars a car, but you will get from ten to fifteen dollars more than the ordinary on each one of these cars, for the rate is excessive."

Mr. Stone thought it over for some time, but before they were thirty miles out of the city, he said,

"All right, Ed., I'll take the business."

By the time the train reached Aurora, Mr. Stone had written out a telegram to his people, and Mr. Ayer had prepared one to send to Lot Smith instructing him to withdraw all propositions made to any of the other railroads, since arrangements had been made with the Burlington to handle the entire business. The two friends went on to Mexico and were gone six or seven weeks.

A day or two after they returned Mr. Ayer said to Mr. Stone: "Henry, what did Potter (president of the road) say to you about that contract when you got back?"

Stone replied, "I went in the next morning after my return, and he said, "You raised the devil on your watch, going off on a junketing trip with Ayer and letting him do you out of a hundred thousand dollars or more.' I said, 'Mr. Potter, this contract is all right; and if you will let me run it, I will stake my reputation on it.' Potter's response was, 'You've got to run it. I won't have anything to do with the blasted thing.' "

Mr. Ayer gave the Burlington that season as many as forty cargoes in forty hours. The company loaded on their dock from ninety to one hundred and ninety-eight cars a day for a period of about six months, and during all of this time not a cent of demurrage was paid.

Not only was pooling the order of the day in big business circles in the early period of railroading in the West; it was the period, too, of unregulated freight rates. Each shipper made the best terms he could with the railroads, and of course the man who supplied the most freight got the best rates. In the railroad-tie pool that Mr. Ayer entered, two portions of the allotment into four parts were given to him. The pool ended on dock in Chicago. Mr. Ayer's associates were content to conclude their part in a given transaction with the delivery of the ties on the Chicago dock, but he nearly always sold at delivered rate; that is, his price included shipment by rail to whatever point the purchaser indicated. As he was a very heavy shipper, he, of course, secured special rates, and in consequence his profits were increased in this way by tens of thousands of dollars a year during the "boom" period of railway building.

The following incident is an illustration of the advantage that came to Mr. Ayer as a big shipper and a skillful manipulator. One of his associates in the pool on a certain occasion went to the traffic manager of the Northwestern Railroad and demanded his rates. The traffic manager sent for Mr. Ayer and said to him:

"Ed. I'm in trouble. Mr. —— has come in here to insist upon knowing what rates I am giving you. I put him off, but I will have to give him an answer."

"Why don't you comply with his request?" Mr. Ayer asked.

"What do you mean?"

"Have I ever in the world asked you for a rate to any point without at the same time telling you how many cars I had to ship at that rate?"

"No," replied the manager (and this was true).

"Now you send for that man and tell him that you have been thinking the matter over and have come to the conclusion that perhaps it isn't fair to give me a rate different from what you give the other tie men, and that you have concluded, under like conditions, to give them all the same rate. He will say, 'There, that's fine, I knew that you would do that when the thing had been presented to you properly.'

"Ask him how many cars he has to ship," Mr. Ayer continued. "He will say, 'Wh-wh-why, I haven't any cars; how can I ship anything when I don't know the rates?' You can truthfully say to him, 'My dear sir, Mr. Ayer *never* has come into this office and asked for a rate without telling me exactly the number of cars he has to ship on that rate. Of course you

EDWARD E. AYER
PHOTOGRAPH TAKEN THE YEAR OF HIS GOLDEN WEDDING

will agree with me that a very large shipper who gives us trainloads is entitled to a better rate than a man who gives only an occasional car or two. And I will say this, any time you or any other man comes here and asks for the rate that Mr. Ayer is having to a given point—if you will supply me an amount of business equal to what Mr. Ayer gives us—I shall be very glad to name Mr. Ayer's rate.' "

During the time that Gould was in control of the Union Pacific Railroad, so far as the work of the purchasing agent was concerned, the company was straight in its dealings. But conditions changed after Adams became president. He brought a new purchasing agent out with him. The Chicago Lumber Company had forty or fifty yards in Nebraska and the Northwest. Mr. Green was president of this company. The Nebraska manager, Mr. Kohlpretzer, was an appointee also of the Government for the supervision of the Union Pacific Railroad.

Soon after Adams took the control of the road, Mr. Ayer received notice as usual that the road would like a price on a certain number of ties. On subsequent occasions similar notices came, and each time Mr. Ayer replied, giving a conservative price. But invariably the answer came back, "Sorry, but your price is too high." Mr. Ayer investigated, and having found out what the trouble was, he said to his manager,

"Lot, when the time comes, we'll fix them up."

Finally the purchasing agent asked for a price on 500,000 railroad ties, to be delivered the following spring on the Northwestern dock in Chicago. That season Mr. Ayer had already sold 3,000,000 ties at thirty-five cents each. He said to Lot,

"Make them a bid of twenty-eight cents. If we are going to hit that man Green, let's knock him right into the middle of Nebraska."

So the bid went in at twenty-eight cents. Three days

after this bid had been made Green came in and asked,

"Ayer, what will you take for 500,000 ties on the Northwestern dock next season?"

Mr. Ayer replied, "Green, your money is just as good to me as anybody's; it is perfectly immaterial who I sell ties to at my price. I'd just as soon have your money as the railroad's, and I have sold already during the last two or three months 3,500,000 at thirty-three cents. If you want half a million, I will give you the same price."

"Ayer," he said, "there's one thing about the tie business I haven't got onto yet, but I'll get there."

"Green, you astonish me! I have been in the tie business now twenty or twenty-five years. If I allowed half an hour to pass over my head without in the meantime learning something about the business, I would consider my time wasted. You have been nibbling at it about four days now, I believe. Will you let me tell you when you will find out that 'one thing' about the business? I'm surprised that during the time you have been in the business you haven't learned it all. Green, the first time there is a shortage in railroad ties is right now."

In June Kohlpretzer came into Chicago. He had telegraphed to ask Mr. Ayer to meet him at the Grand Pacific Hotel. So Lot Smith and Mr. Ayer went down there to meet him. Said Kohlpretzer:

"Of course we got our ties, but we were a little late in getting them out. We will get them in a few weeks now; but rather than run any risk, we should prefer to buy from you and stand the loss. What is your price now?"

"Thirty-six cents, Kohlpretzer."

"All right, I will take 300,000."

"How many ties have you got to get out?" Mr. Ayer asked.

"Three hundred and fifty thousand."

"Kohlpretzer, this is June; I will bet you a seventy-five dol-

LOT P. SMITH

lar suit of clothes that you won't get 75,000 ties out of the
Northwest between now and the first snow-flurries."

Just at the time of the first snowfall he wrote to Mr. Ayer,

"What testimony do you want from me about that suit
of clothes?"

"Just a bill from the tailor with your O. K.," was the reply.

The next day Mr. Ayer received a letter instructing him to
go down to some second-hand store and buy himself a suit of
clothes.

Just as was the case with everyone else, these Chicago Lumber Company people fell in love with Lot Smith. Soon after
the deal with Kohlpretzer the company offered to put up
$200,000 for the purpose of establishing a department in
their business for the handling of cedar. They offered Lot the
presidency of this branch of the business and half the profits
from the sale of cedar, if he would leave Mr. Ayer and come
over with them. His reply was,

"Do you think for a minute I am running this business?"

"Of course we do."

"Well, I'm not. Neither I nor anybody living could get any
of Edward Ayer's business if he wanted it; and if he wanted
it, he'd break us up by getting all the business. Anyway, there
is no proposition anybody could ever make that would influence me for a second to leave him as long as I live."

Matters went along very well until about 1893, when to
his very great sorrow Mr. Ayer suffered the loss of his staunch
friend and able manager. The other members of the pool had
been somewhat dissatisfied, for Mr. Ayer had been selling
seventy-five per cent of the material that came into the hands
of the pool. They supposed that Mr. Ayer's great success was
due to the popularity and enterprise of his manager, for he
himself for six or seven years had been spending a third of
his time in Europe. They thought now that their opportunity
had come; so very soon after Lot Smith's death they notified

Mr. Ayer that all agreements were off. These men did not realize that while Mr. Ayer worked little, he thought much. But they were rudely awakened to this fact. Their energetic competitor went out a month before the usual time for the making of prices and sold to all the people he had been selling to in the past and to others with whom he had had no dealings hitherto. In most cases the contracts were made to cover a period of five years. This having been done, Mr. Ayer placed the business in the hands of his assistant manager, Mr. Watson, and then went to Europe in accordance with his regular custom. When the other three members of the old association went out to look for business at the usual time, they found there was little left to be secured.

It was in 1893 that Lot Smith died; that the Chicago pool was dissolved; and that Mr. Ayer went out in advance of the usual season to make his sales. As has been said, the business was placed in the hands of Mr. Watson during Mr. Ayer's absence in Europe. The cedar branch of his business was very extensive—too large indeed for Mr. Watson to handle successfully. In this emergency Mr. Ayer's mind turned to Mr. Philip Raber who was connected with one of the firms that had constituted the pool. Being fond of Raber, and feeling sure that his employer was now doing little business, Mr. Ayer said to him:

"Phil, come up and spend Sunday with me at Lake Geneva."

"All right," Raber replied.

As the two men were talking together Sunday, Mr. Ayer asked,

"You're not doing any business to amount to anything, are you?"

"No."

"Can you get out of the business—can you get away from your concern—honorably on short notice?"

"Yes, I think they would be glad to get rid of me."

"Would you like to work for me?"

"I can answer you emphatically, yes."

"Well," said Mr. Ayer, "if you can get out of your concern honorably, very soon, as Watson wants a rest, I should like to relieve him of his responsibility for a time. I will put you in charge of my cedar business with him as assistant, and will give you ten thousand dollars a year."

"I accept," was the prompt response.

This arrangement was entered into, and the cedar business was carried on in this way up to 1900. At that time Mr. Ayer felt that he would like to retire permanently from the cedar business. Accordingly, he asked his managers to associate themselves properly as "Raber and Watson, Successors to Edward E. Ayer in the Cedar Business," and when this had been done he turned over a quarter of a million dollars worth of material to them to sell on commission. He then gave them a credit of fifty thousand dollars in the bank and withdrew from all activity in that field. There were few things in life that gave Mr. Ayer more pleasure than the opportunity he had on various occasions of establishing upon an independent footing young men who had won his confidence by long and faithful service. Said he:

"These men (Raber and Watson) made a fairly good success of it, and made money enough to keep them in comfort. Watson was an awfully good fellow and perfectly safe. Matt Riordan, Lot Smith, Raber, and Watson—all good men."

It was that memorable year, 1893, that Mr. Ayer went over the Illinois Central Railroad with Stuyvesant Fish and the Directors and got a tentative agreement to furnish them with ties for a term of five years. Up to this time his business in oak ties had been small. As stated above, he was about to withdraw from the cedar business. There was one competitor in the oak tie business with whom he had dealt to a considerable extent—Mr. John B. Lord of the firm of "Powell and Lord." After returning from his trip over the Illinois Central, he saw Mr. Lord and told him of the advantageous agreement he had entered into, and proposed that they accept this proposition on the basis of an equal partnership. He requested Mr. Lord to take three or four of his best wood-runners and go over the Illinois Central properties, in order to find out how much standing timber there was within ten miles of any of their various branches, and so satisfy himself whether it would be profitable to accept the proposed contract. Mr. Lord's report was favorable, and forthwith the firm of Ayer and Lord was established.

Thirty-four years after this partnership was formed, that is, in April, 1927, both Mr. Ayer and Mr. Lord were in Pasadena, California, where they had been spending the winter as usual. The writer was there at that time, also, and he had the pleasure of drawing from these gentlemen, respectively, the story of their long business connection. Said Mr. John B. Lord:

My association with Mr. Ayer began in 1893. I was not interested with him in the cedar business or telegraph pole business in which he had been engaged before my connection with him began. The starting of our business together was when we made a contract jointly with the Illinois Central Railroad. This contract is still running after a period of thirty-four years. In the meantime we have increased our business to a very large extent.

Our source of supply of ties for other contracts was on the Tennessee, Cumberland, Ohio, and White Rivers. At one time we owned seven steamboats and enough barges to keep these boats busy. Our business began in a comparatively small way, and reached a maximum in the delivery of 12,-600,000 ties in one year.

My association with Mr. Ayer for these thirty-four years was the most satisfactory period of my life. He was always cheerful and optimistic, and his wonderful disposition was an inspiration to me. All this time our relations in every way were most harmonious and satisfactory. I am sure Mr. Ayer had the same feeling towards me.

When we started in business, we handled mostly white oak ties; and as this kind of timber became depleted, we built treating plants at Carbondale, Illinois; Grenada, Mississippi; and North Little Rock, Arkansas. These plants have always been busy and are at the present time. At first we treated ties with chloride of zinc which is a good preservative, but not so good as creosote. Now our treatment is mostly with creosote, which we import from abroad and unload at New Orleans into large tanks with a capacity of 4,000,000 gallons. We import now an average of one cargo a month.

Mr. Ayer's account of this long friendship and partnership was given in a mood of tender reminiscence only three days before his death:

Our business grew from that small beginning with the Illinois Central to a position of prominence. We built up an extensive business. We had no trouble in securing practically all the business that we wanted. During all these years I have grown to love John Lord more and more, as he has me, and never has there been a word of misunderstanding between us—not one. It was the same all those years I was associated with Lot Smith; so I can truthfully say, on this last day of April, 1927—this sixty-seventh anniversary of my leaving home to cross the Plains—I can truthfully say that no man ever had a better time doing business—fewer disappointments and greater joys—and a large measure of this is due to my loving and splendid relations over such a long series of years with Lot Smith and John Lord.

CHAPTER VIII

Travels in Mexico

TODAY, as in the remote past, Mexico exerts some siren spell upon the American traveler. One need not leave this continent to experience all the allurements of foreign travel. Antiquity, mystery, myth, tradition, high tragedy, sunshine, starlight, Nature in tropical luxuriance, and Nature in austere grandeur—Mexico is all this and much more. No doubt fifty years ago this goodly demesne of gold and dreams held even more of magic and marvel for the American youth than it does at present. It was here in this land that Edward Ayer first met pure romance face to face. In an earlier chapter we have seen how by a conjunction of happy incidents (the chance reading of Prescott's *History of the Conquest of Mexico* and the good luck that took him into Sonora on a military expedition of unique historic interest) he awoke to the knowledge that here in Mexico were his "tropics and his Italy."

For more than half a century Mr. Ayer came and went in Mexico. First and last he visited this southern republic at least a score of times. He journeyed through it on horseback and muleback, on foot and in river boat, by wagon, stage, and private car; he traveled in and out, and back and forth, over mesa and mountain, through jungle and plantation, in village and city—all over this realm so full of variety and charm. Nor were the outward scene and the stirring incident any richer in romantic possibilities than the eye that saw and the spirit that felt. Nothing ever continued to be commonplace after Edward Ayer once looked at it or passed by it. No matter how ordinary the experience, how untoward the circumstance, it took on romance, significance, comedy, grandeur, as the case might be, from the moment that this man of imagination and vision encountered it and entered into it.

During the early fall of 1881, Mr. Ayer, Mr. George Sturges, President of the Northwestern National Bank, and Colonel Farrar, Business Manager of the *Chicago Journal,* started on a tour through the Southwest. After they had spent two or three weeks in California, Mr. Sturges said:

"Let's go down and see Al and his outfit in Sonora."

Al was Mr. Sturges' brother, who, with some associates, had bought a gold mine some seventy miles from Caborca and about twelve miles from the Gulf of California. From Los Angeles Mr. Ayer's party went east over the Southern Pacific Railroad as far as Maricopa Wells, which at that time was as far as the passenger service extended. From Maricopa Wells they intended to take a night stage to Tucson and reach that town about noon the following day. As Mr. Ayer did not like the idea of riding inside the coach, he took some cigars and went to look for the driver. He found that dignitary on his seat, muffled up preparatory to the cold night drive. Mr. Ayer looked up at him with all the reverence that an obscure man has for a great man and spoke thus:

"Are you the driver of this coach?"

As weak great men sometimes do, the driver looked down upon his interlocutor with more or less contempt. But at length he replied,

"You better bet I am."

"I want to ride with you, and I have some cigars, and when we get to Tucson, some money besides."

"All right, my covy," came the cheerful response.

At that moment Mr. Ayer felt Mr. Sturges tugging at his sleeve. "Come here," said that gentleman.

He had discovered a freight train standing on the track about ready to pull out for a point fifty miles farther east.

Mr. Gage, a mine inspector from Tombstone, had talked with the conductor and had secured his consent to take five or six of the travelers down the road for a consideration of fifteen dollars per man. Mr. Ayer's party, together with Mr. Gage and two or three others, got into a car loaded to within about four feet of the top with barley. There were in the car, also, about eight or ten kegs of beer and a carcass or two of beef. About midnight the train stopped opposite the stage station and the engineer blew a long whistle. At this a light appeared at the station. The travelers walked over, entered, and made themselves as comfortable as they could on the floor until morning. About eight o'clock the stage came in with a cold, dusty, dreary looking lot of passengers.

The seat by the driver had been occupied all night by a Tucson man named Brown. At breakfast the driver said to Brown, pointing to Mr. Ayer,

"This gent owns that seat from here to Tucson, so you will have to give it up."

With a sure instinct for live comradeship, Brown crawled over the baggage with the remark,

"Well, I'm not going to get far away from you, anyhow."

"Where do you hail from?" inquired Mr. Ayer.

"Tucson."

"When did you first settle there?"

"In 1862. I came out with the California Column."

"What!" exclaimed Mr. Ayer. "Why, I was a trooper in the California Column myself."

Brown was, indeed, a former comrade in arms, and at this time owner of Tucson's most sumptuous saloon and gambling hall—none other than Charlie Brown. Mr. Ayer's tenderfoot friends, Sturges and Farrar, found the remaining miles to Tucson short ones as they listened to Charlie Brown's stories about comrades of the long ago—Red-headed Mike, Six-toed Pete, and Frying-pan Sam.

Early the next morning Mr. Ayer went around to the
Tucson-Altar Stage corral and engaged seats for himself and
his friends. The route they took was the old familiar one he
had traveled on horseback nineteen years before—by the
Cerro Colorado mine, Arivaca, and the spot where, in 1862,
he had nailed up the sign: *Water One Mile up the Canyon.*
At this place a ranch-house had since been established. At
Altar a rig was secured. They drove to Caborca, and learning
that eight miles beyond Caborca a sheep-herder was located
at the last point where water could be secured between Caborca and the mine, they continued the journey until late
afternoon in order to reach this place, and thus cut down the
last sixty-mile waterless stretch—a hard enough day's journey
that they needed another mount, so they sent this man back to
Caborca to secure another horse and saddle. Their four-in-
hand the next day consisted of two little mules hitched to a
high *Democrat* wagon, the guide and the driver on horseback
leading the way with a lariat attached to the end of the
wagon-pole, Mr. Ayer driving, Colonel Farrar whipping, and
Mr. Sturges riding behind. An early start was made, and the
journey was completed before dark. They found their friends
in tents, doing very well, and making good headway in the
development of their mine.

After a visit of three or four days, at six o'clock on a Monday morning, with a good team of horses and a wagon owned
by the mining company, the return trip was begun. Mr. Ayer
now determined to test the mettle of his two tenderfoot friends
—to "give them a run for their money" as he expressed it.
They were in Caborca by six P.M. Exchanging the horses for
a pair of mules, they drove on to Altar, reaching there at two
o'clock Tuesday morning. They were up again by six o'clock,
and by half past seven were ready to start north in a two-
seated wagon drawn by two scraggy horses and a pair of
diminutive mules. No stop was made until about two o'clock

Wednesday morning when they arrived at the ranch near the Arizona border.

Once more they took the road in the early morning, and though delay was occasioned by the straying away of some of their animals, they got as far as Arivaca by six o'clock Wednesday evening.

About half past seven the stage arrived, and the Chicagoans offered to pay the driver fifty dollars if he would turn around at once and get them back to Tucson by one o'clock the next day. He accepted the proposition, and, as soon as possible, away they went. It was nine o'clock, and the night was very dark when they left Arivaca. The first stop was at the Cerro Colorado mine where Mr. Ayer was stationed for three months during the Civil War. They traveled all night and until noon the next day, securing only such sleep as could be snatched in a stage as it bumped along over a rough road. At four o'clock in the afternoon, after a good dinner, the three friends started for the railroad about twelve miles away, hoping there to hire a hand car to take them to Maricopa Wells where they would be able to catch the morning train for San Francisco. But no hand car was to be had. It looked as though they would have to return to Tucson and wait there until the work-train should come down the next day.

A happy thought came into Mr. Ayer's mind. He remembered that the Disstons of Philadelphia had come down into Arizona on a private Pullman car with the thought of buying the Schieffelen and Gird mining properties; and upon inquiry he learned that the car was about ten miles down the road at a place called Point of Rocks. He suggested to his friends that they go down there and stay all night. Someone said that probably they would not be allowed to occupy the car. Mr. Ayer replied that he did not believe there was a porter in any Pullman car at that time whom he did not know, as he was using Pullmans about a hundred nights a year, so he felt sure that there would be no trouble about getting aboard the sleeper. By this time it was almost sundown. Their way was impeded by mesquite and sage brush, as the road was but poorly broken. They had borrowed a lantern, and after dark one man went ahead to guide the team. Finally, at eleven o'clock, they reached Point of Rocks. Said Mr. Ayer to the others,

"I had better go alone to the car."

Accordingly, he mounted the platform and knocked on the door. An emphatic voice came from within:

"Who dar?"

Mr. Ayer called out, "Come to the door, I want to see you."

The answer came back, "You go way from hyar. You can't get in tonight; we all's done gone to bed."

"Don't be a fool," said Mr. Ayer, "come to the door. I want to see you a minute. Nobody is going to hurt you."

The voice replied, "Who am you, anyway?"

"Edward Ayer from Chicago."

"From Chicago! You ain't Edward Ayer from Harvard, is you?"

"Yes, from Harvard."

At this the door slowly opened, and Old Bill Bassy stood there with a candle in one hand and a six-shooter in the other. Behind him were his cook and waiter, altogether as scared a lot of colored persons as one can imagine.

"For God's sake, Mistah Ayer, wha did you come from?"

"Bill, I have been down in Sonora. I have a couple of friends with me, and you have got to take care of us."

Said Bill, "I don't care if you have a whole regiment; you jest bring them in."

The invitation was promptly accepted. "The first thing

we want is some whisky, then a bath, and after that the best meal you can get us."

After a fine night's sleep they took the work-train the next day for Maricopa Wells, and soon they were back in California. Mr. Ayer declared that, though his city-bred friends were constantly on the move from the time they got up Monday morning at six o'clock until Thursday night at eleven o'clock, there was never a minute that they were not having a good time, and that the experience was one they would remember until the last day of their lives.

The first time that Mr. Ayer went beyond El Paso into the interior of Mexico was in 1886, when with Mr. Daniel Robinson, then General Manager of the Mexican Railroad, he traveled to the City of Mexico. This was one of the most memorable of his many romantic journeys into the Southern Republic. It was necessary on this occasion to travel two hundred and fifty miles by ambulance, as there was a gap of that extent between the terminus of the road projected from the north and the end of the line that had been built from the south as far as Zacatecas. In Mr. Robinson's party on this trip there were twenty-four people. Part of the time the company camped, but at other times it enjoyed the princely hospitality of the great haciendas—a hospitality hardly to be surpassed in graciousness and splendor.

The picture of the lordly and lavish manner of living on the vast ranches in the remote interior as portrayed by Mr. Ayer is fascinating. It is like a page from the *Arabian Nights*. Mr. Ayer goes into some particulars in his description of life on the Mesquite Ranch: A courier had been sent ahead twenty-four hours in advance of the arrival of the American party. However, when the travelers reached the hacienda at five o'clock in the afternoon, the courier had not put in his appearance. Consequently they arrived unannounced. They were informed that their prospective host was out riding with his boys, but that he was expected home very soon. In a little while he rode into the yard with his two boys—one twelve, the other fourteen years old. They rode magnificent Kentucky horses. As they dismounted, attendants removed their spurs, etc.,—"one man for each leg," as Mr. Ayer expressed it. The strangers were promptly and cordially welcomed by the man of the house. At six o'clock the guests sat down to chocolate and sweet bread of several kinds. At nine o'clock dinner was announced. The company at the table consisted of the host, his wife, his grown daughter, his eldest son, a Catholic priest, a French teacher for the children, his head man, and the twenty-four Americans. The dining room, as may be imagined, was spacious. The dinner consisted of nineteen courses; there were seven or eight different kinds of wine; and the feast did not end until about one o'clock in the morning. A band played throughout the evening.

The next morning the strangers were conducted about the place. They found that there were one hundred and sixty horses in this gentleman's private stable and corral. All together the central establishment covered about twelve acres. Among the various buildings there was a church, and, indeed, everything else that went to make up a civilized community. The host, they learned, was not the owner of the estate, but the manager, the proprietor himself being in Paris at that time. There were four outlying ranches from fifty to seventy miles distant from this central hacienda. The manager used to visit each of these ranches about once in three months. He would start out with a coach drawn by eight horses or mules and escorted by fifteen or twenty men on horseback, dressed in leather garments ornamented with silver bands and silver lace, wearing large sombreros, and riding in costly and ornate saddles. Coach and horsemen would all go on the run for about twelve miles when they would come to a fresh relay of horses or mules that had been sent on ahead. The horses and mules would be changed, and again the company would be off at a run. They would change about five times in a journey of fifty or sixty miles, so they always traveled at full speed with fresh animals.

This great ranch consisted of two million acres of land, one hundred thousand head of cattle, seventy thousand sheep, one hundred thousand goats, and fifty thousand horses. There were many such ranches as this over the plateaus of Mexico —though perhaps none that surpassed it. Very likely there is no private estate at present that can compare in wealth, extent, and isolated magnificence of life, with these vast estates visited by Mr. Ayer and his associates on this trip into the interior. The party finally reached the City of Mexico, and after spending about ten days in sight-seeing, Mr. Ayer and two others returned to the terminus of the railroad where the ambulance and a four-mule team awaited them. They spent another night at the Mesquite Ranch, where they were again entertained in sumptuous style, and then made the two hundred and fifty mile drive to the railroad connection for the North.

In 1887 Mr. Ayer with his friend Mr. Henry Stone, General Manager of the Burlington Railroad, went to Mexico for a six weeks vacation. The journey from Chicago to Aguas Calientes was made in Mr. Stone's private car. Mr. Wharf, a civil engineer employed by the Mexican Central Railroad, had invited Mr. Ayer to look over the country between Zacatecas and Tampico with him, as the Mexican Central was then projecting a branch road between these two cities, which was afterwards built. Mr. Wharf and Mr. David Mac-Kenzie, who was general superintendent of the road, met them at Aguas Calientes for the five-hundred-mile horseback ride. At Aguas Calientes one day was spent in looking about the city. They took with them in the walks about the town a little Mexican boy, Irjuano, who peddled oranges. Mr. and

Mrs. Ayer had employed him on visits to Aguas Calientes, and they were fond of him. On this occasion Mr. Ayer took him to the theater, and later gave him a suit of leather clothing ornamented with silver braid, and a Mexican hat to match.

MacKenzie and Wharf arrived in due time with camp out-fit, mules, ambulance, and everything required for the trip across the country. The first stopping place was to be the Salinas Ranch—so called because there was a salt lake there and salt works. As the road was dusty and their animals in poor condition, their progress was slow. About the middle of the afternoon their attention was attracted to an unusual amount of dust that moved steadily toward them. This phe-nomenon was soon explained by the appearance of three or four Mexicans in charge of fifteen or sixteen fine horses. After salutes and greetings had been interchanged, Mr. Wharf, who spoke Spanish, informed his friends that the owner of the Salinas ranch and salt works, thinking that their stock might not be good, had taken the liberty to send them some of his. They mounted the fresh horses and went on at a fine pace into the magnificent estate.

The travelers found themselves in a foreign and mediaeval world. The buildings on this hacienda had been erected in the remote past at a time when civilized settlements had to be defended constantly by force of arms against savages, out-laws, and revolutionists. The home, or central plant of this hacienda, occupied several acres of ground and was sur-rounded by a stone wall twenty-five feet high, with bastions at the corners. There was a moat around the whole enclosure, with drawbridges to give entrance to the fortification. Inside were spacious houses with dozens of spare rooms. Everything was on the patriarchal scale. The houses were well furnished, and the Americans were entertained in sumptuous style here for two nights and a day. Mr. Ayer, an eager sportsman in those days, went shooting on the lake the morning after his arrival and got a fine bag of ducks. As they were about to leave, the gentleman of the house said to Mr. Wharf:

"I notice that your stock is not good; and I have taken the liberty of sending relays ahead of you for three or four days travel, so that once a day, at least, you may have fresh animals."

"I am sorry you have taken so much trouble," Mr. Wharf replied.

The Mexican gentleman shrugged his shoulders and said, "Ah, no trouble to me, only trouble to the mules."

As long as the relays held out the company made fifty miles a day. Each night they stopped at some hospitable hacienda where they were royally entertained. At one place there was a great deal of game, including deer, and they stayed there long enough to enjoy some shooting. The owner of this ranch sent out a hundred and sixty men and boys to beat up the mountain and drive out the deer and other game for his guests. The visitors did not get any deer, but they could not help wondering at the unbounded hospitality of the people. A stop of one day was made at San Luis Potosi, a fine city on the eastern edge of the plateau of Mexico. The route down into the tropics passed through a remarkable canyon. It was very deep. Some places the walls rose to a height of two thousand feet in almost perpendicular ascent. A railway from Aguas Calientes to Tampico was to be built down this canyon, and already a trail had been made over which supplies and materials of all kinds might be carried in. They went down this trail. It was a horseback ride that tried men's nerves, as the road for considerable distances was not more than four feet wide. In some places the eye of the traveler glanced down through space a sheer thousand feet to the bottom. In the late afternoon they came to a narrow river that ran down the canyon. At one place they found a pool a hun-

dred and fifty feet across into which a mighty waterfall came
tumbling. Soon they found themselves in a tropical jungle
with ferns and luxuriant foliage all about sparkling with spray
that arose from the falls. After a refreshing swim the party
rode on to the headquarters of a coffee plantation and there
spent the night.

The following day Mr. Ayer had occasion to make use of
experience gained on the plains and in the army. A Mexican
undertook to guide them to the sugar plantation of Señor
Rascom, that lay a little distance off their route. About noon
their guide led them into a palm forest where the soil was very
rich and soft, and where the palm trees were covered with
vines that had stickers on them from two to four inches in
length. They found that they were lost and that their guide
was drunk. He undertook in this soft soil to cross a creek
about ten feet wide. His horse floundered in the black mud
and threw him. He managed to get out on the other side, but
his horse struggled helplessly on the bank. None of the other
members of the party were used to that sort of thing, so Mr.
Ayer had them tie one lariat to the halter of the horse and
another to the horn of the saddle. Then, after stamping down
the soft earth, there being eight or nine men in the party,
with a strong pull and a pull all together, they hauled the
animal out on their side of the stream. Next a lariat was
thrown to the Mexican, and he was drawn back across the
creek. As they were now between two rivers, Mr. Ayer sent
some of the Mexicans ahead to cut a path through the briars
and clear the way somewhat. Guiding themselves by the sun,
they were able finally to extricate themselves. They reached
the river, crossed it, and arrived at the sugar plantation about
five in the afternoon.

After a day at the plantation the company struck out east
across the plains. About forty miles from Tampico they came
upon an abundance of game—deer, avocets, and all kinds of

water fowl. Of game that was fit to eat, they killed as much as they wanted. One joyous day was spent on an excursion to the mouth of the river, where a famous Italian caterer served fish dinners. The trip was made in a boat about forty feet long. Having to row against the wind, the oarsmen grew very tired. There was a sail in the boat; and to the delight of the natives and to their surprise, too, for they did not know that a boat could be made to sail against the wind, Mr. Stone rigged this sail to the mast, and sailed the boat down for them. The dinner of hard shell crabs and fish cooked in many different ways was delicious, especially as their appetites had been well whetted by the day's labors.

The following day a party consisting of Mr. Stone, Mr. MacKenzie, Mr. Ayer, Señor Rascom, who had come down with the Americans from his plantation, and ten Indians, as rowers, went out into the Gulf of Mexico to a point about ten miles southeast of Tampico to fish for red-snappers. The sea was perfectly calm, but the day was very hot and there was a heavy swell. Before they were a mile out Señor Rascom was in the bottom of the boat. Mr. MacKenzie had a more than Scotch seriousness of expression. He stood a good deal of chafing from Mr. Stone, who, being an Atlantic coast yachtsman, supposed himself to be immune. The party had breakfasted early, and about ten o'clock Mr. Stone thought he would get a little lunch. Leaning over in the boat, he reached into the pail, but quickly came up looking white, without any lunch.

"Darn that lunch!" he ejaculated.

When they were ten miles out, they all fished as best they could in their state of health, but nobody got a bite. As this did not seem to pay, they all lay down in the bottom of the boat and went to sleep. The Indians, in the meantime, proceeded to get drunk on sugar cane rum; at least they were all feeling good.

"Get up here. The wind is coming up!" shouted Mac-Kenzie after they had all been asleep for some time.

Sure enough, "a Norther" had descended upon them. It was a rather dismal situation. The greatest danger was that they might not be able to cross the sand bar at the mouth of the river, as the water there was only ten feet deep. But they got up their sails, and while Mr. Ayer went forward to trim them, Mr. Stone took the tiller. If they had had to make one tack, they could not have reached the harbor; but by sailing close-hauled all the way, they managed to shoot across the bar. It was none too soon; thirty minutes later it would have been impossible to cross. The day's outing was concluded to everybody's satisfaction with another excellent fish dinner at the café of the Italian.

The next lap of this adventurous trip took the travelers through a dense tropical country to Pachuca. The Indians in the numerous villages through which they passed had never seen a wheel. There were no vehicles of any kind; everything was carried on pack mules. These primitive inhabitants were exceedingly interesting. The travelers remained over Sunday in an Indian village called Huayutla. There was a large cathedral in this place, and this Sunday happened to be an important feast day. There were about four hundred Indians in the village. Some of the men wore sandals; others were barefoot; and all of them wore shawls. The women were dressed in low cut chemises with broad embroidery of bright-colored wool around top and bottom. Over their shoulders both men and women wore a coarse cloth called *esquino,* with a hole cut through for the head. This garment came down ten or twelve inches below the neck, was folded away from the shoulders, and usually was beautifully embroidered. True to his instincts as a collector, Mr. Ayer bought two of these garments and later presented them to the Field Museum, where they may still be seen.

As they came out of the tropical country heavy with vegetation, up onto the plains of Mexico, they traveled over an immemorially ancient road known as "The Hidalgo Trail." It was used by the natives, probably, hundreds of years before Cortes the Conqueror came. The weather was intensely hot. Mr. Ayer rode a large, very rough-gaited mule. Most of the time the company moved at a slow trot, and Mr. Ayer averred that his friends estimated—an estimate that he himself considered correct—that he bounced four inches from the saddle ninety thousand times each day. He was somewhat stout at that time, his weight being about two hundred pounds, but fortunately he was only forty-five years old and was in prime condition. One day, as they began to approach the end of their long journey, they stopped at a little hotel just about noon. They had now been away from home about five weeks, and Mr. Ayer was beginning to feel eager to return to civilization. They had intended to allow themselves two and a half days more to reach Pachuca.

The game "Follow Your Leader" is an old one; and every boy knows how irresistibly the impulse sometimes comes to give a dare. Mr. Ayer was the oldest man in the party, and by far the heaviest, but there was much of the boy in him. He decided to give a dare.

"If you fellows had any nerve," he said, turning toward his companions, "you would go through to Pachuca by tomorrow noon."

The rest all laughed, and Stone said to the others, "Boys, let's go to Pachuca under Ayer's guidance, just as he wants us to go."

They all agreed to do this.

"Will you mind me in every way—in regard to meals, sleeping, traveling, and everything?"

"Yes," they said.

"All right. We start now."

A chorus arose, "For heaven's sake, you are not going out in this sun, are you?"

"Yes, in ten minutes. But before we go, I will map out a little schedule. We will travel about ten miles to the station where we had intended to spend the night. At five o'clock this afternoon we will go down to the river and take a bath. At 6:00 we will have our supper. At 7:00 we will go to bed. At 11:30 you will be called. At 11:45 you will have coffee and bread. At twelve o'clock, sharp, we will start for Pachuca."

The distance to Pachuca from the place where they were to have their few hours of sleep was about fifty miles; the train was scheduled to leave Pachuca at one o'clock the next day; so they were allowing themselves only about twelve hours on the road. As the pack train was to return over the same route it had just come, it was now left behind, except for a few mules to carry baggage. They carried out the program to the letter and the minute. Said Mr. Ayer,

"It was a bright and starry night. First, we went down across the narrow valley, and then up a steep trail over a range of mountains three thousand feet high. At seven in the morning it commenced to get hot; at eight, it was intensely hot; and the heat grew more intense every hour. I never stopped for anything, but kept on and on in that awful glare of heat and dust. We arrived at Pachuca at noon, about as tired a lot of men as anyone ever saw. After a quick lunch there we took the train on the narrow gauge railroad at one o'clock. We went down to the junction of the main line of the Mexico and Vera Cruz Railroad, reaching there about four o'clock. At five "a Norther" came on, and the weather grew very cold. Huddled up around the station, our weary group waited for the train in much discomfort."

As the train drew near the station, Mr. Ayer noticed a yellow car at the rear end; which he recognized as a private car belonging to the Chicago and Northwestern.

"Who is in this car?" he inquired of the colored man who stepped down onto the platform.

"Mr. Marshall Kirkman and some of his friends," the negro replied.

Mr. Kirkman was treasurer of the Northwestern at that time, and was an intimate friend of Mr. Ayer's. Rushing into the car, Mr. Ayer found Mr. Kirkman and his wife, Mr. Volney Foster, Mr. Kirk, and another gentleman—all personal friends from Chicago. They were amazed to see Mr. Ayer here. The rest of the party was promptly invited into the car; the colored man was soon busy preparing food for the cold hungry wayfarers; and in this special car, enjoying all the luxuries of civilized life, they made their entrance into the City of Mexico. Mr. Stone's car had been sent down from Aguas Calientes, so a few days later the friends started for home.

CHAPTER IX

World Travel

THERE are many ways of securing "a higher education." Experience is a great educator; a man may become wise and cultivated through the reading of books; and by means of travel he may acquire knowledge, power, poise, and polish beyond anything that a college course can offer him. Says Emerson, "What we do not call education is more gracious than what we do call so." Mr. Ayer was a fine example of the cultivated man in contradistinction from the formally educated or college bred man. His grammar school training he secured on the Plains and in the army. He found the equivalent of a high school course in business and on the railway trains. For four years in college he substituted wide reading and the expansive joy of collecting. Finally, in middle life, he entered the University of European and World Travel, and in this institution spent twenty-six spring quarters in postgraduate work. He was a research scholar, too, if ever there was one. He specialized in collecting; and, though he wrote no thesis and sought no degree, in his own field he submitted every necessary credential, and in the substantial document known as *The Ayer Collection* he added to the sum of original knowledge.

It was long before Mr. Ayer had any Ulysses-like longing to "sail beyond the sunset and the baths of all the western stars." He seemed to dislike the thought of an ocean voyage, and his vision only gradually expanded to the vast sweep of European culture available through travel. Mrs. Ayer had been abroad twice before Mr. Ayer was willing to give a thought to such a remote new world of experience. But in due time Mrs. Ayer's enthusiasm for foreign travel overcame his reluctance; and having once come under the spell of the Old World, his ardor knew no bounds. For a quarter of a century the spring months invariably found him abroad.

He took his first trip to Europe in company with his wife, his daughter, and Miss Marion Sturges. There was nothing wanting to make this first experience abroad memorable, stimulating, enlightening. He seems to have made the conventional European tour—how far from conventional to him and to every eager American who enjoys it for the first time! He marveled at Chester, with its Roman ruins, ancient walls, splendid cathedral, and old timber buildings. He found London, indeed, "a man's town, with power in the air." He was impressed with its tremendous size, its river thoroughfare, the ceaseless roar and stir of its traffic, and, perhaps, more than anything else, with its museums and collections. If London overwhelmed him, Paris fascinated him—cathedrals, monuments, art galleries, arches, avenues, and boulevards— how much more glorious than he had imagined! He was entranced with the Milan Cathedral, Venice, Naples, Rome, Pisa—each of these cities laid its peculiar spell upon him. In Florence Mrs. Ayer was stricken with typhoid fever and they were detained three months. During this time Mr. Ayer came and went repeatedly among the almost incomparable art galleries and architectural monuments of that city. Seventy-two times that season he wandered through the Uffizi and Pitti art galleries.

It is exceedingly interesting to study the mental impressions and aesthetic reactions of this American business man, reared in the rough and ready schools of the West, the far West, and the remote Southwest, when thrown now for the first time into the center of the world's most famous museums and proudest achievements in art. Here is the real test of his fitness to enter into and enjoy these priceless, universal gifts of the

human spirit. He was equal to the opportunity, for there was
in the soul of Edward Everett Ayer inherent greatness. There
was simplicity, sincerity, susceptibility to beauty, capacity to
recognize and enter into the truest and the best. His response
to these new values and revelations was untutored, but it was
genuine and discerning.

His chief interest from the first was in museums and art
collections. He had himself already made creditable beginnings as a collector, so he was prepared at once to enjoy the
world-famed museums, aquariums, and natural history collections of Europe. He was struck with the collection of armor
and crown jewels in the Tower of London, with the South
Kensington Museum, the Natural History Museum, the Indian Museum, and like places. When he got to Naples, he
was thrilled with wonder and delight. Here was one of the
greatest museums in all the world. He found here fourteen
thousand remarkable specimens of bronzes from Pompeii and
Herculaneum, a rare collection of Roman glass and antique
jewels in the gem room, and, most magnificent of all, Pom-
peian mural collections more numerous than the sum of those
contained in all the other museums of the world. In the Vatican at Rome he gazed with amazement upon books, bronzes,
statues, tapestries, Egyptian antiques, and natural history
specimens such as he had never dreamed of before.

During this first tour he saw many of the most sublime
cathedrals of Europe, and from the first he was subdued by
their beauty and uplifted by their grandeur. He was awed by
their "antique pillars massy proof," and he loved their "sto-
ried windows richly dight, casting a dim religious light." On
subsequent trips he was to see many others equally beautiful
and impressive. During his lifetime he visited nearly all the
chief cathedrals of Spain, England, France, Germany, and
Italy, and he entered with keen appreciation into everything
about them—the spirit of worship and aspiration that brought

them into existence, the variety and quality of the material that entered into their construction, and the marvelous architectural genius revealed in their erection. Said he: "Some people say they get sick of looking at cathedrals, but it fills me with disgust that anyone could be so stupid as to get sick of a beautiful architectural cathedral. Think of the Milan cathedral with its one hundred and twenty-five spires! Conceive of the fact that it was in process of building for a hundred and twenty years!"

Up to the time that he visited Europe, he had seen almost no great paintings, and in consequence his taste in art was unformed. The first canvases by the old masters that he ever saw were in the National Gallery in London and in the Louvre. He was impressed by the art collections that he saw in Milan—particularly with *The Last Supper* of Leonardo da Vinci. Rubens' *Last Supper* elicited his praise, also. "Rubens' rough and rugged figures," he said, "coincide more with my idea of the fishermen of Galilee than any others I have seen." However, at that time he got comparatively little pleasure from art galleries, for he was not used to them. It was not until he reached Rome that he had his real awakening. One day with Mrs. Ayer and the two young ladies he went to visit the Vatican. Mr. Ayer had traversed the whole length of the gallery before the ladies had completed their survey of the first room. In the very last room he came upon the picture of a saint upon her knees with her hands uplifted. In the clouds toward which her eyes were cast two or three little cherubs could be seen indistinctly. Never before in his life had he been so impressed with anything. He exclaimed to himself, "My Lord, that's a fine thing!" He looked at the name of the painting and found that it was Barocci's *Saint Michaelina*. He hurried back at once to find Mrs. Ayer and the girls.

"For heaven's sake," he said, "come and see this *Saint Michaelina*."

They, too, shared his enthusiasm. From that moment he became a lover of pictures. When he learned that in Rome there was a room named for Barocci in which several of his pictures were hung, he was much gratified; for he felt that his first great adventure in art appreciation was in the right direction. Four years later when he next visited Rome, he went straight to the Vatican; and rushing up three flights of steps, he walked directly to the *Saint Michaelina* to see if it had lost its appeal for him. It had not, nor did it ever cease to interest him.

Just on the eve of his departure for America, as Mr. Ayer was making a farewell visit to the Louvre, he discovered a second painter who was to remain a favorite with him all the rest of his life. He had got as far as Room 22, when suddenly he came upon six or seven canvases that depicted certain cathedrals and ruins in Southern France. They were the work of the French painter Robert. At that time Mr. Ayer did not know that Robert was celebrated throughout Europe for his architectural and landscape paintings. There was something about these pictures that thrilled and uplifted our traveler. He could breathe the very atmosphere that surrounded them, and he felt that he had never seen anything like them before. These were among the first pictures that really interested him, and as with the *Saint Michaelina,* this interest never wore away. He was so excited over his discovery that he went back at once to find his companions, so that he might share his enjoyment with them.

Nearly always Mr. Ayer's startling adventures with books, pictures, and antiques had their sequel and climax. Twenty years after the experience just related, Mr. and Mrs. Ayer were in Paris in company with their intimate friends Mr. and Mrs. Martin Ryerson and Mr. and Mrs. Charles Hutchinson of Chicago. Mr. Ayer secured an illustrated catalogue of several very large canvases by Robert that were to be sold in

Paris at auction. He went at once to Mr. Ryerson and Mr. Hutchinson, and after showing them the catalogue, easily persuaded them to go with him to the gallery where these pictures were on exhibition. All three of the gentlemen were fairly captivated by them. Four, in particular, interested them keenly. They decided to secure one of them for the Art Institute in Chicago at any cost. They debated half a day trying to determine which one they would buy, for they admired all four so very much that it was difficult to make a choice. Finally the decision was reached to buy all four, if they could be procured at any reasonable price. M. Raoul, an expert, was engaged to bid for them. M. Raoul's instructions were that they would go as high as 60,000 francs, if necessary. The pictures were finally knocked down to the Chicagoans at 59,900 francs; but as the bidding went on they had gradually worked themselves up to such a pitch that they would have paid another 100,000 francs if necessary. Others were bidding against them all the time, and it was impossible to tell how high they might have to go. These wonderful paintings were brought to Chicago and hung in the Art Institute. The first four men who viewed them there paid for them.

These very large canvases—about twelve feet high and five or six feet wide—may now be seen at the head of the stairs in the Art Institute. They depict with massiveness of impression the Ruins of Rome. They were meant originally for a very large room in a French chateau, and were designed to produce the effect of spaciousness. Mr. Ayer relates that a man who was ascending the stairs in the Art Institute stopped in astonishment when his eyes fell upon these pictures and exclaimed:

"Now I know where these Robert pictures are that have been lost to the world for so many years! I have known them all my life in the chateau of my friend, and they are of great value."

The Ayers were among the first Americans to tour Europe in an automobile. Mr. Ayer owned an automobile in France before he had one at home. His first car was a Darracq, purchased through Mr. Dallaba, head of the American Express Company in Paris. Though it had its peculiarities, as all things French have, it was a good, comfortable car. The chauffeur was French, too, and he proved to be both dishonest and disagreeable, as well as peculiar. Worst of all, he was a poor driver and a poor mechanic. So far as the pleasures of touring were concerned, the trip was a failure. They limped along from day to day and from city to city with some new disaster to record at every stage. In his notes Mr. Ayer gives about equal attention to mishaps to the Darracq and to illuminating comment on history and art. The following typical extracts from Mr. Ayer's journal tell the story:

"About five miles out of Paris the ignition gave out; and after working for hours, the chauffeur finally got us to Versailles where we stayed all night, having made twelve miles that day."

"We had a good deal of trouble all the way along and finally stopped in Orleans before our hotel, stock still. The gasoline had given out.

"That afternoon a little before dark the car stopped again, and we found that the gasoline was entirely gone. The chauffeur got a team and went back several miles to a small town to get some gasoline; and we at last reached Bourges in the evening, the car red hot and in bad order.

"We worked on from there to Vichy and then across the mountains to Lyons, where the car gave out entirely, and the chauffeur had to go back to Paris for some parts.

"When we were four or five miles out of Nîmes the car stopped again. We were hauled back into Nîmes with a pair of horses and it took the chauffeur the whole day to fix up the ignition. We then went on to Arles for lunch. It took the chauffeur two hours to get the car started after lunch. Just at night something gave out again and it took two and a half hours to get started. We landed in Marseilles about nine o'clock that night. From here the chauffeur had to go back to Paris for some new parts, and we had to wait two days.

"We finally got to Genoa all right and stayed all night. Going out of there the next morning the chauffeur was arrested for fast driving and I had to pay a fine of ten dollars.

"At four in the afternoon as we were going up the hill the car again balked. Some men came along and we hired them to push the car to the top.

"He concluded something might be wrong with the carburetor, and found that it was filled with wax.

"He worked the next afternoon on the car and we started for Rome and arrived there in bad condition. We had smashed both of the lamps bumping into a building in a narrow place and the top was all loose and tied on with ropes. After working on the machine for three days we started for Florence. We remained there a few days and then went on to Bologna. We had gone only about twelve miles when the whole differential of the hind axle gave way and we had to be hauled into Florence with two yoke of big white oxen. I then sent the chauffeur to Paris for a new hind axle. He was gone two days and it took two more to fix the car.

"We were sailing along toward Mantua all right when the whole back end gave way again. . . . In despair I sent the car back to Paris by rail."

If there were nothing more to relate than this, it would have been a lugubrious experience, indeed. But, as has been intimated, the route lay through Chartres, Orleans, Tours, Avignon, Nîmes, Orange, Marseilles, Genoa, Nice, Pisa, Sienna, and Rome; so there were days of delight as well as hours of annoyance, and the account glows with references to cathedrals, museums, chateaux, Roman arches and theatres, towers, palaces, and temples. Mr. Ayer was so constituted that nothing in which he was engaged could possibly turn out a failure. And surely there are worse hardships for the lover of art than to be stranded for a few hours in Chartres or Avignon, or doomed to a delay of two days in Florence or Rome. And, indeed, our travelers found so much joy in this first attempt to tour Europe in an automobile that before sailing for home, despite the disasters that had dogged their way, they determined to buy a new and better car the following season and again ramble at will wherever fancy might direct.

October 22, 1904, in company with Mr. Daniel Burnham and his wife, Mr. and Mrs. Ayer sailed on the sixteen thousand ton ship *Mongolia* for the Orient. Mr. Burnham, the distinguished Chicago architect, was going to the Philippines to lay out new summer residences up in the mountains a hundred and twenty-five miles from Manila for the American officials. Major General Corbin and his wife were also passengers on the *Mongolia*. The General was going out to take command in the Philippines. The company went ashore at Honolulu and for one day enjoyed its tropical beauty. The next stop was Yokohama. General Corbin and his wife went on up to Tokyo to pay their respects to Mr. Griscom, the American Minister. Immediately an officer came back from Tokyo with a message from General Corbin requesting the Ayers and the Burnhams to come on to the capital to attend a dinner party that the minister was giving the next day.

The dinner was a stately affair. There were thirty guests at the table—Japanese officials for the most part; but there were present, also, the ministers of France, Germany, and England, as well as other men of international distinction. The war between Russia and Japan was then at its height. On Mr. Ayer's left was seated General Terruchi, Secretary of War, and on his right, the wife of the famous Japanese Marshall Oyama. This lady had been educated at Vassar College, and she spoke excellent English. She was modestly and very beautifully attired in Japanese costume. A few days later the Americans were invited to the Mikado's garden party, held in one of the great parks. The Japanese ladies on this occasion were dressed in French costumes—not so becoming as their native garments, Mr. Ayer thought—and the men were arrayed in Prince Albert coats and silk hats. The visitors were invited to attend the annual military review, also. Thirty thousand splendid, well-dressed soldiers on this occasion passed before the reviewing stand of the Mikado.

At Nikko Mr. Ayer was struck with the cypress trees of enormous size that grew about the temple and for miles along the chief avenue. At Kamakura he saw the famous bronze statue of Buddha. The figure is in a sitting posture, and is sixty feet high and twenty feet across the shoulders. In the temple city of Nara his interest was aroused by the four thousand stone lanterns that lined all the avenues and surrounded the courts of the great temples. He wondered, too, at the hundreds and hundreds of tame deer in the woods about the temples. He saw chrysanthemums—a thousand lovely blossoms on a single plant. Several happy days were spent, thus, sightseeing —and collecting; for he carried away from every city he visited some rare article characteristic of Japanese life and art. Lovely lacquer and embroideries, sonorous-sounding temple gongs, a long blue manuscript in gold letters—a part of the Buddhist bible—specimens of *cloisonné* made by Nama Kawa, the most skilful designer and maker of *cloisonné* in the world, and many other fascinating articles.

At Kobe the party took boat for the Philippines, sailing two hundred miles down through the inland sea of Japan to Nagasaki and then on by the Island of Formosa, and at last into the harbor of Manila. General Corbin, who had preceded them to the Philippines, sent his steam yacht out to meet them and then entertained them most hospitably in his home during their stay in Manila. Mr. Ayer was intensely interested in everything that he saw, but especially in the work of the American Commission then in charge of the civil affairs of the Islands. It was during this trip that he made the acquaintance of Mr. Dean C. Worcester and secured from him the remarkable series of photographs and descriptive notes mentioned in Chapter VI.

About ten days after the Ayers arrived in Manila, General Corbin invited them aboard the Government's three thousand ton yacht, to accompany him and his staff on a cruise of the Islands. They went in and out among the numerous islands until they came to Iloilo, headquarters of the army division under Brigadier General W. H. Carter. They next sailed south to Zamboanga, where Major General Leonard Wood's division was stationed. They had lunch with General Wood and then under his direction took a trip into the country. He had the natives climb the cocoanut trees and throw down cocoanuts for his guests. They closed the day by attending a school entertainment and reception at the Club. That evening they went south to Jolo, where Lieutenant Colonel Hugh L. Scott, an expert in the control of primitive peoples, was in charge of the fanatical Mohammedans who lived on this southernmost point of the Islands.

Returning to General Wood's headquarters at Zamboanga, they started out anew. Mr. Ayer's own words best describe this picturesque part of the journey:

The next morning General Wood and his wife, part of his staff, and ourselves sailed east on our steamer for about two hundred miles along the south end of the Island of Mindanao. We stopped at a little fort called Fort Lapitan. General and Mrs. Corbin, General and Mrs. Wood, Mrs. Ayer and I, took an ambulance and, accompanied by the staff on horseback and six or seven cavalrymen as a guard, we started into the tropical jungles that had been the stronghold of the Moros. It was a most interesting ride of twenty-four miles up the hills above the shores of Lake Lanao. The jungles of this far-south tropical district were most wonderful, with birds, monkeys, or some other interesting thing in sight every minute. We had to walk down a steep path two miles to the lake. Here we found a little steamboat ready for us, and embarking we went fifteen miles to the fort on the west end of the lake. There we were distributed among the officers of the fort. We stayed all night and part of the next day. It was here that I bought the splendid knife with ivory and silver handle that I now have in my library.

We left this fort about ten o'clock in the morning, again in an ambulance, and went north, coming out about three o'clock in the afternoon on the north end of the island at another small fort. Shortly before arriving at this fort, we left our horses and went into the jungle about half a mile where we came to the river that runs from Lake Lanao. Here it runs through a canyon five or six hundred feet deep, and right where we came out it makes a perpendicular fall of two hundred and fifty feet. It was a large river and the sides of the canyon from top to bottom were covered completely with immense ferns and other tropical foliage. The mist rising from the water in a cloud sprayed all parts of this foliage, so that in the bright sun it seemed that each and every leaf held millions of diamonds. The size of the leaves in this tropical jungle are almost beyond belief; I know we saw several that were ten feet long and five or six feet wide.

After lunch and a little reception at the fort General Wood, his wife, and the staff went back to Zamboanga by steamer, while the Corbins and the Ayers steamed north among the innumerable islands to Manila. General Corbin once laughingly said, "Mr. Ayer has done more than anyone to disarm the Moros by buying their weapons for the Field Museum."

The day before Christmas Mr. and Mrs. Ayer sailed on a tiny steamer for Hong Kong. During the next few weeks they traveled widely in China and India, viewing with intense interest the strange customs and grim rites, "the splendor and the havoc" of these Oriental countries. In Hong Kong they took a sedan chair and visited the tea factory; they bought quantities of embroidery and white grass cloth in Canton; they disembarked at Singapore, only a few degrees from the equator, and here bought a rare collection of shells; they sailed across the Indian Ocean to Colombo on the Island of Ceylon, where the loveliest pearls are gathered. At Kandy a visit was made to the Botanical Garden—the most famous one in the world. They marveled at the temples in the cities of Tuticorin and Janjore in the extreme south of India; Madras was remembered for its size and its miserable hotels.

In Calcutta they witnessed the burning of the dead, in accordance with the custom of the country—several bodies being burned at a time in a large open court. At Darjeeling, day after day for five days, they gazed out upon the splendor and majesty of the Himalaya Mountains. A visit was made to Benares in the valley of the Ganges, where they saw the dead burned, after the bodies had been immersed in the waters of the sacred river. To their amazement the country about Benares was overrun with birds and animals. These creatures are preserved because of the superstition of the people, so they multiply without limit. In Benares they visited a special temple where from fifteen hundred to two thousand monkeys are kept all the time. At Cawnpore, Lucknow, and Delhi the terrible realities of the Sepoy Rebellion were brought vividly to their minds. Agra—located three miles from the Taj Mahal, the loveliest of all lovely buildings erected by the hand of man—was visited at the full of the moon. Day after day and night after night they drank in its beauty. They could not get enough of it. Mr. Ayer pronounced the tombs of Agra the architectural gems of the earth. There are many of them, and they are encompassed by walls a mile square. There are wonderful gates and gardens "and most curious and unique carving—all built at great expense and a cost of untold labor." At Bombay they visited the strange temple where the Parsees expose the bodies of their dead to be devoured by vultures.

From Bombay the travelers steamed across the Arabian Sea and entered the Gulf of Aden. Thence they moved on into the Red Sea; passed through the Suez Canal; crossed the Mediterranean between Sicily and the mainland of Italy;

went between the islands of Corsica and Sardinia through the Straits of Bonifacio, and so into the harbor of Marseilles. Disembarking at Marseilles, they went to Paris by rail, expecting there to find the new automobile that had been ordered the previous year all ready for their use. But owing to a protracted strike in France their car was not ready for them. However, Mr. Ayer's good friend Dallaba put his own automobile at their disposal, and they soon set out to enjoy numerous tours about Paris. In fact, before their own car was delivered to them, they traveled in all about two thousand miles, returning frequently to Paris as a center. With the car they were able to reach many places not easily accessible to the casual tourist. They stopped at the Normandy Inn at Dives, in which William the Conqueror spent the night before he sailed for England; they ate one of Madame Poulard's omelettes in her noted inn at Mont Saint Michel; and at Nantes they saw the fine chateau in which Anne of Brittany was married. They went to Carnac; studied the forty pieces of beautiful tapestry at the cathedral of Angiers; and felt the spell of enchantment at Rheims that the cathedral there exercises over every one who sees it.

As soon as they could secure their own car they started for Italy, going by Fontainbleau and the little cathedral town of Sens. In the church treasury here they were shown a small tapestry ten feet in length and not more than three in width that was valued at more than a million francs. They started for Turin by way of Chambery, expecting to reach Turin over the Mont Cenis pass. But the snow near the top of the mountain was three feet deep, and they had to go back to Modena and ship the car to Turin. They went by Milan and the Italian lakes and then climbed the Saint Gothard pass as far as was possible with an automobile. At the east end of the tunnel they put the car on a railway train and shipped it through to the west end. One day they lunched at Altdorf, the home of

William Tell; went by way of Basel, Strassburg, and Nancy; and then sped two hundred miles, over roads that are a delight to the tourist, into Paris. A few more Parisian days and then homeward! They had traveled around the world and in so doing had enjoyed to the brim much that the old world had to offer.

The spring of 1906 found our travelers still unsatiated. This season proved one of the most satisfactory they had yet experienced. Added to all the other attractions of a foreign tour was the joy of congenial companionship. On the same steamer with them sailed their close friends Mr. and Mrs. Charles Hutchinson, Mr. and Mrs. Martin Ryerson, Mr. and Mrs. Daniel Burnham, Mr. and Mrs. Wells, Mr. Wheeler, his wife and daughter, and Mr. Chauncey Blair and his family. They all sat at the same table on board the great ocean liner—the captain's table, of course, and there was continually "a feast of reason and a flow of the soul"—each day vying with the last in pleasure and good fellowship. Mr. Ayer had ordered a new car. It was ready for him when he arrived in Paris. He had secured a new chauffeur, also, and a fine one, Adrian Golet.

On this tour they saw many cathedrals—Chartres, the Byzantine cathedrals at Périgueux and Poitiers, the church at Rodez with its fine campanile, the church at Albi, distinguished for the loveliness of its stone entrances and its screen of delicately carved stone. In the cathedral at Aix they saw tapestries of extraordinary beauty and value, two rare paintings, and a pair of carved wooden doors as fine as any in Europe. In the dirty little mountain town of Conques they were shown, in the remarkable church treasury, a collection of books in silver bindings set with jewels, priests' hats, capes, and coats, and tapestries of fabulous value. Six million francs had been offered for this collection. They visited the church at Assisi. Giotto devoted twenty-two years of his life to the

decorating of this cathedral sacred to the memory of Saint
Francis. At Padua they saw the church of Saint Anthony,
celebrated for the Donatello bronzes, the tomb of Saint
Anthony, and the chapel painted by Giotto. In the cathedral
at Innsbruck they were shown the tomb of Maximilian I, one
of the most perfect specimens of monumental bronze in the
world. The Cologne cathedral, thought by many to be the
finest example of Gothic art in existence, was a fitting climax
to their study of church architecture.

On this trip, too, they saw romantic castles, ancient colleges,
and places made memorable by heroic or tragic deeds—Car-
cassonne, that most remarkable of mediaeval fortresses;
Arezzo, where fine specimens of the handiwork of Luca della
Robbia were seen; Ferrara, with its impressive moated castle;
the old Roman town of Verona, with its strange tombs and
the haunting pathos that Shakespeare has thrown over it with
the tragedy of *Romeo and Juliet;* ancient Nuremberg, with its
red roofs and mediaeval torture chambers; Bingen, "fair Bingen on the Rhine"; and cloistered Heidelberg; and mighty
Worms, dominated by a colossal statue of Luther. Set in the
midst of the chalk hills about Lebau they saw the stronghold
of the robber barons of long ago. The houses are cut out of
chalk cliffs and are reached through stone entrances. At one
time this town had a population of four thousand, but now it
has only about two hundred inhabitants.

As the years went by, the Ayers were continually entering
new fields of travel. One of the most unusual of all their many
trips was that extending over several weeks through Algeria
and Tunisia in Northern Africa, in the year 1910. In a volume
of unique interest, entitled *A Motor Flight through Algeria
and Tunisia,* Mrs. Ayer has recorded the experiences of this
tour. This book is full of stir and color. It is written with zest
and is illustrated with more than a hundred excellent photographs made by Mrs. Ayer during the journey. With the com-

bined aid of pen and camera the reader is able to follow the
travelers over highway and through byway in strange and
remote places. In these vivid pages one feels the glamour of
Oriental life—sometimes, the squalor too. The tour was made
in a six-cylinder car that was the pride of Mr. Ayer's heart,
over roads not surpassed by the best roads in France. Their
chauffeur, Adrian, was to the manner born, one who "felt
every throb of his engine, and loved his car as one loves a fine
horse." Mrs. Ayer took as much delight in her two kodaks as
Mr. Ayer did in his automobile and his driver. She was somewhat annoyed because there was little literature available
concerning the places to be visited, but nothing could cloud the
eager expectancy of her husband.

"As for me," he said, "If I can't read up and do not know
much about the country through which I am passing, I am
content to be going on good roads with a beautiful panorama
of hills, mountains, and sea unfolding before me; with the
sight of the curious people on the road, the fresh, pure air
blowing in my face, and the throbbing of a fine engine under
me."

The tour included Algiers, Cherchel, Bou Saâda, Tlemcen,
Laghouat, Constantine, Tébessa, Timgad, Biskra, Touggourt, Tunis, Carthage—these and a score of other fascinating cities in addition. In Algiers the splendid mosques and fine
old Moorish palaces delighted them. Mr. Ayer remarked,
discriminatingly: "I like the style of architecture here. It
suits the country better than the ugly modern French style.
When they conquer a country and begin to erect new buildings
they can't do better than to copy the style of architecture of
the first occupants. White Moorish buildings in our country,
with its changing climate are much out of place; here they are
admirable."

On the way to Cherchel they passed the famous Tombeau
de la Chrétienne. They were charmed with the site of the old

Roman city of Cherchel and with the ruins of temples, aqueducts, arches, statues, and luxurious baths that they saw all about them. The walled town of Bou Saâda, set in its green oasis, is notorious as the home of the Ouled Naïl dancing girls. The ever eager collector secured from one of the dancing girls four or five highly desired articles of jewelry; and afterward his companion considered herself more fortunate than her husband when for a small amount she got the privilege of "a snapshot at one of the girls with all her jewelry hung on her." Two glorious days were spent on a trip to the ancient city of Tlemcen, once a Moorish capital of Western Algeria. Here are three beautiful mosques; one of them, the mosque of Aboul Hassan, has been made into a museum, into which are gathered many of the antiquities of Tlemcen. The doors and minarets of these mosques are of exquisite beauty.

Laghouat, in the country of the Mozabites, was the next objective. It is a fortified outpost of civilization on the edge of the hot wind-swept desert, built on the low hills in a palm oasis. After a night in Laghouat the travelers set out for Ghardaia, the head city of the Mozabites, two hundred kilometers distant across the burning sands. Here they encountered the actual life of the desert. "The large white square was filled wtih a tumultuous, seething jumble of natives, camels, sheep, and goats—all ebullient and bubbling with excitement; the air was full of guttural speech, cries, bleating of sheep, snarling of camels—all lighted with the hot rays of a brilliant sun, with the most intensely blue sky above."

Constantine, built on an isolated rock that rises a sheer thousand feet from the bed of the Rummel River, fascinated them as much by its location as by its romantic history. They visited the strange little town of Tébessa, a place of no mean importance even as early as 300 B.C. It had been a crossroads of the nations. Under Trajan it became the richest city in Africa, next to Carthage. Mr. Ayer was amazed at the beauty, size, and good degree of preservation of its arches and temples. Most splendid of all, he thought, were the ruins of the Temple of Minerva, and the great basilica—the noblest Christian monument of North Africa. He was equally interested in the ruins of Timgad. It was a very ancient city, and at one time it had been a superb one. At the height of its glory it had been the home of rich men who had taken pride in adorning it with temples, statues, monuments, a library, a forum, and costly baths. On a tile in the pavement of the forum the guide called attention to this inscription: "To hunt, to bathe, to play, to laugh—this is life." It seems strange that these ruins, the finest in Africa, should have remained unknown to the modern world until the year 1888.

Biskra they approached with eager anticipation. It is called by the Arabs "The Queen of the Desert." Mrs. Ayer had looked forward to the delights of its climate and Oriental color. Nor was she disappointed. All was as she had pictured. Here was an oasis filled with one hundred fifty thousand palm trees and arched by the bluest of skies. Here were all beautiful Oriental things. Mrs. Ayer writes:

The white buildings, with a dome or two showing beyond; the golden sunshine; the palms raising their feathery fronds along the road; the warm air; the natives in their white burnouses crowding around the car; the indolent tourists lounging on the balconies above; the general air of languor; the feeling that nothing need be done today—that the morrow would suffice—all this gave our motorists the impression that at last they were in the land of *dolce far niente*.

Mr. Ayer made the somewhat daring decision to run from Biskra one hundred fifty miles farther south to Touggourt, in the real Sahara Desert. He was told that he would have to go through heavy sand sometimes; but the guide informed him that rolls of common matting might be carried which could be unrolled and spread in front of the car when the sand became so heavy that the automobile could not plough through it. It was a six days' trip for the strongest and swift-

est camels, but the powerful automobile covered the distance
in two days. The travelers arrived in Touggourt on the eve
of a popular fair to which the natives flocked from remote
places, some of the wild tribes coming even from far down in
the Desert. Added to all the strangeness of the human spectacle (and the equally strange impressions made by a visit to
the old town, with its buildings constructed of sun-dried mud
bricks, and its shops—mere holes in the walls) were the mystery of the Desert at sunset, and the solemn splendor and
silence of the starlight night.

The tour was soon to end, but there was no falling off in
charm. Tunis and Carthage offered a fitting climax. It was the
White City, Oriental Tunis, that they wished to see, not the
modern French town with its conventional shops, *cafés*, and
showy pedestrians. Not until they passed through *Bab-el-
Bahar*, the Old Sea Gate, did they come into the midst of the
color and the glamour, the stir and brightness of the Tunis
they had imagined. Their guide took them first to the *souks*,
or bazaars. Each street is given over to a particular business
or occupation—jewelers, perfumers, saddlers, silk merchants,
shoemakers, embroiderers—each within its own precincts. It
was a motley crowd that they saw here: Tunisians, Algerians,
Jews, Moroccans, Negroes, Bedouins, and Moors. There was
lovely architecture to enjoy—especially the minarets of Sidi-
Ben-Ahrous and Sidi-Ben-Ziad, and the palace of the Bey.
They particularly admired the tiled corridors of the court-
yard at the palace, and the Moorish arches in black and white
stripes of marble. Passing through the cool, vaulted streets
they came to the Great Mosque and admired the beautiful
doors with their Moorish arches. Mr. Ayer was never for a
moment forgetful of his beloved museum in Chicago. The
principal treasures that he acquired here "were some old Bedouin fibulae of fine chased silver; some wonderful old earrings, big as hoops, all hung with little bells; a chased silver
necklace set with mountain garnets; some bracelets of Moorish work in gold and rough emeralds; and Moorish earrings,
a wonder of fine gold filigree and set with many colored
stones."

Carthage impressed them profoundly. Here they passed a

day of pure delight. Carthage is the most famous historical city of Africa. It is associated with Rome in the thought of every student of the Classics. Fable has it that Carthage was founded by Phoenician Dido about 850 B.C. From that legendary time down through Punic, Roman, Christian, and French occupancy it has always been a place of wonder, power, and fascination. The survey of what once was Carthage was an experience never to be forgotten, for these tourists were prepared to enter into the full significance of the past as it here lay spread before them in the form of ruins as majestic and eloquent as any that the world can offer to the inquiring traveler. Fortunately in the College Museum, named for Cardinal Lavigerie, who here, in 1881, inaugurated the Grande Seminaire as a College for the "White Fathers," are collected and preserved all objects from the Punic, Roman, and Christian tombs. An afternoon of enchantment spent in the garden of the "White Fathers" and in the Museum rounded out for the Ayers a perfect tourist day.

At last the travelers were back in Algiers. The time had come when they must return to America. Regretfully, yet with deep satisfaction, they summed up the whole romantic experience as it now unrolled itself in memory.

"Well," said Mr. Ayer, "it is all past—those long delightful rides on perfect roads, over the mountains with glorious scenery of green valleys and snow-capped peaks, across the Desert, by curious villages and always among a strange and picturesque people. . . . And for the archaeologist, what interesting ruins of Roman times, of temples, aqueducts, baths, cisterns, arches, and columns! I would begin the trip over again tomorrow, if I could!"

With a sigh Mrs. Ayer answered: "I would, too, were it possible! What a country for an artist to visit! Such color in tones and half-tones; such subtle gradations in tints of which he never dreamed before, in the color on the mountains in early morning and in the sunset glow at night, in the sands of the Desert, in the creams, blues, reds, and yellows of the costumes of the Bedouin women and in the azure and turquoise of this ever-changing sea!"

And, finally, in the person of the man of affairs now, the railroad builder, the practical American, Mr. Ayer rejoined:

"And the French administration in Africa—how marvelous it is when you think that for several centuries before they came to Africa this country had been suffering from the worst sort of government; that there were no roads that could be called such, no schools, no justice, and no agriculture to speak of! Now, the splendid roads, reaching all parts of the mountains and deserts; the fair system of railroads; the thousands of acres of vines, the thousands of date palms and the millions of olive trees they have planted; the hundreds of artesian wells they have sunk; the paternal interest they take in the people in giving them schools and a fair and just taxation, and in many other ways looking after their interests—all this makes the French occupation and its results the best colonization scheme yet devised."

EDWARD E. AYER AT EIGHTY-TWO
FROM THE PAINTING BY
RALPH CLARKSON

Hawaiian Islands; and more than 900 on the Philippine Islands; and 450 manuscript maps. Not less interesting are the illustrations contained in the collection. There are 3,000 photographs of individual American Indians; 400 prints and 8,000 photographs of the peoples of the Philippine Islands; 900 water color drawings and 600 black and white drawings; 1,232 red chalk drawings of Western Indians from life by Elbridge Ayer Burbank; and finally, forty-eight oil paintings, two by Charles Bird King, and one by Grace Hudson. In addition to all the books, pictures, and manuscripts listed above, there are in this library 200,000 typewritten pages of transcripts from the archives of Spain and Mexico.

In order to make still more impressive the variety and extent of the Ayer Collection, the following extracts are quoted from the descriptive pamphlet alluded to above:

"So rich is this special library in early printed editions, in original manuscripts, in transcripts of unpublished archive material, in original drawings, photographs and other pictorial presentation, that no serious student can afford to overlook its resources or fail to avail himself of them who is concerned with the discovery, settlement and early history of America, or with the customs, habits, manners, language or history of the native races of North America, or of the Hawaiian or the Philippine Islands.

"Geography: Included in this section are many early books on cosmography as well as geography, all with more or less reference to America; atlases and maps, both manuscript and printed, the former including thirteen portolan atlases and eleven portolan charts, all exceedingly valuable material for the early history and development of cartography; also early voyages and travels.

"Indians of North America—Their Origin, Prehistoric Life and History: In this section are grouped the books treating of the origin of the Indians, all the way from the point of view of those who considered them the descendants of the ten lost tribes of Israel, to that of the modern scientific anthropologist. The fascinating story of their prehistoric life is just be-

America, Mr. Ayer had employed his niece, Miss Clara A. Smith, to catalogue it and care for it. To this day it is still under the same intelligent and painstaking supervision, and as a result its usefulness is much enhanced. Fortunately up to the very close of his long life, Mr. Ayer was able in person to direct and administer his remarkable collection. His vision and inspiration were felt to the end; no item was added without his approval; and so keen was his instinct for historical value, so wide his knowledge of men and books, that his judgment was rarely at fault.

The Ayer Collection is essentially a body of source material on the North American Indian and the native inhabitants of the Hawaiian and Philippine Islands. It includes, however, abundant matter on the discovery, exploration, and colonization of the North American continent. In 1927, realizing that the resources of his library were not well enough known to students and research workers, Mr. Ayer requested the Newberry Library to send out to a selected number of libraries and scholars a pamphlet containing brief descriptive notes on the volumes, manuscripts, and other accessioned items in his library. He liked to point out that this document was unique as a guide or catalogue in that it did not contain the title of a single work of the forty-nine thousand that it described. The material is listed under certain group headings, and to indicate the extent and comparative importance of a particular group he had the number of items in each group recorded. There are 3,000 volumes on the Origin, Prehistoric Life and History of the Indians of North America; 800 volumes on Indian Warfare; 1,900 volumes on Geography; 180 Trips Across the Plains; 430 Accounts of Captivity Among the Indians; 1,200 volumes on Spanish North America; 800 volumes dealing with the French Colonies in America; and 2,700 with the English, Dutch, and Swedish Colonies in America; nearly 500 volumes on the of good design and workmanship, glassed (and curtained when desirable), reaching to a height of six or seven feet. Solid, ample tables, comfortable chairs, and large show cases in which are displayed rare maps and drawings, are distributed conveniently about the outer room. There is no sense of crowding; everything seems to be within reach. Yet one feels that everything is precious, that nothing is to be profaned, and that the secrets of this storehouse of wisdom and beauty will reveal themselves in proportion to the seeker's ability to enjoy them.

When the Newberry Library was incorporated in 1892, Mr. Ayer became a member of the Board of Trustees. About 1897 he decided that eventually he would give his collection of books on the American Indians to the Newberry Library, and by this time his home was becoming so overcrowded with books that he found it difficult to shelve them all. Accordingly, cases were provided in the Librarian's office and in the room set aside for the meetings of the Board of Trustees to hold the overflow, and many of the books were transferred from his home to the Library. By 1910 the collection had been augmented to such an extent that it became necessary to provide permanent and spacious quarters for it. To meet this need a doorway was cut through from the exhibition room of the Library on the first floor, and two rooms to the west adjoining the exhibition room (at that time used as the Medical Department of the Newberry Library) were taken over, also. Finally, in 1911, Mr. Ayer's entire collection was placed in these three rooms, and in the course of that same year he made an outright donation of the Ayer Collection to the Newberry Library, reserving to himself, however, the direction and management of it so long as he should live.

During all these twenty or twenty-five years that Mr. Ayer's collection had been expanding from a private library in a single room into one of the most notable collections in

CHAPTER X

The Edward E. Ayer Collection
of
The Newberry Library

THE NEWBERRY LIBRARY, in which the Ayer Collection is housed, is a sedate and substantial building in Spanish Romanesque style, constructed of Connecticut granite. The partition walls are built of brick and tile, and the floors are of red English tile. It occupies a spot of historic interest—the site of the old Ogden house, the only residence in the fire-swept district that was not destroyed in the great fire of 1871. It is situated on Walton Place, facing Washington Square, an attractive little park on the North Side, between Dearborn and Clark Streets.

The Ayer Collection occupies three spacious, well-lighted rooms on the first floor just to the left of the main corridor. It is a bright and inviting place to work. On the wall, directly in front of the visitor as he enters the first room, hangs a portrait of Mr. Ayer by Ralph Clarkson. It was painted when Mr. Ayer was approaching his eighty-second birthday. The atmosphere of these rooms is very agreeable. There is a sense of fitness and beauty. One feels immediately that the treasures which he seeks here are both secure and accessible. This collection is scarcely less notable for its pictorial resources than for its printed material, and one is immediately reminded of this fact upon entering the room. The walls are hung with portraits of famous Indian chiefs, done in colors, and there are exhibited, also, remarkable examples of native Indian art. All available wall space is lined with uniform bookcases

155

THE NEWBERRY LIBRARY

THE ROOMS AT THE LEFT ARE WHERE THE AYER COLLECTION OF AMERICANA IS KEPT —FIRST FLOOR

delineation of the red man. In 1832 he left friends, wife, and aged parents and departed for the western wilds. "I started out," he writes, "inspired with an enthusiastic hope and reliance that I could meet and overcome all the hazards and privations of a life devoted to the production of a literal and graphic delineation of the living manners, customs, and character of an interesting race of people, who are rapidly passing away from the face of the earth—lending a hand to a dying nation who have no historians or biographers of their own to portray with fidelity their native looks and history; thus snatching from a hasty oblivion what could be saved for the benefit of posterity.

"I set out on my arduous and perilous undertaking with the determination of reaching, ultimately, every tribe of Indians on the Continent of North America, and of bringing home faithful portraits of their principal personages, both men and women, from each tribe; views of their villages, games, etc., and full notes on their character and history. I designed, also, to procure their costumes, and a complete collection of their manufactures and weapons, and to perpetuate them in a *Gallery unique,* for the use and instruction of future ages."

How these words and the four hundred pictures that accompanied them, in the two large volumes that Catlin later published under the title, *Letters and Notes on the Manners, Customs, and Condition of the North American Indians,* must have thrilled our book collector when they first came under his eye and into his possession! May not the sentences quoted above be the very inspiration and chart that guided Mr. Ayer as he set out on his career as a collector?

It must have been about 1880 that Mr. Ayer definitely decided to take the North American Indian as his particular field of study and investigation. About this time too, he secured a book that proved a boon to him in the succeeding years and that perfectly supplemented Catlin, Lewis and Clark, School-the first and relate each incident in order. There is magic in the narrative, and the reader will remember that the source of this magic was the three volumes entitled Prescott's *History of the Conquest of Mexico.* In exquisite binding and encased with loving care these books rest in the inner vault at the very center of the shrine, side by side with other books far more costly, though not so precious. What the second book that he acquired may have been, it seems impossible to state. Strange to say, Mr. Ayer never wrote his name in his books or indicated the date of purchase or cost of a particular acquisition. His friends like to think that after the Prescott volumes the next book to come into his possession was a Lewis and Clark, a Catlin, or a Schoolcraft. Certainly the works of these authors are in full evidence on his library shelves. But who can say which one of these many volumes he acquired next? Beyond question Catlin must have been known to him early, and without doubt this author excited his imagination.

George Catlin was a young man of good family, born in Wyoming, Pennsylvania, in 1796. His parents entered the Wyoming Valley soon after the Revolutionary War while the memory of the terrible Indian massacre was still fresh in the minds of the people. He early had a desire to be a painter. However, he studied law and was admitted to the bar. He soon sold his law books, gave up his practice, and diligently took up painting, though without teacher or adviser. He was seeking some field of art in which to display his powers when there arrived in Philadelphia, where he then lived, a delegation of a dozen noble and dignified-looking Indians from the wilds of the Far West. "In silent and stoic dignity these lords of the forest strutted about the city for a few days, wrapped in their pictured robes with their brows plumed with the quills of the war-eagle."

Young Catlin's imagination took fire. His decision was made at once to devote his life and his art to the study and with the English, they are for convenience or classification grouped together here, and this grouping follows them not only through their Colonial life, but in their conquest, exploration and settlement of the country from the Atlantic Ocean to the Golden Gate."

Before turning from this general account of the founding of the Ayer Library and the somewhat detailed description of its resources, it seems fitting to quote three or four paragraphs from a very friendly and illuminating letter written by Mr. Albert H. Wetten, a member of the Board of Trustees of the Newberry Library.

The task Mr. Ayer undertook was most timely. If he had delayed, much of the material that his collection now contains would have gone elsewhere, or would have perished completely. As it stands today, the student of Southwestern colonization cannot afford to ignore the Ayer Library. My acquaintance with him did not become intimate till 1918, when I went upon the Board of the Newberry Library and was assigned to the Committee on Administration. It then became my duty to look after the safeguarding of the Ayer Collection, which is the outstanding department of the Newberry Library; and from this time on till the date of his death, I was in constant and confidential communication with him.

The inspiring motive of his work on his library was a great sympathy with the pioneers who had colonized the Southwest —perhaps more of interest in the men than in their achievements. He sought human experiences; not sophisticated abstractions. He loved the diaries of a trip across the Plains, filled with the things, often commonplace and sordid, that made up the day's adventure. This same interest in the human document inspired his most ambitious task; the acquisition of transcripts from the Archives of the Indies, of reports and correspondence pertaining to the Spanish Colonies of the United States and of Mexico. This is the source material that stirred his imagination, and from which he hoped that the history of the Southwest might be rewritten.

Every word and act of Mr. Ayer falls naturally into story form; so, to give an account of his library, we must begin at

ginning to be unraveled and told, and every year brings new
revelations from archaeologists in all parts of the country.
The history of many tribes is yet to be written and much can
be done from sources found here. Under this grouping are
books dealing also with the following matters: Indian arts and
industries, trade, money, mythology and religion (including
ceremonies and dances), music, physical anthropology, health
and disease, missions and schools, and the biographies of
individual Indians.

"Indian Languages and Graphic Systems: One hundred
and eighty-eight different languages or dialects are represented in the Ayer Collection. The books illustrating or treating of them include grammars and grammatical treatises,
vocabularies and dictionaries, and some few school books;
translations of the Bible, prayer books and catechisms; all
very largely done by missionaries, both Catholic and Pro-
testant. Of more recent date are books containing folk-lore
and myths with both free and literal translations. Supple-
menting these are some fifty-five original manuscripts, and
50,000 pages of photographic copies of manuscripts, prin-
cipally in the Mayan and allied languages.

"Indian Warfare: In this section are included books relating to the French and Indian Wars, the American Revolution,
the War of 1812, the various colonial wars, and later the
Indian warfare with the United States. Here are included
430 volumes containing narratives of Indian captivity, and
seventy volumes containing Indian treaties. There are also
several manuscript treaties.

"Spanish North America: This section includes the early his-
tory of the discovery, the conquest and the settlement of
Mexico, Central America, the West Indies, and Florida,
Texas, New Mexico, California, and the Spanish period in
Louisiana.

"French Colonies in America: Includes Canada and New-
foundland, the early exploration of the Mississippi Valley and
the founding of Louisiana. This section also is supplemented
by many original manuscripts and by transcripts relating to
the fur trade from the archives of the Hudson Bay Company.

"English, Dutch and Swedish Colonies in America: As the
colonists from both Holland and Sweden soon became merged

ROOMS OF THE EDWARD E. AYER COLLECTION IN THE NEWBERRY LIBRARY

craft, and similar books. This volume was Thomas W. Field's *An Essay Towards an Indian Bibliography*. It was a catalogue of the books that Mr. Field had in his own library, "relating to the history, antiquities, languages, customs, religion, wars, literature and origin of the American Indians." It contained critical and descriptive notes of an illuminating character and synopses of the contents of some of the least known works. Field was an earnest and intelligent bookman with high and definite aims; so his essay was and still is a significant one—particularly because of its complete and instructive bibliography. In this book Mr. Ayer took great delight. Its influence upon his activities as a collector was of first importance. No other bibliography or catalogue quite took its place. We cannot lay our hands on the first copy of this book that he owned—a misfortune his biographer feels keenly. That copy was destroyed, and the one that replaced it was bought much later. If only that first copy could be recovered, what accidental glimpses might we not get, from some checkmark or annotation, of his dawning interests, his first excited predilections in the field he was later to occupy!

A book collector's "will is the wind's will and his thoughts are long, long thoughts." What ordinary man can weigh the motives and measure the ardor of a book-lover who will calmly pay thousands and even tens of thousands of dollars for a few old printed pages that could be purchased for five or ten dollars in far more readable print and perhaps in much better binding. Yet original manuscripts, first editions, and solitary surviving copies of certain books shake the collector with the fever of desire or the ague of disappointment. And even for the ignorant these literary nuggets and diamonds have their fascination, as the writer found when he was admitted to the vault in which are locked the chief treasures of the Ayer Collection and handled among other documents the works now to be described.

There was *A Brief Compendium of Processiones* (Vn cōpēdio breue que tracta d'la manera de como se hā de hazer las pcessiones) by Dionysius de Leuwis. It is interesting primarily as a very early example of American printing. It came from a press in the City of Mexico in 1544. Europeans had not been on the Continent very long at that time. Indeed it was the seventh book printed in America. It is not known where Mr. Ayer got it nor what he paid for it. Zaehnsdorf of London bound it, using the Le Gascon design. Another was John Eliot's translation of the Bible into the Massachusetts Indian language and printed at Cambridge, Massachusetts, 1661–63. Mr. Ayer bought it for a pretty round sum in 1897. Undoubtedly there is a strong appeal in the fact that it was the first Bible ever printed in any American Indian language, and the additional fact that it was the first Bible to be printed in America in any language.

The *Memorial of Fray Alonso de Benavides* is not a very stirring document to read, yet it is a source book of the utmost importance on the history of the Southwest. It was written in New Mexico in 1628 and published in Madrid in 1630. Mr. Ayer secured one of the few extant copies of this original Spanish edition. He later paid Dr. J. A. Munk for an original French edition of this little book, published in Brussels in 1631, its weight in gold many times over. This rare piece of Americana interested him so very much that he bought every edition of it that he could secure; and he had photostats made of such as he could not purchase. On the shelves of the Ayer Library and the Munk Library, and scores of other public and private libraries, this book can now be read to much better advantage in the translation made from the 1630 Spanish edition by Mr. Ayer's wife, Mrs. Emma Burbank Ayer, and annotated in the most scholarly manner by Frederick Webb Hodge and Charles Fletcher Lummis. One of the three hundred copies of this privately printed translation by Mrs. Ayer could be bought for about fifty or seventy-five dollars, but it, of course, lacks the glamour and the flavor of the original Spanish and French editions.

It gives one a strange sense of pleasure to take into one's hands two volumes "in an olive-green morocco pull-off case, gilt and lettered, *The Verie Two Eyes of New-England Historie.*" These two tiny volumes that nestle luxuriously in their cradle of olive-green are Gosnold's and Waymouth's Voyages. Diminutive as are the books (the first contains forty-eight small pages; the second, twenty), the titles have something of the spaciousness of the Elizabethan Age. "A Briefe and true Relation of the Discouerie of the North part of Virginia; being a most pleasant, fruitfull and commodious Soile. Made this present yeere 1602, by Captaine Bartholomew Gosnold, Captaine Bartholowmew Gilbert, and diuers other gentlemen their associats, by the permission of the honourable Knight, Sir Walter Ralegh, &c. Written by M. Iohn Brereton, one of the voyage. Whereunto is annexed a Treatise, of M. Edward Hayes, etc. London, Geor. Bishop, 1602." The title of the second account is: "A trve Relation of the most prosperous voyage made this present yeere 1605, by Captaine George Waymouth, in the Discouery of the land of Virginia: Where he discouered 60 miles vp a most excellent Riuer; together with a most fertile land. Written by Iames Rosier a Gentleman employed in the voyage. Londini, Impensis Geor. Bishop, 1605." The note in the sales catalogue following the description of these two volumes as given above is: "EXCESSIVELY RARE, severally, and, when united, of MATCHLESS RARITY."

As a collector's item there is perhaps nothing in the whole Library so precious as Father Junipero Serra's holograph diary of his journey from Loreto to San Diego written in 1769. There was something of the characteristic Ayer good fortune in the securing of this manuscript. In 1900 he bought from Quaritch a number of manuscripts that had formerly been a part of the Ramirez library. Among other things were included three volumes that had been listed in the Ramirez sale catalogue in 1880 as: "918. Yucatan. Misiones del Norte y de Yucatan." A full table of contents followed this entry. In Quaritch's catalogue these three volumes are described as: "901. Misiones y viages" . . . with the same table of contents. Vol. 3, No. 2, is listed: "Expedicion a California en 1769." Neither Ramirez nor Quaritch seem to have realized that No. 2 was the diary of California's celebrated priest and pioneer.

Claudius Ptolemaeus was the most famous geographer of the early Christian world. For thirteen hundred years his geography was recognized as authoritative. It is a distinction known to book collectors all over the world that there is in the Ayer Library the most nearly complete collection of Ptolemy editions ever brought together. Perhaps Mr. Ayer's outstanding achievement as a book collector was the acquisition of this Ptolemy collection.

About 1848 Henry Stevens set out to procure as many editions of Ptolemy's Geography as he could obtain. It was his purpose "to illustrate cartographically the progress of modern geographical discovery and knowledge from pre-Columbian down to comparatively recent times." He was especially eager to show by a series of maps the gradual "evolution of America from the sea of darkness." By 1886, when he died, he had collected about thirty different editions of Ptolemy. It seemed to Mr. Stevens' son, Henry N. Stevens, a pity that a series of books so valuable as this that his father had brought together by long and patient labor should now be dispersed. He accordingly determined, if possible, to complete the series and name it the Henry Stevens Memorial Collection. During the next decade he was able to add about sixteen more editions; and, believing now that the collection would be greatly enhanced in value and far more likely to remain intact if bound uniformly, after consultation with Mr. Pratt of London, who with his father before him had bound books for Mr. Stevens and his father for more than half a century, a substantial binding was decided on, of olive-green morocco of the very finest quality, tooled in blind and gold.

By 1898 the forty-six volumes had all been bound thus, uniformly and elegantly. By this time the enterprise had grown too expensive for Mr. Stevens' means, and there were still costly editions that he very much wished to acquire. He decided, therefore, to seek a patron who would co-operate with him in his cherished undertaking. As good fortune would have it, Mr. Ayer was in London at just about this time; and, the matter being broached to him, he gladly and promptly purchased the collection. That the Chicago collector concurred in his desire to perpetuate the Henry Stevens Memorial and to augment it particularly delighted Mr. Stevens. In a fascinating book that he printed privately in London in 1908, entitled *Ptolemy's Geography,* Mr. Stevens writes: "Since it was transferred to him in 1898, Mr. Ayer has nobly redeemed his promise, with the result that fourteen most valuable editions or variations have been added, bringing the total number of volumes up to sixty. At the present time only one or two editions of importance are still wanting." Since these words were written, in 1908, Mr. Ayer has still further closed the gap, so that now only one edition of prime importance, the Bologna, is wanting.

Up to 1475 the geography of Ptolemy was preserved in manuscript form only. The first printed edition bearing a definite date was produced in Vicenza, without maps. Very soon editions began to appear with maps copied from the manuscripts. These manuscripts were no doubt all drawn from the rules and directions laid down by Ptolemaeus for the drawing of maps. Four books with maps appeared in rapid succession—three in Italy and one in Germany. In the Rome edition of 1478 there are twenty-seven maps; in a version by Berlinghieri in metrical form printed about 1480, there are thirty-one maps; in the Bologna edition, issued, supposedly, in 1482, but dated 1462, there are twenty-six maps; and there are thirty-two in the Ulm issue of 1482. By 1730 fifty more editions had come from the press.

At the time the forty-six volumes of Ptolemys were transferred to Mr. Ayer a special Memorial Bookplate was designed. The main features of the Bookplate are alike in each volume, but each one differs from every other one in "recording briefly the salient points of the particular edition to which it appertains. The border of this Bookplate, in the Holbein style, has been copied and adapted from one of the map borders of the Basle Edition of 1540." In the center is reproduced Henry Stevens' private bookplate, representing the tree of Bibliography growing from a well-spring in the desert. Thither wayfarers came to refresh themselves, and to carry away life-giving knowledge. In each corner of the border is a shield. On these four shields are inscribed the monograms, respectively, of Claudius Ptolemaeus, Henry Stevens, Henry N. Stevens, and Edward E. Ayer. Twenty copies only of this Bookplate were struck off. A set of them appended to Mr. Henry N. Stevens' little privately printed book *Ptolemy's Geography* "forms a chronological index to the whole Collection. From these Bookplates it will be seen how marvelously full the Collection is, and it is to be hoped that the very few remaining 'desiderata' may yet be acquired."

At the end of his Essay on *Ptolemy's Geography*, printed in London in 1908, Henry N. Stevens writes thus, gracefully and generously:

In conclusion it is very gratifying to learn from Mr. Ayer, while this Essay has been in the Press, that when in the fullness of time the Collection must necessarily pass into other hands, he has already arranged for it to be preserved intact, by transferring it to the Newberry Library at Chicago. But let us hope he may long be spared to enjoy the personal possession of this grand set of books, which in the distant future, as the

STEVENS-AYER PTOLEMY COLLECTION

may well form a lasting memorial to

HENRY STEVENS OF VERMONT

who conceived the idea, and to

EDWARD EVERETT AYER OF CHICAGO,

by whose generous patronage it has been
brought to a successful Completion

The Henry Stevens Ptolemy Collection as it now exists in the Ayer Library consists of:

   I. Eight manuscripts. Of these five are geographical, the earliest being a Greek codex of about 1260-70. Three are astronomical: one in Arabic, one in the Catalan language, and one in Latin.
   II. Fifty-three printed editions, beginning with the first edition, 1475, and of the early editions there is lacking only the one printed at Bologna.
   III. Fifteen supplementary volumes—Berlinghieri, Stobniczy, Blundeville, Wytfleet, etc.

Mr. Ayer took great delight in his eleven portolan charts and thirteen portolan atlases. No one can examine them without feeling a like pleasure. Supplemented as they are by many printed facsimiles of old manuscript maps and charts, photostats of the Henry E. Huntington Collection, and photographic copies of American maps secured from the French, Spanish, and Mexican archives, they offer to the student valuable material for the study of early geographical science. They were made by practical navigators and explorers at the time of the new discoveries when the earth was daily expanding before men's eyes. Here for the first time the gates open

into the New World—Africa, India, and America. The charts
all seem to be based upon some common original, so closely do
they follow the same pattern. Only slowly do they enlarge
their scope to take in the expanding world and the results of
new knowledge, yet we must recognize them as the first modern scientific maps. At the period when these portolan charts
were most in use they included the Mediterranean, its shores
and islands, the Atlantic coast of Europe as far north as the
Scandinavian Peninsula, with, perhaps, a part of the Baltic
Sea, and the British Isles. As they were made for the use
of seamen, little attention was given at first to inland geography.

So far as is known, there is not in existence a portolan chart
that was made before 1300. The oldest one that is dated and
signed was drawn by Pietro Visconte, in 1311. There are extant one hundred made previous to the year 1500. Contrary
to the Roman and Arabic practice of orienting these charts
from the south and contrary, likewise, to the early mediaeval
custom of placing the east at the top the portolan charts
have the north at the top. It may be that the inven-
tion of the compass had something to do with the rapid
development of portolan charts, but this is not certain. The
learned map-makers of the sixteenth century seem to have dis-
regarded the value of these charts made by navigators until
by actual astronomical measurement Ptolemy's maps were
shown to have been inaccurate. After that they came to be
prized more highly. As for the seamen, they continued to
prefer them long after printed maps came into use.

These maps combined beauty with utility. In the early
period not many of them were done in color, but in the course
of time it became common to use colors of red, blue, green,
yellow, black and gold, and as a result many of them are fine
examples of the miniaturist's art. They are drawn mostly
upon parchment—sheepskin, goatskin, and calfskin. Some are

on single sheets; many are in the form of atlases, several sheets being folded and glued together back to back. They vary greatly in dimension, the size being determined usually by the size of the skin that could be procured. Often the entire skin was used, even including that of the neck.

The oldest geographical manuscript in the Ayer Collection was written about the year 1400 by Leonardo Dati, a Florentine diplomat. It is entitled *La Spera* and is in the ottava rima stanza form. The poem is a treatise on cosmography and geography. It is written on vellum in blue and gold with splendid initials. In the border at the bottom of the first page is depicted the coat-of-arms of an ancient Italian family, and, throughout, the borders are ornamented with numerous globes representing the earth, the sky, and the heavenly bodies. There are maps of the sea, also, including the Mediterranean, the Canary Islands and their surrounding waters, and the shores of Egypt and the Holy Land.

Two portolan atlases, both unsigned and undated, yet both confidently assigned to Baptista Agnese, are exceedingly interesting. Both are on vellum. The first is believed to have been made about 1550. It is in fine condition—clean and bright—in binding of old leather, with simple gold tooling. It had metal clasps, but only fragmentary bits remain. At the center, inside of the back cover, is a wind rose in colors, and beneath this ornament, set into the thick cover, is a small compass still active after the lapse of centuries. The charts include waters, islands, and coast lines all the way from the Baltic Sea to the Black Sea, and from the British Isles to the Holy Land.

The second atlas, about 1560, contains ten charts and five maps. The charts and maps are placed back to back and folded, thus forming a book without binding or cover other than the backs of the first chart and the last. Agnese was best known as an ornamental cartographer, his artistic charts being prepared chiefly for libraries; but this atlas has apparently suffered many a sea change. It has manifestly seen actual and hard service. It is stained, weather-beaten, soiled, and scorched. Finger prints and fly-specks indicate that the navigator has had it open before him on deck. There are, too, dim marginal notes.

None of the portolan atlases in the Ayer Collection is so interesting as the one containing five charts on vellum, executed by Giovanni Martines in 1583, bound in modern russia leather with stamped border. The charts show the Mediterranean and Black Seas, the coast of Africa, the Cape of Good Hope, and the western and northern coasts of Europe and the British Isles. The historic interest and value of this atlas is much enhanced by reason of the fact that it was successively the property of Lord Charles Howard, High Admiral of England; William Cecil, Lord Burleigh, Secretary of State to Queen Elizabeth; Charles Bailly, Governor of Hudson Bay; and Pierre Esprit Radisson. The following inscriptions may be read on the verso of the last chart:

14 Avgusti 1595. This Book is gyven to me W. L. Burghly by ye Lo Charles Howard high Admyral of England.

Ce livre Ma donné par Charles Bailly gouuerneur de la Bay d'udson En 1673 (here an illegible word) J'apartiene a pierre Esprit Radisson serviteur du ,Roy de la grande Bretaigne a tous sont qui ces presente.

Ce liure ma este donne par le nomme cy dessus Nomme Radisson pour lamour du quel Je le gardere toute ma vie Jusque a ce que Je trouve a man de faire en faveur d'un autre. 1675, Morpin (last letters not quite legible).

Il la rendu a Radisson a qui est apartenant. [1690.]

More inclusive and ornate than any of the volumes mentioned above is an anonymous Portuguese portolan atlas prepared about 1600. Its distinction is that it was planned as an atlas. It is not merely a number of charts brought together

and bound. The drawings, throughout, are on both sides of
the sheets of vellum. This is true of no other atlas in the Ayer
Collection. There are twenty-four highly decorative charts,
the work of a Portuguese seaman. The volume is bound in calf
and is in an excellent state of preservation. "The prominence
given to Lisbon and the Portuguese escutcheons would seem
to show that the work was done before 1580, but it was probably somewhat later. . . ." There are large illuminated initial letters and painted leaves and roses in the borders. Rules
for the movable feasts are given with conventional floral borders in brilliant colors. The first drawing is a full page picture
of the crucifixion. The whole atlas is profusely ornamented
with colored drawings of ships, castles, desert caravans, escutcheons, banners, wind roses, and mythological figures. Its
creation must have relieved the tedium of many a dreary day
at sea; and it is the kind of thing that might easily "keep a
child from his play or an old man from his chimney corner."

Some years ago Mr. Ayer bought of Jacques Rosenthal a
massive volume containing more than one hundred large maps
and sketches illustrating French trading-posts, expansion, and
settlement in various parts of the world. The title *Cartes
Marines—A la Svbstitvtion dv Valdec, proche Solevre en
Svisse. MDCCXXVII,* and the caption of the table of contents, "Table des feuilles rassemblées dans ce volume en
1727," give the only clue to the meaning and purpose of this
collection. The maps are beautifully executed in water colors
on heavy, durable paper. In some instances the cartographer's
name is given, but nothing is indicated as to the originals from
which they were copied. They are arranged in the atlas with
respect to the region which they illustrate rather than alphabetically or chronologically. Starting with the Peyssonel map
of Tunis and Algiers, they proceed in regular order down
the west coast of Africa, around to Madagascar and the adjoining islands, along the coasts of India and China, then by

the Moluccas and the Philippine Islands to the Strait of Magellan, and so up the coast of the Americas. There are a few maps of South America and the West Indies, and many very fine ones of Louisiana, Nova Scotia, Cape Breton, Labrador, and the St. Lawrence River. Just what they were intended for is a mystery. They constitute such a complete and orderly series, and are such good examples of French map-making that they pique one's interest; the more so as Mr. Ayer has in the library, also, from some other entirely unrelated purchase, several volumes of manuscript memoirs that seem to belong with the maps. Indeed, it seems likely that the maps were made to illustrate the manuscript.

It is a striking coincidence that in 1927, exactly two hundred years after this very cumbersome atlas was bound, the maps were detached from each other by Miss Smith, the custodian of the Ayer Collection, and placed in boxes for easier use and better preservation. It is strange that such a bulky volume should have remained intact after the wear and tear of two centuries.

One of the most famous chroniclers of the expanding New World was Pietro Martire d'Anghiera, commonly known as Peter Martyr. He was a contemporary of Christopher Columbus. His chief works are *De Rebus Oceanicis et Novo Orbe Decades* (a History of the New World), and *Opus Epistolarum* (a very important collection of eight hundred sixteen letters dealing with the events of his own day). Mr. Ayer took much pride in his fine collection of Peter Martyrs. It includes eighteen editions published before 1600, among them being the editions of 1511, 1516, and 1521.

A body of publications known as *The Jesuit Relations* should be noted here. *The Jesuit Relations* is a series of annual reports made between 1632 and 1673 by Jesuit missionaries serving on the frontiers of New France. Each year the superior made up a journal, or *Relation,* from these docu-

A CORNER OF THE SAFETY VAULT IN THE NEWBERRY LIBRARY WHERE THE RARE BOOKS OF THE EDWARD E. AYER COLLECTION ARE KEPT. THE BOOKS ON THE TABLE ARE PRESCOTT'S CONQUEST OF MEXICO

ments submitted by the heroic priests at the front. These annual *Relations* were sent by the superior to the provincial of his order in France, by whom they were carefully edited. These reports, being first-hand and graphic accounts of what the Jesuit missionaries in New France actually saw and experienced, are "our first and best authorities" on the region and the period with which they deal. The first volume issued by the authority and under the direction of the provincial was published in Paris, in 1632, in a duodecimo volume bound in vellum, by Sebastien Cramoisy, and each succeeding year up to 1673 a similar volume came from the Cramoisy press. The Ayer Collection contains all but two of this series—*Copie de deux Lettres envoiees de la Nouuelle France,* being the *Relation* for 1655, and *Lettres envoiees de la Nouuelle France* for 1659. The messenger bearing the 1655 *Relation* was attacked by highwaymen after he reached France, and his letters were all lost or mutilated. He recovered two, however. These two were printed. The report of 1659, consisted of only three letters, dated respectively, September 12, October 10, and October 16, 1659. The first tells of the arrival of a bishop; the second of the Algonquin and Huron missions; and the third of the Acadia missions.

Few Americans knew that John Howard Payne, whose name has been made immortal by his song, "Home, Sweet Home," spent much time between 1835 and 1841 in diligent research into the traditions and customs of the Cherokee Indians. He visited John Ross, at that time the chief of the Nation, and for a long time carried on a correspondence with individual Cherokees, with missionaries who had long served among them, and with white people who knew their history and their ways intimately. He himself spent much time in the Cherokee country, and in 1841 was employed by the War Department upon business connected with a proposed treaty with the Cherokee Nation. It was his purpose to write a his-

tory of this tribe; and, indeed, he partly accomplished this
task, though his work was never published. He left fourteen
manuscript volumes dealing with the Cherokees. Some of this
manuscript is in finished literary form; much of it consists of
letters, jottings, and lively anecdotes about particular members of the tribe; all of it is written in a clear, distinctive handwriting and methodically arranged in well-bound specially prepared notebooks. Here is a most inviting mine ready for the
exploring hand of the student.

The wealth of source material of a pictorial character in
the Ayer Collection is, indeed, astonishing. Of exceeding value
and interest are the maguey drawings, the Waldeck drawings, and Mr. W. H. Holmes' archaeological panoramas of
the Mayan cities. All of these pictures have to do with early
civilization in Mexico. The maguey drawings are examples
of Aztec picture writing. The crude paper on which the pictures are drawn is made by pounding the pulp of the century
plant into flat, thin sheets. One very old manuscript was found
at Teotihuacan, an ancient ruined Toltec city near the City of
Mexico. Another manuscript tells the story of a great battle
between the forces of two rival rulers. This pictograph is confidently referred to a period before the coming of the Spaniards, and is believed to reveal, therefore, the characteristic
writing of the Aztecs before they came under the influence of
European civilization.

Not until recently was it known, even among American historians and archaeologists, that the rare Waldeck collection
of drawings and water color paintings was in existence. Since
it has become known to scholars that they form a part of the
Ayer Collection, much interest has centered on them. The
English ethnologist Professor G. Eliot Smith, F.R.S., points
out in an article published in the *Illustrated London News,*
of January 15, 1927, which he accompanies with photographic reproductions from Frederic de Waldeck's water

color drawings in the Ayer Collection, that these Waldeck
pictures of elephants' heads drawn from the relief of the
Temple of the Cross at Palenque offer decisive evidence of
the cultural connection between Central America and Asia in
the eighth century.

The following letter, dated December 26, 1926, written
to Mr. Ayer by Dr. Sylvanus G. Morley, the distinguished
specialist in Mayan hieroglyphic writing and Middle American archaeology, throws further light upon the extraordinary
value of some of these documents as source material:

I am on the point of leaving for Mexico City, but before
I go I wish to thank you very deeply for the privilege of seeing your splendid collection at the Newberry Library. I do not
feel competent to pass upon . . . most of the material that
I saw, as it lies in other fields than my own, but I was simply
dumbfounded at the wealth of unpublished source material
which you have gotten together on my own field of Middle
American Research. You showed me there the other morning
material which I did not know even existed. I refer to the
splendid Waldeck Collection of drawings and paintings.

Waldeck was in Central America and southern Mexico
nearly a hundred years ago and had an opportunity of copying
sculptures, paintings, etc., which have since been destroyed
or largely defaced. The copies made from the originals are
now, therefore, of priceless value. Some time I hope I may be
permitted to really study some of the material you have there
at the Newberry Library. It will be a rare privilege.

Not the least of that amazing collection was the group of
Mexican post-codices. A number of these at least I am
confident are genuine, and will shed much light on conditions in Central America during the first half of the 16th
century. Here again is a rich body of unpublished source
material.

Take your originals of Mr. W. H. Holmes' drawings, his
large archaeological panoramas of Mayan cities in southern
Mexico. They are the finest drawings of their kind in existence
and some day will have an immense value actually, as they
have scientifically and sentimentally now.

But time and space are lacking to enumerate other of
the wonders I saw. Permit me, Sir, as a student in this field to
felicitate you on the gathering together of such highly important scientific material, and to thank you for the generous
offer of its use, which you made.

In addition to the three hundred colored drawings by Indians and the three thousand photographs of individual
American Indians, many of which were taken in the '70's,
the Ayer Library has an abundance of remarkable illustrative
material on the American Indian. Notable among the collections of drawings and paintings that were made on the plains,
under the open sky, in the very heart of the tribes that they
depict, are Catlin's pencil sketches and portraits of American
Indians, and his *North American Indian Portfolio* showing
hunting scenes and Indian pastimes on the prairies and in the
Rocky Mountains; the sketches and paintings of Karl Bodmer; the portfolio of Frank Blackwell Mayer, containing
sketches, drawings, and some water color paintings; and the
very large collection of red chalk drawings of well-known
Indians of our own day by Elbridge Ayer Burbank. The way
in which Catlin pursued his work among the red men has already been related. The common feature in the pictures of all
these artists is the exactness of detail with which they present
every aspect of Indian life and the impression of vividness
and immediacy that they impart to all their representations
of Indian faces, figures, and activities, as well as to the scenes
of Nature. These artists are in the midst of what they paint
and are a part of it, and they are able to make us see just
what they see.

Mayer was present at the Treaty of Traverse des Sioux in
1851, and one of his best-known canvases is entitled *The
Treaty of Camp Traverse des Sioux*. The Ayer portfolio contains many detached and tentative sketches made on the spot.
They are specialized impromptus with pencil and brush of

weapons, ornaments, lodges, animals, and individual men—red and white. In his completed work these are assembled and unified with striking effect.

Perhaps no pictures in the Ayer Collection show such excellent draughtsmanship and coloring—are so artistic and so marked with high distinction—as the series of thirty-four sketches, drawings, and paintings in the volume of *Illustrations to Maximilian Prince of Wied's Travels in North America,* done by the young Swiss artist, Karl Bodmer. Maximilian engaged Bodmer to go along with him on his famous journey into the Northwest, in 1832-34, to paint the primitive landscapes and the Indian inhabitants. Bodmer later rose to eminence in France, receiving medals of honor in the Paris salons of 1851 and succeeding years, and finally the ribbon of the Legion of Honor. One of his paintings was bought by the French Government and placed in the Luxembourg Gallery.

Mr. Elbridge Ayer Burbank is a noted contemporary painter of Indians. He was born in Harvard, Illinois, in 1858, and is the grandson of Elbridge Gerry Ayer, the founder of that town. Mr. Burbank received his art training in the old Chicago Academy of Design, and in Munich. Portrait painting attracted him from the first. His earliest success in this field was won through a series of carefully executed Negro studies. There was prompt and popular response to his work in this vein, as his subjects, for the most part, were rendered with humorous intent. His *American Beauty*—a little Negro boy holding in his hand an American Beauty rose of the most perfect variety—was reproduced as a chromo and circulated widely in Sunday newspaper supplements. In the 1893 exhibition of the Society of Chicago Artists Mr. Burbank was awarded the Yerkes Prize. His work was exhibited at the Paris Exposition and at the St. Louis World's Fair.

It was not until 1897, however, that Mr. Burbank found his distinctive field as an artist. At about that time he was encouraged by his uncle, Mr. Edward E. Ayer, to take up the painting of Indian portraits and was commissioned by Mr. Ayer to paint the Apache chief, Geronimo, then living at Fort Sill, Oklahoma. He later made extended trips into the territory of the Sioux, Crows, Nez Perces, Cheyennes, Utes, Navajos, Moquis, Zunis, Apaches, and many other tribes, with the purpose of securing a series of exact delineations from life of the most famous Indian chiefs then living in America. Proof that he carried out his ambitious project with a large measure of success may be found in the Ayer Collection.

His first portraits of Indian chiefs were done in oil, but his later work is mostly in red chalk. However, he did not limit himself to warriors; he drew the portraits of typical squaws, also. Both by his extended practice in portrait painting and his sympathy with Indian character he was well fitted for the task. "His long training in painting heads," says his friend Charles Francis Browne, "had given a facility and an unfailing ability to catch a likeness at once. This is necessary in making Indian portraits from the difficulty of getting them to sit; and it is important to finish as quickly, as there is no surety that they will hold out as long as the painter wishes." In Mr. Burbank's Indian pictures there is a clear delineation of individual character; and he reproduces with scrupulous accuracy every detail of tribal and ceremonial dress. The Ayer Collection includes a very large number of his best portraits—for the most part red chalk drawings, though some are in oil.

It is difficult to determine just when Mr. Ayer first thought of augmenting his ever-growing collection of Americana with transcripts from the archives of Spain and Mexico. Very likely the idea came to him at the time that Mr. James A. Robertson was laboriously searching in Spain for source material on the Philippines to be used in the writing of *The*

Philippine Islands, which Miss Emma Helen Blair and Mr. Robertson published in fifty-five volumes in 1903. After the completion and publication of this history Mr. Ayer purchased a considerable quantity of the transcripts made by Mr. Robertson in Spain. No doubt the publication by the Carnegie Institution of Washington, in 1910, of a "List of Documents in Spanish Archives, relating to the History of the United States, which have been Printed or of which Transcripts are Preserved in American Libraries" further stimulated Mr. Ayer's desire to add to his library as many transcripts as possible dealing with Spanish history in the Southwest.

Somewhat later, perhaps about 1912, while Mr. Ayer was traveling in Spain, he found in Seville two young men from Berkeley, who had been sent over by the University of California as honor graduates to go through the piles of Colonial manuscripts preserved in Seville and note in each bundle of papers examined what documents pertained to Spanish American history. It was their duty to make a list of all items that bore upon Spanish American affairs and paste these lists upon the bundles, respectively, for the guidance of future students. These lists were afterward published in America and were of great service to research scholars. The thought immediately came to Mr. Ayer that he could get a lot of interesting material through these men. So he said to them:

"Wouldn't it be a good scheme for you to have a thousand dollars or so with which to hire Spanish scribes to copy from the documents you are noting anything that is especially interesting on Spanish American history that has never been published?"

"It would be a very good idea, indeed," they replied; and accordingly Mr. Ayer entered into such an arrangement with them.

As a result of this and like enterprises carried steadily on through the years, and still in operation, the Ayer Library has built up its great repository of 200,000 pages of transcripts dealing with Spanish affairs in the Southwest. The archives of Mexico as well as those of Spain have, of course, been utilized.

In this account little emphasis has been placed on the money value of Mr. Ayer's acquisitions. This is as he would have it. He made slight mention of the cost of particular items and only rarely is there a record of what he paid for a book. He spent lavishly for articles and documents upon which he had set his heart, but never recklessly or ostentatiously. In his collecting he was not prompted primarily by personal and selfish motives—certainly not by the mere vain desire of possession or the pride of outbidding a competitor. Through all the years he placed before himself a lofty ideal of service to his fellowmen, and, particularly, of continuing service through coming generations; for he did have a characteristic dominant in our early Anglo-Saxon ancestors—the desire to achieve glory by high deeds and generous works. He was modest, but he was not unaware of the fact that his name would be remembered and honored by scholars and lovers of beauty for centuries because of the accumulated riches of art and literature that he had brought together for their enjoyment and profit. As a man of vision, able to forecast prophetically the increasing, the ultimate desirability of this or that book or object of art, he bought betimes and bought opportunely. His collection could not be purchased now for three times the outlay that it cost him; indeed, most of it could not be secured at all today. Many documents for which he paid five, ten, or twenty dollars could not be had for a thousand now.

At the very time this chapter was being written in the rooms of the Ayer Collection two incidents occurred that are apropos here. A well-known book buyer from the East, who often drops in to regale himself with a look at Mr. Ayer's

literary treasures, remarked to the custodian that he had just
come from an auction where the Bologna edition of Ptolemy
was placed on sale. He stated that he failed to secure it, as he
was not willing to bid more than seventeen thousand dollars
for it. No doubt if Mr. Ayer had had a like opportunity,
keenly as he desired this book, he would have refrained from
going to an unreasonable limit to gain possession of it. The
second incident is a good example of how romance and utility
join hands on this enchanted ground—that is, within the precincts of the Ayer Library. Professor John Cornyn, of the
University of Mexico, a specialist in the primitive Mexican
language, came in one day to inquire whether the Library contained any manuscripts in the Aztec language. Many years
ago Mr. Ayer bought of Quaritch, in London, several books
by Sahagún and a few manuscripts, one at least, *Sermones en
lengua mexicana,* written on maguey paper made by the Indians. This last is, perhaps, the most interesting and valuable
volume in the Mexican language ever acquired by a collector.
Among the manuscripts was a dictionary prepared by Sahagún
in three languages, Latin, Spanish, and Aztec. All these rare
items duly accessioned and locked in the vault, were shown
to Professor Cornyn by Miss Smith. What was his amazement to find here the great Sahagún tri-lingual dictionary
made not more than fifty years after the conquest of Mexico
by the Spaniards! It was known to the Professor that Sahagún
had prepared such a dictionary, and long had he conjectured
what might have become of it; but not until that moment did
he know that it was still in existence. So here across the gulf
of four centuries the modern linguist from Mexico City
clasped hands with Father Sahagún, who came to Mexico in
1529, and died there in 1590, and whose knowledge of the
Aztec language and literature has, perhaps, never been surpassed.

The Ayer Collection is impressive. Within its special field

it is unequaled by any private library ever brought together. It deserves the most serious consideration of scholars and writers. As the generations come and go its value as a depository of source materials will be more and more fully recognized, and its riches will be sought from all quarters of the world. A chapter is all too brief to set forth the extent and variety of its resources. Mr. Ayer was first and chiefly a collector, and in the long run his title to greatness will rest upon the inspiration and discernment that led him to gather these scattered treasures of man and the mind of man and provide a secure home for them where all future generations can enjoy them.

CHAPTER XI

Connection with Field Museum of Natural History

BEFORE narrating in detail Mr. Ayer's individual part in the creation and development of the now world-famous Field Museum of Natural History, it may be well to relate briefly the incidents that led up to its organization. The Field Museum "is both the outcome and the monument" of the Chicago World's Fair. As early as May 31, 1890, Professor R. W. Putnam, of Harvard University, in a letter to the *Chicago Tribune,* pointed out the desirability of a Museum of American Ethnology for Chicago, as an outgrowth of the Columbian Exposition; and at the invitation of Mr. William T. Baker he spoke before the Commercial Club on the same subject in November, 1891. Director Goode, of the National Museum, in conversation with Mr. J. W. Ellsworth, in April, 1891, recommended that a committee be appointed immediately to arouse interest in a local museum; and from that time Mr. Ellsworth himself actively advocated the founding of a museum at the close of the World's Fair. The proposal was early favored, also, by Mr. Baker, Mr. Ryerson, Mr. Lefens, and Mr. Higinbotham, all members of the Foreign Affairs Committee of the Exposition; and Mr. F. J. V. Skiff states that this committee almost from the first kept in view the thought of the museum that they hoped would grow out of the exposition. Mr. S. C. Eastman published a letter in the *Tribune* in July, 1893, definitely proposing the museum, and the entire press of Chicago supported the project.

In August, 1893, at a meeting of the Directors of the Exposition, a committee consisting of Mr. George R. Davis,

Mr. H. N. Higinbotham, and Mr. J. W. Scott was appointed
for the purpose of crystallizing community sentiment in favor
of a museum. This committee issued a call on August 11,
1893, for a meeting of all citizens who thought it desirable
"to adopt measures in immediate aid of the project to establish in Chicago a great museum that shall be a fitting memorial of the World's Columbian Exposition and a permanent
advantage and honor to the City." In response to this call a
hundred leading citizens of Chicago met on the evening of
August 17, in the Administration Building of the Exposition.
Director-General Davis presided, and Mr. S. C. Eastman
served as secretary.

It was first proposed that the scope of the Columbian Historical Society be enlarged so that it might include the museum, but this suggestion was voted down for the reason that
this society was incorporated in Washington. The next plan
brought forward was to have the new organization operate
under the charter of the Academy of Sciences of Chicago.
This proposal, also, met with opposition, particularly from
President H. N. Higinbotham, who spoke very earnestly in
favor of "a new and strong organization, independent of educational institutions, locality, creed, or calling, strong enough
to stand alone, and large enough to take in everything."
As Mr. Higinbotham's remarks met with general approval, a
committee consisting of the following gentlemen was appointed to incorporate a museum; G. E. Adams, E. C. Hirsch,
J. A. Roche, C. H. Harrison, S. C. Eastman, A. C. Bartlett,
General A. C. McClurg, R. McMurdy, and C. Fitzsimmons.
General McClurg withdrew from the committee shortly
afterwards and his place was filled by the appointment of
Mr. Edward E. Ayer.

During all these months Mr. Ayer had been one of the
most active promoters of the growing project, and at this
point his personality became one of the decisive factors in

bringing the undertaking to a successful issue. Since no one is better able than he to set forth all the circumstances in connection with the founding of this remarkable institution, his own words are here set down with all their intimacy and narrative charm.

Previous to the Chicago Exposition in 1893, I had collected very extensively material on the North American Indians, putting myself in touch with all parts of North America through Indian traders wherever I could hear of them; and I finally got in contact with most of them. I had bought Indian paraphernalia in considerable quantities, and in the World's Fair my private collection exhibited in the Department of Anthropology constituted quite an important section of that exhibit.* During the Fair I often went to see the different collections and, indeed, studied everything very carefully; and as a result I early saw that there would be a tremendous amount of material from different countries, as well as from all parts of America, that could be secured at a minimum price at the end of the exposition. I had collected a good deal in the Americas and had already collected a little here and there in Europe during the several years that I had been going abroad, and I felt that the time had come to start a natural history museum in Chicago at the end of the World's Fair and that the opportunity should not be allowed to pass.

At the various Chicago clubs I came into familiar association with the leading men of the city at the table and at card games, so I began on all occasions to urge the importance of our getting material for a museum at the close of the World's Fair. There were several others who thought as I did—among the principal ones being George M. Pullman, Norman Ream, and James Ellsworth. These men endorsed and backed up my remarks. Of course Marshall Field was the richest man we had among us in those days, so during our fishing trips and on social occasions when I would meet Mr. Field I began to talk to him (and others did, too) about giving a million dollars to start with. He always responded,

---

*Director S. C. Simms states that this Collection, in its field, was unsurpassed in interest and value.

"I don't know anything about a museum and I don't care to know anything about a museum. I'm not going to give you a million dollars."

It went on this way, but we were all good enough friends to permit of our talking about it whenever the opportunity arose, so it was broached to Marshall Field a good many times before the end of the Fair, but he persistently answered as at first. Finally, when it was only a month now until the end of the Fair, a meeting was called and a committee of about twenty was appointed to see what could be done about a museum. I was not present at the first meeting, but I was at the second. By this time the widespread business panic of '93 had developed, and those present at the first meeting saw plainly that we were going to have a difficult time to raise the money for the museum. They knew that Marshall Field had repeatedly been unsuccessfully approached for a gift of a million dollars—the amount considered necessary to make a start—so at this first meeting they had concluded the only thing they could do would be to raise two or three hundred thousand dollars, buy what they could with that small amount of money, get donations of as much of the material exhibited as possible, and store everything until with the coming of better times they could secure the museum.

I was asked my opinion and replied that I thought the plan would be impossible for the reason that ninety per cent of the natural history material, such as feather-work and leather-work would deteriorate and in time be destroyed. They then asked what I would suggest in place of the plan they had presented. My advice was that, in view of the impossibility of starting our museum, we raise as much money as possible, purchase what we wanted, and from this make four working collections—one for the University of Chicago, one for Northwestern, one for Beloit College, and one for the University of Illinois. I was asked what I would do in that case with my Indian collection. I said I would give that to the University of Chicago, or dispose of it in any other way that the members of the committee thought best. I went away from the meeting and that very night got a letter from James Ellsworth asking me if I would not see Marshall Field once more.

I wrote back that I would do so, but that I did not believe it would do an atom of good.*

The next morning I was in Mr. Field's office when he arrived at about half past nine. I said:

"Marshall Field, I want to see you tonight after dinner."

"You can't do it," he replied, "I have a dinner party and shall be late."

"Well, the next night."

"No, I have another engagement then."

"Well, I have to see you right away; it is important."

"You want to talk to me about that darned museum," was his reply to this.

"Yes," I admitted.

"How much time do you want?"

I replied, "If I can't talk you out of a million dollars in fifteen minutes, I'm no good, nor you either."

"He got up, closed the door, came back, and said, "Fire ahead."

I commenced in this way, "Marshall Field, how many men or women twenty-five years of age or younger know that A. T. Stewart ever lived?"

"Not one," he replied.

I continued, "Marshall Field, he was a greater merchant than you, or Claflin, or Wanamaker, because he originated and worked out the scheme that made you all rich; *and he is forgotten in twenty-five years.* Now, Marshall Field, you can sell dry goods until Hell freezes over; you can sell it on the ice until that melts; and in twenty-five years you will be just the figure A. T. Stewart is—absolutely forgotten. You have an opportunity here that has been vouchsafed to very few people on earth. From the point of view of natural history you have the privilege of being the educational host to the untold millions

---

*Mr. Ayers was Chairman of the Finance Committee of the preliminary organization. It was very natural that Mr. Field should have been conservative in his attitude toward an undertaking that was still tentative or problematical. At that time a million dollars was a very large sum for a single benefaction, though gifts of this magnitude have become common during the last two decades. In view of these things Mr. Field would, of course, want Mr. Ayer to justify fully the need of such a large amount as was being solicited by the ardent promoters of the proposed museum.

of people who will follow us in the Mississippi Valley. There is practically no museum of any kind within five hundred miles; and these children who are growing up in this region by hundreds of thousands haven't the remotest opportunity of learning about the ordinary things they see and talk about and hear about every day of their lives, and it does seem a crime not to provide them with the information they need."

I talked fast and steady. Finally, he took out his watch and said ,"You have been here forty-five minutes—you get out of here."

I replied, "Marshall Field, you have been better to me than you ever have been before; you have always said No, and you haven't this time—yet. Now I want you to do me a personal favor: I want you to go through this World's Fair with me and let me show you the amount of material that is there—I mean exactly what there is that can be used in a natural history museum; for the collections can be gotten very cheap, much of the material for nothing. I want you to go through the World's Fair with me before you say No."

"Well, Ed," he replied, "I should like to go through with you. George Pullman told me you had shown him through and that he had been astounded himself at the quantity of material that was there. My brother Joe is here and I should like to have you go with us. We will do it tomorrow morning at ten o'clock."

We went through the whole exhibition. When we came out a little before one o'clock, I said, "Can Norman Ream and I come to your office tomorrow morning at half-past nine and see you about this matter?"

"Yes," he answered.

We were there promptly, and he gave the million dollars with which to start the Museum. George Pullman gave a hundred thousand, Mr. Harlow Higinbotham gave a hundred thousand, my friend Mrs. George Sturges gave fifty thousand, and I put in my collection which was estimated to be worth a hundred thousand. In addition to all this the great concerns that had provided money for the founding of the World's Fair contributed their shares of exposition stock and, as we realized about fifty cents on the dollar on this, we had about a million and a half dollars to begin with, besides a large amount of stuff that was given to us from the various exhibits. And so it was the Field Museum had its beginning.

During all the remainder of his life Mr. Field's interest in the Museum increased. He left a bequest of eight million dollars at the time of his death, and he had in mind a final magnificent gift when he suddenly passed away. He, personally, enjoyed the Museum very much and from time to time made large contributions toward the current expenses of the Institution; so, naturally, his relatives and friends became interested. A nephew, Mr. Stanley Field, is, and has long been, president of the institution; and Marshall Field's grandson annually gives very large amounts for its support.

The Field Columbian Museum, as it was then called, was formally opened June 2, 1894. Mr. Ayer presided, having been elected as its first president. It was a notable occasion. The orator of the day, Mr. Edward G. Mason, closed his inspiring address with these words:

The first museum, from which the name has been handed down through the centuries, established by the old Egyptian king in the once proud city of Alexandria, was set apart for the use of one privileged class alone. But this museum knows no distinction of class or condition of men. It holds for all its wealth of opportunities for instruction and for research, and its treasures are to be had for the asking. No man can measure the amount of pure and elevated pleasure, of real and lasting benefit, which will be derived from it by the multitudes who will throng its halls from this time henceforth. Nor can we lightly estimate the continuing tribute of thankfulness which they will gladly pay to its benefactors and especially to those whom we honor as its founders. To them it is not easy to render a fitting meed of praise. But they already have a reward in that consciousness of a grand deed grandly done, of which nothing can deprive them. This great creation is due to a munificence far more than princely. A prince can only give his people's money. These donors have given of their very own freely, lavishly, for the good of their city and of their

race. As we enter into their labors there enter with us the rejoicing shades of the philanthropists of all time to welcome
this latest exemplification of the spirit of those who love their
fellow men, and in their shining list will forever appear the
names of the founders of the Field Columbian Museum.

At the close of this eloquent peroration, President Ayer,
who was to live to see the whole vision and prophecy come
true, with raised gavel said, "I now declare the Field Columbian Museum open."

As president of the new Museum, Mr. Ayer lost no opportunity to add to its resources and extend its usefulness to the
public. In the autumn of 1894 the German Ship *Bismarck* was
chartered for a cruise across the Atlantic, through the Mediterranean and into the Black Sea, with opportunity, of course,
to visit the interesting ports in Southern Europe, Egypt, and
the Near East. Mr. and Mrs. Ayer were members of the
party who made this voyage, as were, also, their Chicago
friends, Mr. Lyman Gage and his wife, and Mr. Daniel
Burnham and his wife. The travelers were supposed to have
about five days in Egypt. They arrived at Cairo in the evening and went at once to the hotel for the night. The next
morning Mr. Ayer got up early and went down to have a first
look at this Egyptian city. As he strolled out in front of the
hotel, he noticed that the street was lined with shops where
were displayed all manner of Oriental ornaments, ancient
relics, and even mummies. In fact here was offered for sale almost every archaeological specimen to be found in Egypt.
Mr. Ayer was not unmindful of the fact that he was president
of the Field Museum, and at once the instinct of the collector
asserted itself. What followed must be related in his own
words, for no other narrator can do justice to incidents of this
kind :

I stood on the porch for a few minutes and then went back
to our room and said to Mrs. Ayer, "Emma, I'm not going on

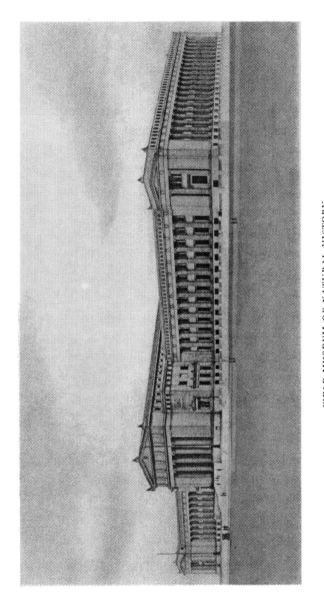

FIELD MUSEUM OF NATURAL HISTORY

this steamer. I'm going to stay right here for a month or six weeks and make a collection for the Field Museum."

After breakfast I took a cab and went out to the Gizeh Museum, devoted, of course, to Egyptian antiquities. I sent my card in to the director, Mr. Emil Brugsch-Bey, an Austrian. He received me kindly, and I explained to him that I was just taking my first lessons as president of the new museum in Chicago that had been started from the things left over from the Columbian Exposition. I said that I had come to Egypt expecting to stay only a few days but had changed my mind and now wanted to remain long enough to make a collection of Egyptian material for the Field Museum. I continued:

"Now, Mr. Brugsch-Bey, there is nothing in the world you can do for me—individually—nothing; but I do not know anything I would not expect you to do here in Egypt to help in building up this new museum in the United States. I do not suppose that any grown man ever came to Egypt so ignorant of everything that is Egyptian as I am. I have collected a good deal in America and to some extent in Europe, but I am completely at sea here. Now, Mr. Brugsch-Bey, I appeal to you to help me. As I said before, there is nothing you can do for me, personally; but there is nothing that I would not ask you to do to help me understand the situation here so I may make as few mistakes as possible in securing articles here in Egypt for our collection."

He replied, "Well, Mr. Ayer, what do you want me to do?"

"First, I want you to go through your own great museum with me and I want you to answer my questions, so that I may gain an idea of what all these things mean and the relative value of the various articles, so far as you are able to indicate it. I want to know what all these things mean, what they are here for, and how I can begin to make a suitable collection. Then I want you to go up town with me a couple of times and stroll along with me while we look into the windows of all the shops of these dealers in antiquities, and I want you to tell me what these things are and what would be a fair price for them. After that I want you to show me the frauds so I may guard myself against them as much as possible. Next,

I want you to let me buy anything in Egypt whatsoever that I care to purchase subject to your approval—and with the understanding that I won't pay for anything unless you say so. And, finally, when we get all through, I want to bring everything that I have bought to this museum and spread it out on tables in some room you can let me have here, and I want you to come and look everything over and give me your opinion about it all."

"Well, Mr. Ayer," he replied, "you have laid out a nice job for me."

"I know that just as well as you do," I responded. "I understand both how big an undertaking it is and how interesting it will be for me; but, as I have intimated, I don't think you, as a museum man, have any desire to let me blunder around here when you can set me straight."

So he said, "Well, Mr. Ayer, I'll do it."

I started right in and collected things all over town. Then I went up the Nile, got acquainted with all the dealers up there, and brought back a lot of stuff. Then I assembled all my purchases in a room set aside for me at the museum, and going to Mr. Brugsch-Bey's office asked him to come and see it. He looked over and checked everything, and was good enough to say to me that I had made a very good selection, and that he was astonished to find nothing that did not appear genuine. I spent about twenty thousand dollars there in Egypt on this first trip, and the stuff that I got would cost ten times that much now.

With the exception of the Coptic material and a few other purchases that the Museum has added during recent years, the entire Egyptian collection was gathered by Mr. Ayer. To enter upon an enumeration or description of the particular acquisitions made by Mr. Ayer would be out of place here. They may be studied in the Museum, where they are easily accessible, set forth as they are with unique skill and attractiveness in the recent strikingly modern arrangement. However, attention may be directed to a few very remarkable objects: the Egyptian Tomb Sculptures and Paintings, representing the Old Kingdom, the Middle Kingdom, and the Empire; numerous Grave Tablets on which are inscribed mortuary prayers; statuettes and fragmentary portrait statuary; a predynastic body, in the "embryonic" posture, dating back farther than 3500 B.C.; and two wonderful sarcophagi. A few words concerning these two tombs may not be amiss. One is the sarcophagus of Amenemonet, of the 19th Dynasty or later, taken from Sakkara, Egypt. The lid is gone. At the lower end of the drainage there is a hole which leads the experts to suppose that this sarcophagus was used in Roman times as a bathtub. The other is the massive, highly decorated tomb of Pefthaukhonsu. It also was excavated at Sakkara, by a representative of the Egyptian Government in 1910-11. Worthy of special note, also, are the *Funeral Papyrus of Khonsurenpe,* and the *Facsimile of the Funeral Papyrus of Ani.* The original of the object last named, one of "the finest known examples of the Empire *Book of the Dead,"* is in the British Museum.

One of the most remarkable of the Egyptian relics is an Ancient Egyptian Boat of the 12th dynasty. It was secured by Mr. Ayer and purchased and presented to the Museum by Mrs. Cyrus H. McCormick, of Chicago. The display card in the enormous showcase that protects the boat has the following description:

It is constructed of cedar and was propelled by oars. It is one of the five oldest boats known to exist, having been in use 4,500 years ago. This with four others was excavated near the Dahshur Pyramids, which are twenty miles above Cairo and several miles from the Nile. It was employed in an important mortuary ceremony and buried after such use.

Continuing his account of his experiences as a collector during the tour begun on the Bismarck in 1894, Mr. Ayer said:

I should say that I did not rejoin my friends on the Bismarck at all. I was going to meet the party again in Egypt, but

I came down on another boat to Naples. I was already aware that there was in Italy a great amount of ancient Roman bronze material—ninety-five per cent of it in Naples. There are in Naples, from Pompeii and Herculaneum alone, seventeen thousand specimens of original bronzes. No one who studies these collections can fail to be surprised at the beautiful forms represented there, and at the love of artistry even at that early time revealed in workmanship of every kind— even in the designing of steel-yards, weights, measures, and cooking utensils. These as well as vases and candelabra and everything else these ancients used are nearly always exquisitely ornamented.

While I was in Naples on this trip I found in stores and other places copies of quite a number of the original bronzes from Naples and Pompeii. They were made by a man named Angeles. I hunted him up and had him go to the museum with me; and with the aid of the Directors I selected five hundred representative artistic pieces and had him reproduce them for me in facsimile, so that I could have for our museum a consistent and beautiful exhibit illustrating how every common article was ornamented by the early Romans. I may say here that all the bronzes found at Herculaneum were buried about seventy-five feet deep in soft rock or mud, so that they are preserved in as fine condition as they were when the lava rolled over them. At Pompeii, on the other hand, they were covered to a depth of only a few feet, so that the sulphur has gone through and formed a patina on the bronze changing it to striking colors, but often destroying the finer hues. So if one sees an Etruscan art relic that is dark—almost black— he may know that it was found at Herculaneum, whereas those that come from Pompeii are covered with a patina of lovely greens, etc. Every one of these articles that I selected I had modeled from the originals with the proper color effect; and in consequence our bronzes in the Field Museum are exact replicas. One time as I was returning from Europe on the same ship with Mr. Carnegie I told him about these bronzes, and he telegraphed me later requesting me to have a full set made for the Pittsburgh Museum. This I did.

Then, too, during the early days of the Museum, about 1895, it was my good fortune to be collecting in Italy when

LOOKING SOUTH IN EDWARD E. AND EMMA B. AYER HALL, FIELD MUSEUM OF
NATURAL HISTORY

Boscoreale, a suburb about a mile and a half from Pompeii, was excavated. It was then that modern people first realized that Pompeii had the same kind of rich suburban homes that our cities of today have. In this aristocratic countryside was found "The Treasure" of Boscoreale. The skeleton of a man was discovered, face downward, in a pit underneath the room occupied by the wine-presses in the chief suburban home that was uncovered. In his fingers were clutched an ornamental gold chain and bracelets of gold, and all about him lay scattered a thousand gold coins—the contents of his purse. Near him were found a hundred and seventeen pieces of silverware which he had carried away in a bag. These discoveries at Boscoreale became famous when Baron Edmond de Rothschild bought the coins and some of the other more precious articles for 500,000 francs and presented them to the Museum of the Louvre in Paris.

My chief purchases from the relics found in this villa consisted of two remarkable bronze bathtubs; eight pieces of bronze, including a table; and a hundred pieces of beautifully ornamented silverware. I secured, besides, all the mural decorations that were found in this villa. All these things I bought; and Mr. H. H. Porter, Mr. D. H. Burnham, Mr. Charles Singer, and I presented them to Field Museum. They are now in Edward E. and Emma B. Ayer Hall; and, with the exception of the five hundred reproduced bronzes described before and now displayed in twelve cases, everything in that room is genuine original material.

I also secured three of the five early Etruscan decorated tombs—the only ones of this kind ever found in Italy. I bought them from Alessandro Jandolo in Rome. They came from either Toscanella or Civita Castellana. The decorations on these sarcophagi suggest the influence of Greece or Egypt. I got one of the leading sculptors of Rome and Dr. Nevin, a distinguished Episcopal minister and a recognized expert in antiquities, to go down with me and examine the tool-marks; for I thought there might have been certain tools peculiar to this or that epoch which might give some clue to the antiquity of these specimens. Both of these gentlemen said that the indications from the tool-marks would place these sarcophagi eight hundred years before Christ.

During the first twenty years Mr. Ayer was in the contracting business, he worked very hard and took almost no recreation. He began to realize that his health would suffer if he did not seek some means of relaxation. Reverting to his boyhood love of a gun, he took up shooting, and for the next twelve or fifteen years annually spent several weeks in his favorite sport. At the same time he began to buy illustrated books on birds, his fancy running chiefly to color plate books. Though prompted in this merely by his own taste, his instinct as a collector was in the right direction as usual; for, as one of his friends recently expressed it, "neither ducks nor colored plates are growing more common as the years go by." After he began to go to Europe each year, he discontinued shooting. By this time, however, he had brought together a magnificent library worth perhaps forty thousand dollars, consisting mostly of colored plates of birds. One of the first things he did after the Field Museum was organized was to present this library of ornithological books to that institution.

His business was very prosperous during those years; and he told the officers of the Museum that since it was his desire to make as complete a collection of books as possible on ornithology, he would like to have the zoological department examine catalogues dealing with ornithology and buy every book on that subject that turned up, whether at auction or private sale, and send the bills to his office until he gave instructions to the contrary. He himself was continually examining catalogues that came to him from everywhere; and all the lists of material on birds that came he sent to the specialists at the Museum. Mr. Wilfred H. Osgood, curator of zoology at the Museum, wrote about this collection as follows in the "Preface to the Catalogue of this Library."

Since effort had especially been directed to the acquisition of books illustrated in color, the proportion of such books in the library was very large, and it was found that the literature of ornithology was not comprehensively covered. . . . This deficiency has been largely overcome during the past five years. . . . Books have been added rapidly and continually and, as the Catalogue goes to press, it is evident that additions in the future will consist mainly of scarce items and of such new books on the subject as may occur.

It was about five years ago that the Field Museum decided to publish the catalogue, referred to above, of the Edward E. Ayer Ornithological Library. This book contains seven hundred pages, and in it are listed one thousand one hundred fifty authors. No expense was spared to make it a perfect book of its kind. The finest experts were secured to prepare and edit it. In particular, Mr. John Todd Zimmer has left his scholarly impress upon it. The layman can form some conception of the extent of the collection and the significance of this catalogue from the following note at the end of the book: "In the works catalogued in the foregoing pages, exclusive of the periodicals and the General Dictionary of Natural History which are listed separately, there are, approximately, 50,995 plates of birds (39,888 in colors and 11,107 plain), 39,347 text figures of ornithological subjects (987 in colors and 38,360 plain), and 1,981 plates of birds' eggs (1914 in colors and 67 plain)."

Distinguished bibliographers refer to this catalogue in words of high praise. Mr. George Watson Cole said concerning it, at the time of its appearance: "It is the greatest bird bibliography in the world." Mr. J. Christian Bay wrote at about the same time: "This work will prove one of the most important bibliographical sources in ornithology and, indeed, is far more important than its most modest title indicates. Each work is described fully, and the annotations in many cases are the last word in bibliographical research in this field." The frontispiece of this catalogue is a reproduction in color of the Ralph Clarkson portrait of the collector. Perhaps none of the complimentary expressions about this book pleased Mr. Ayer so much as this comment in a letter from Mr. Milton J. Ferguson, Librarian of the California State Library at Sacramento: "I have never seen such a fine cata-logue: but, really, the finest thing in it is the old bird on the first page."

There seemed to be no limit to Mr. Ayer's breadth of interest as a collector. His latest large gift to the Field Museum was a unique collection of pewter, consisting of about eight hundred pieces. An attractive room, easy of access, sixty feet long has been set aside for the exhibition of these specimens of pewter, gathered from many lands and representing several centuries. When the writer asked Mr. Ayer how he became interested in pewter, his reply was in the form of a quotation:

"The only things in the world which are without interest are the things of which we are ignorant." Intuitively I had always recognized that truth. The moment we know a little about a thing it becomes interesting to us, and then we are led on indefinitely in pursuit of it. In my many years of travel-ing in North America, and in Europe, and around the world, I became interested in a great many subjects—in fact I do not know of any subject that has not appealed to me—and the result is that, in my relations with the Field Museum, the Newberry Library, the Art Institute, and in the making of acquisitions for my own private enjoyment, I have collected in a great many fields.

So it was with this wide interest that I began to take note of the pewter in the museums of Europe. I found that very early, and even up to a comparatively late date, pewter had been used for all sorts of purposes—for table-ware of every description, flagons, tankards, and guild cups, communion plate, baptismal ewers and basins, swinging censers, etc. I did my first collecting in Germany, Austria, and England. Then I got some things from France, Sweden, Holland, and America. Much later I collected a great deal of Chinese pewter, some of the pieces being very elaborate. It was not used to any great extent in Japan.

One half of the exhibit consists of specimens from China, some of them dating back to the Ming period (1368-1643) and others as recent as the Kang-hi period which closed in 1722. There are a great many very large pieces, mostly in the form of candlesticks designed as New Year's presents. They are all very ornate and highly symbolical. The Eight Immortal Genii figure conspicuously. They are to be found in almost every household, for they are supposed to bestow many blessings, long life in particular, upon the members of the family. Strikingly appropriate for its purpose as a New Year's gift is a piece representing the Twin Genii of Harmony and Union. One holds "a sceptre of good luck, the other a silver bullion. The jar between them surmounted by a bat, which is a symbol of luck, is supposed to contain blessings for the recipient of the gift." A very interesting gift for use at the New Year's Festival is a "pair of pewter candlesticks resting on caparisoned stags (the spotted deer) carrying a vase and holding a fungus of immortality under their feet"; and still another is a "pair of candlesticks in shape of double dragons, each with three figures of Taoist mythology on the base under the leadership of the God of Longevity."

The casual visitor enjoys very much the display of Chinese teapots, ewers, chafing dishes, finger bowls, and other articles for common household use; for they are all exquisite in design and proportion. Quaint and fascinating are the various table dishes with their embossed covers, on which are moulded the particular viands to be served. The bowl that contains a duck is surmounted by the figure of a duck, that in which a fish is to be served, by a fish. The carp dish is the exact shape of a carp. One large chafing dish, the cover of which is surmounted by two peaches with leaves, is separated into five compartments; each with a cover ornamented, respectively, with a goose, a duck, a crane, a carp, and a deer. On this dish is engraved the motto: "May you rise as high as the sun." One beautiful piece designed for the serving of chicken has a rooster embossed on the cover—his comb represented in red coral or flint.

Dr. Berthold Laufer, Curator of the Department of Anthropology, who himself secured many of the choicest specimens of Oriental pewter for the Ayer Collection, states in the 1927 *Annual Report* that up to the last Mr. Ayer was making notable additions to this collection. Among the objects thus acquired, but not yet placed in the public exhibit, he lists the following:

The new gifts consisting of twenty-one objects, all except one from China, include a fine altar set of five pieces (censer, pair of flower vases, and a pair of candlesticks) inlaid with decorations in brass of dragons, birds, flowers, and Buddha-hand citrus; a pilgrim bottle with copper inlays; pewter boxes with scenery and figures of the Eight Immortals in brass inlays; a pewter cash-box, and a number of exquisite teapots and water-ewers. There is a very artistic pewter bowl, lined with a coat of cracked porcelain, and engraved with a spray of phoenixes; and large candlesticks supported by figures are likewise deserving of special mention.

A letter to the author from Miss Grace Nicholson, whose Oriental Shop in Pasadena is well known to collectors and art patrons, contains informing items about Mr. Ayer's interest in pewter and throws light also upon other aspects of his work as a collector. One season Mr. Ayer called at Miss Nicholson's shop soon after his arrival in Pasadena and mentioned that he had added to his collection of European pewter in the Art Institute a small private collection of American and other pewters, and had then transferred the whole lot to the Field Museum. Turning to Mr. Hartman, Miss Nicholson's buyer, he said:

EDWARD E. AYER PEWTER COLLECTION, FIELD MUSEUM OF NATURAL HISTORY

"Charley, I want to make the Ayer collection of old pewter world renowned."

"That is easy," Mr. Hartman replied. "Why not start right now and buy our old Chinese pewter?"

"But there is no such thing," said Mr. Ayer, astonishment in his voice. "I want real pewter—rare pieces—for I won't get much encouragement from the Museum unless they are unusual."

Mr. Hartman left the room and soon returned with four odd-shaped pewter dishes and a candlestick.

"Are you sure these are pewter, Mr. Hartman?" Dr. Laufer would laugh at me if I sent them to the Museum and they proved to be imitations."

Miss Nicholson handed him a glass and requested him to scratch one of the articles on the base. He did so; satisfied himself that this was genuine pewter, and forthwith bought more than forty pieces. From that time on he cared little about Europe and American specimens, but bought every Oriental piece he could secure. These purchases from Miss Nicholson formed the basis of the extensive Chinese collection of which he was so proud.

Said Miss Nicholson, "For a number of years Mr. Ayer was interested in my private collection of old rhinoceros horn libation or so-called poison cups. He had my promise that when I felt that I had added all the types and designs to the collection that would enrich the artistic or educational value, I would give him the first chance to purchase the collection for the Field Museum, as I insisted it must go to some museum. He had never viewed the collection as a whole, so I promised to let him bring some friends to see it when he came the next season. Walking with crutches, in 1924, he informed me the first day he called that as soon as he could throw away one of them he would hobble up the stairs to my private gallery to see the collection."

It was only a short time before he came, accompanied by about a dozen of his personal friends—among others, Mr. Edward Butler, Mr. John J. Mitchell, and Mr. John B. Lord. Everyone in the party was interested in the collection and all declared that the specimens should be added to the Field Museum. But no one volunteered to buy them. After a considerable time Mr. Mitchell said that he must leave. There was manifest disappointment on the part of both Miss Nicholson and Mr. Ayer.

"Never mind," said Mr. Ayer in an aside to the owner of the collection, "I'll buy it myself."

But the outcome was to be different. As Mr. Mitchell passed Mr. Hartman on the stairs he informed him that he would buy the collection, but he requested that neither Mr. Ayer nor Miss Nicholson be told of this until all the rest had gone. It was an hour before the good news could be conveyed to Mr. Ayer, but when he learned of the generous action of his friend he was filled with excitement and delight and expressed his deep appreciation.

This collection of Rhinoceros Horn Cups is a very rare possession. During the winter of 1927 the writer was in Pasadena, and there met and interviewed several of Mr. Ayer's prominent Chicago friends—among others, Mr. Mitchell, Mr. Lord, and Mr. Butler. They all spoke of Mr. Ayer's skill as a collector and the contagious quality of his enthusiasm.

"For example," said Mr. Mitchell, in illustrating Mr. Ayer's ability to enlist the interest of others in support of the Museum, "he had got on the track of the Rhinoceros Horn Cups and he persuaded me and other friends to go and look at them with him, the result being that it cost me $15,000. He once telegraphed me from some place in Egypt that he had found two tombs that could be had at a wonderful bargain ($4,000) and was drawing on me for that amount. I replied, 'Will honor your draft, but have no use for a tomb just now.' "

Mr. Edward B. Butler related a number of similar incidents: "Ayer had much to do with the discovery of the prehistoric monsters in the pit of oil or asphalt near Santa Monica. There were thousands of these creatures that perished in the pit two hundred and fifty thousand years ago. He wanted some for the Field Museum. He jumped right in and bought them and then came to me and said, 'I want two hundred and fifty dollars.' In the same way he went to Mitchell and other friends, and so he got a thousand dollars and paid for them. Ask Miss Nicholson about the Libation Cups. Ayer asked her to keep them for us and wasn't satisfied unless she kept them all for him. He called on me, Mitchell, and the others and said, 'Let's call this collection the Stanley Field Collection.' This is just an example of how he would get us stirred up. He would say, 'Do you realize there is only one other in America?' 'Do you know what this means to Chicago and the Field Museum?' and so he would stir up our enthusiasm."

Since so many references have been made to the collection of Rhinoceros Horn Cups—about one hundred in number—this description, copied from the Museum card, may interest the reader.

The cups in this collection range from the Ming (1368-1643) to the Manchu dynasty (1644-1911). It was an ancient belief that the rhinoceros devours with its food all sorts of vegetable poisons and that its horn was capable of neutralizing poison. A cup carved from the horn was therefore credited with the ability to detect poison, and was regarded as an efficient antidote. In the court ceremonial of France as late as 1789, instruments of "unicorn-horn" were employed for testing the royal food for poison. A great variety of forms and designs is displayed in these cups; the natural conditions of the horn are admirably adapted to the artistic intentions. In many cups the shape and designs of ancient bronze and jade vessels are reproduced; others assume the shape of lotus-leaves and lotus flowers, with admirable carvings in high and undercut reliefs. The collection contains excellent material for a study of Chinese decorative motives, as developed during the last five centuries.

Mr. Ayer was familiar with every aspect and detail of the educational work of the Museum. On April 27, 1927, six days before his death, without notes, he gave this account of what the Museum is doing:

Today it has become one of the very great museums of the World. Our building is a white marble temple with twenty-six acres of floor space. Our collections in many ways are superior to any of the other museum collections in the city that are being used in educating the young, and the Field Museum is doing more in this direction than any of the other five great natural history museums in the World. The first important step in public school extension work was made possible by the N. W. Harris gift of $250,000 in 1911. Since that time members of Mr. Harris' family have given more than another $100,000 for the purpose of carrying the Museum into the schools. Mr. S. C. Simms, one of the leading men in the Museum, was put at the head of this work, and he designed small portable cases to illustrate subjects in natural history and economics. For example, he takes one of these cases and in the left hand corner places a little stick of wood three or four inches long. That piece of wood is put through ten or twelve operations and the finished result in the form of a skein of thread is shown in another corner of the case. There are four hundred schools in Chicago, and we have enough of these cases to keep three of them in each school for a period of three weeks each school year. Two automobiles, each in charge of two men, go all over the city delivering these cases, making the changes, and bringing them back to the Field Museum.

But that was only the beginning. We have a theater that holds from fourteen to seventeen hundred people. During more than three-fourths of the year a lecture is given Saturday morning in this theater on natural history. There have been as many as eight thousand children some mornings waiting for the lecture room to open. Sometimes the lecture has to be given three times over during the morning to provide for the overflow. Saturday afternoon the same lecture is given to adults. Each child who attends the lecture is given a sheet or pamphlet describing the lecture, which he takes home to his parents. In addition to this, arrangements have been made whereby teachers in the various schools can hold regular sessions of their classes in the Museum. The pupils are provided with regular question forms on which they can set down their answers after they study the exhibits. They are transported in great busses that hold fifty, seventy-five, or a hundred pupils; and at times we have had classes from as many as ten or fifteen schools in one day, with the teacher there and the actual material for study before them.

About a year ago a lady came into the Museum and said, "I want to make it possible to carry this extension work for the schools still farther. I have brought with me here securities valued at $500,000, and I should like to have you train a group of people to give lectures in the schools themselves on subjects illustrated in the Field Museum. What I desire is to have lecturers with lantern slides go right into the school-rooms. All of the schools have halls equipped with lanterns, etc., so this will not be hard to carry out. It will take about two thousand lectures a year for the four hundred schools—fifty or more in each school—and interest on $500,000 will carry on such a program."

Of course it takes a great deal of money to carry these things on. To show the effect this work has had on the people of Chicago, I need only point out that they have found it necessary to provide more money for the Art Institute, the Aquarium, and the Field Museum. So the bill was introduced into the Legislature of Illinois asking that body to authorize the South Park Board to levy a tax, the income from this tax to be apportioned equally among the Field Museum, the Art Institute, and the Aquarium, sufficient to furnish $200,000 a year to each of them perpetually. This bill passed the Legislature almost unanimously. The Governor signed it in a minute, and there was no referendum. The whole state and the whole Mississippi Valley endorsed it. That is interest at four per cent on $15,000,000.

Mr. Ayer's personality and deeds are written indelibly into the structure of the Field Museum. What he did for this institution will carry his name to distant posterity. For a full generation his heart and soul, to say nothing of his time and money, were wrapped up in this splendid monument to humanity. He helped to bring it into existence; he was its first president and continued to be a member of its Board of Trustees until the day of his death; he gave freely of his most cherished possessions as a collector to build up its various departments; he ransacked the earth for treasures to add to its ever-growing wealth of materials; he inspired and persuaded his friends and fellow citizens to emulate his own unfailing generosity in adding to its rare objects, its scope, and its usefulness; and to the very end of his life he kept in almost daily intimate contact with every detail of its organization and administration, even to the extent of personal acquaintance with the staff and friendly solicitude for their welfare. He never grew weary of visiting the Museum for repeated study and inspection of its endless wealth of information and illustrative specimens of the history of the World and the struggle and growth of man. He took delight in bringing his friends and acquaintances to view the exhibits with him; and wherever he was, there was continually on his lips eloquent discourse concerning its wonders, its benefits, and its ultimate value as a monument of expanding civilization.

The Museum held a deep emotional interest for him, also; for wrought into its very fibre were reminders of his friends and intimate associations: Mr. Norman Ream, Mr. George Pullman, Mr. Charles Hutchinson, Mr. Daniel Burnham, Mrs. Mary Sturges, Mr. Martin Ryerson, Mr. John Mitchell, and a score of others with whom he had worked and planned in the early days. On every hand as he came and went through the various collections, there came to warm his heart reminiscences of social enjoyments, of sports, of travel, and of excited pursuit and then triumphant acquisition of archaeological spoils from the Old World. Certainly no man ever invested his substance more remuneratively. He had found joy in acquiring these things, happiness in bestowing them, and through all the long later years delight in physical and intellectual contact with them.

By way of summary and conclusion it is fitting that the Resolution adopted by the Board of Trustees of the Field Museum as a tribute to Mr. Ayer's memory should here be quoted in full. It is to be found in the *Annual Report* of the Director for the year 1927.

Mr. Ayer gave generous and effective assistance in the initial organization of the Museum. He was in the fullest accord with its purpose, and contributed to its progress an ever wakeful enthusiasm which counted far in the councils of the Trustees, and became reflected in a large number of his contemporaries. For five years, from 1894 to 1899, Mr. Ayer served the institution as its first president, and it fell to his share to formulate and pronounce many of the fundamental principles which originated with its founders. Continuing his service as a member of the Board of Trustees throughout the remainder of his life, Mr. Ayer gave liberally of his time and efforts to strengthen and develop the Museum in every way. His participation in its active management was dictated by his strong faith in the great future of Chicago as an educational center and in the importance of organized museum activities as an integral part of this development. This conviction prompted Mr. Ayer in contributing time and again large collections and groups of important objects, some of which served in the upbuilding of several unrivalled units in the library, others in extending materially the organized collections in other fields. From year to year his contributions, chiefly anthropological interests, continued, and all departments of the Museum give some evidence of his zeal as a collector.

Mr. Ayer was notably successful in enlisting the aid of others in an effort to extend and supplement the collections, and in this way adduced much material which otherwise might have been lost to the institution. His enthusiasm inspired many of his contemporaries to follow his example in this public service.

The most important gifts made wholly or in part by Mr. Ayer include several thousand specimens illustrating the archaeology and ethnology of the North American Indians, large Egyptian collections, valuable antiquities illustrating Greek, Roman, and Etruscan archaeology, an important collection of fossil vertebrates from the Rancho La Brea beds of California, and, in his later years, a large and exhaustive collection illustrating the history and uses of pewter in all parts of the world. He also made many contributions to the gem exhibits in the H. N. Higinbotham Hall.

The Museum Library benefited in many ways by Mr. Ayer's contributions, but his chief service consisted in building up by his donations exceptionally complete collections of books and manuscripts on the subjects of ornithology and ichthyology, including numerous works of superior excellence and rarity, which, as a whole, would be a notable attraction in any institution.

Mr. Ayer's personal character expressed itself in an alert interest in even the minutest details of the Museum, from its personnel to the administrative details. He confessed himself in a privileged position as a member of the Board of Trustees. His sympathies included the care of the collections as well as the welfare of every employe. He remained in close personal contact with the members of the Museum staff and inspired all with his generous, intelligent response to earnest work, his high ideals, his reverence of true service, and his confidence in that form of public enlightenment which remains the cultural foundation of Field Museum.

CHAPTER XII

Service as a Member
of
The United States Board of
Indian Commissioners*

By Malcolm McDowell

MR. AYER was so enthusiastically and diversely interested in the American Indians that to think of him without, at the same time, thinking of them is well nigh inescapable.

As a young soldier in the early '60's, wearing the uniform of the United States Army, he fought the hostile Red Men of the Southwest. As a lumberman in Arizona he employed Navajo and Apache, men of tribes he had faced in armed conflict during earlier times. He studied their peculiarities and learned how to handle them. This practical knowledge of their working capacities enabled him in after years to carry out plans for encouraging Indians to seek and get gainful

---

*When Mr. Ayer was interviewed concerning his public service for the Indians, he referred the author to Mr. Malcolm McDowell, Secretary of the Board of Indian Commissioners in Washington, for information concerning this aspect of his life. In response to the inquiry, Mr. McDowell prepared this excellent paper based upon the official records of the Board. He writes: "In selecting this material, I went all through the office files and gathered reports, letters, notes, and telegrams written by Mr. Ayer and the carbon replies. I also searched the annual reports and the minutes of the Board meetings." When he wrote the article, Mr. McDowell had no thought of its being incorporated in a book just as it stood. He offered it, rather, as source material. But the result of his careful work is so adequate and well-ordered, so full of literary charm and understanding sympathy, that the author sought and secured his consent to include it as a chapter of this biography.

employment. As a student of American history he went back
to aboriginal beginnings to locate the causes whose effects are
observable in the present condition of our Indian folk. As a
collector he gathered under one roof a world-famed library,
with its tens of thousands of volumes, manuscripts, drawings,
photographs, paintings, maps, and other source material on
the North American Indians—the Ayer Collection in the
Newberry Library of Chicago. As a philanthropist he not
only relieved individual distress, but contributed generously
to organizations established for the welfare of Indians. As
a lover of the fine arts he sought to develop the native arts
and crafts of several tribes. As a friend he visited the red
people in their primitive homes, gained their confidence, en-
deavored to protect them from exploitations, and ever stood
out for their rights before the Nation. He was recognized
as high authority on all things pertaining to aboriginal and
contemporary Indians, and was regarded as a prolific source
of accurate information concerning them.

While young Edward Ayer, the soldier, was campaigning
against the hostile Navajo, Apache, Ute, and other Indians
in the Southwest, the tribes of the Great Plains were on the
war path. During and immediately after the Civil War the
Sioux, Arapaho, Comanche, Kiowa, Cheyenne and others
of the Plains Indians were the cause of much anxiety to the
national authorities in Washington. President Johnson sent
into the Indian country a commission, headed by General
William T. Sherman, to inquire into the cause of Indian hos-
tilities and to submit recommendations for changes in Federal
policy and methods of handling Indian affairs which might
lead the warring tribes back to peace.

Among the recommendations submitted by this body was
one calling for the establishment of a commission of private
citizens to be appointed by the President of the United States,
to make a thorough survey of the whole Indian situation and

to deal with the tribesmen. This report, with its findings and recommendations, was passed on to President Grant who, almost immediately after his inauguration in 1869, sent a special message to Congress urging the adoption of the recommendation for what then was called a "Peace Commission." Congress was favorable to the President's suggestion and enacted legislation creating the United States Board of Indian Commissioners to be composed of ten citizens, "men eminent for their intelligence and philanthropy and to serve without pecuniary compensation."

Since 1869 this Board has been functioning as an independent establishment of the Federal Government, serving as an adviser on Indian affairs to the President, Congress, the Secretary of the Interior and the Commissioner of Indian Affairs. Cooperating with the Interior Department and the Bureau of Indian Affairs, it is independent of each. It has the authority of law to go upon and into any Indian reservation or any other branch of the United States Indian Service for inspection and survey; and Congress makes an annual appropriation for its traveling expenses and for the conduct of the Board's office in Washington.

President Taft appointed Mr. Ayer on the Board of Indian Commissioners, or the "Indian Commission" as it is often called, November 18, 1912, and he was an active and influential member of this unique Government organization for nearly seven years, resigning his commission to President Wilson, January 29, 1919. Before relinquishing his commission he requested President Wilson to appoint as his successor Major General Hugh L. Scott, U. S. A. Retired. He thus named his successor, a most unusual diversion from customary procedure.

Shortly after his appointment by President Taft, Mr. Ayer qualified by taking the oath of office, and on January 15, 1913, he attended his first Board meeting, an annual session held in

Washington, and there first met his fellow commissioners. They received him with open arms; for his reputation as a philanthropist and a practical idealist and a man whose wide knowledge of Indians and their affairs had been gained by personal contacts with the Red Men, had preceded him. He found himself in a congenial atmosphere, one of a group of what he said was "the finest bunch of men in the country."

All the members of the Board of Indian Commissioners were men of national, some of international, reputation in the law, church, science, journalism, philanthropy, and business. The Presbyterian, Catholic, Quaker, Unitarian, Universalist, Congregational, and Episcopalian churches were represented in the Board's membership at that time, as well as the republican and democratic parties.

But denominationalism and partisan politics have no part in the work of this Board; church fealty or party loyalty are never permitted to intrude their potentialities for dissension into the common cause, the good of the Indian, which is the chief objective of the Board's activities. The members give what time they can from their private affairs to go into the Indian country to make surveys of conditions, investigate administrative activities, and, particularly, to inquire into the family life and the economic, educational, and health conditions of the Indians. Their reports are transmitted to the Secretary of the Interior and thence to the Commissioner of Indian Affairs, and ofttimes to the President and Congress. They receive no salaries, nor any other compensation excepting the satisfaction which comes from disinterested endeavors to help some fellow creatures who need help. Their bare traveling expenses are paid by the Federal Government; and each year the Board, as a Government establishment, is received at the White House by the President in conjunction with the Chief Executive's reception to the National Judiciary.

This was the Board of which Commissioner Ayer was a member for nearly seven years, during which he "officially" visited the Menominee Indians of Wisconsin; the Apache, Navajo, Hopi, Mohave, Walaupai, Pima, Papago, and Maricopa of Arizona; the "Mission," "Digger," Mono, Paiute, Chemehuevis, Yuma, Cocopa, Hupa, Shasta, Concow, and other Indians of California; the Modoc, Klamath, and Warm Springs Indians of Oregon; and the Yakima, Clallam, Tulalip, and others of the Puget Sound bands in Washington.

His colleagues practically turned the Board's activities in behalf of the Indians of Arizona and Southern California over to Commissioner Ayer, and most of his investigations and official visits were confined to the tribes and the Indian Service schools and hospitals in the Southwest. His recurring trips through this section of the Indian country kept him in close touch with all matters pertaining to these Indians, and whatever he had to say about them received the thoughtful consideration of the Department and of the Indian Bureau.

The Board of Indian Commissioners lost no time in putting him to work. He knew lumber from the roots of the standing timber to the ultimate point of consumption, and shortly after he became an Indian Commissioner a situation arose in the Menominee Reservation in the Green Bay section of Wisconsin which called for a man of his kind of business and experience. During the second Board meeting he attended, in November, 1913, it was stated that there had been certain serious complaints made against the administration of this reservation and of the operation of the large saw mill which the Government had built for the Menominee Indians by authority of Congress, out of tribal funds. By formal motion Commissioner Ayer was requested and authorized to inquire into the complaints and submit a report of his investigation. He promptly accepted the task and arrived on the reservation November 28, 1913.

Ordinarily an inspection of this character would be made by a member of the Board alone; but Commissioner Ayer, having received some information which indicated that the complaints emanated from outsiders who had ulterior motives of a "shady" character, decided to be well prepared for any contingency. He, therefore, took with him and at his own expense Mr. L. P. Holland, one of his mill superintendents; Mr. Philip R. Smith, secretary and treasurer of his company; and Mr. William Anderson, one of his stenographers. At his request Commissioner Cato Sells of the Bureau of Indian Affairs detailed Mr. J. P. Kinney, Supervisor of the Forestry Service of the Indian Bureau, to assist him.

Under the leadership of Commissioner Ayer this inquisitorial body made a most searching investigation, not alone of the saw mill, but also of the Menominee Indian forest and of the selling system, accounts, and other fiscal matters. They also scrutinized the superintendent's administration of the whole jurisdiction, which included a reservation boarding school, hospital, and other units. During the days he was on this reservation, Commissioner Ayer went about among the Indians, visiting them in their homes, inquiring into their conditions, and making many friends. He also viewed the Government school and the Catholic mission boarding school for Indian children.

The result of his investigation is set forth in his report which made a book of 151 pages, and which he had printed at his own expense. He disproved entirely the charges which had been made against Superintendent Nicholson of the Menominee Reservation, and ever after stood back of Mr. Nicholson as a friend and admirer. He showed conclusively that the lumber mill instead of losing money, as the malcontents had claimed, was actually operating at a substantial profit. He made certain recommendations for changes in the Government's merchandizing policy; and these recommendations were approved by the Department of the Interior and, later, were made effective by Congress. "That was one of the meanest jobs ever wished on me," said Commissioner Ayer, "but we certainly discovered the Ethiopian in the woodpile."

The Menominee Indian Reservation report, because of the nature of the investigation, was largely technical; it dealt with logging, lumber manufacturing, contracts, balance sheets, and merchandizing. There was nothing of the human element in it. Supplemental reports, however, took up other matters more nearly related to the human equation of the Indian problem. Mr. Ayer was puzzled to find that Indians who stood in the relation of wards to the Federal Government were not subject to state laws, and that the only laws which applied to them were certain Federal criminal statutes. He found, for instance, that the Menominee Indians were not subject to the marriage, divorce, educational, and health laws of Wisconsin.

He wrote a letter to Chairman Vaux of the Board of Indian Commissioners, March 1, 1915, in which he called attention to this curious situation and suggested "that legislation would have to be had to remedy these evils; and it should be done, of course, at the earliest possible time."

Here he put his finger on one of the most complicated and embarrassing of the many complicated and embarrassing problems which the Federal Government had vainly tried to solve. The situation he noted at Menominee was common to all Indian reservations. Mr. Ayer's letter was laid before the Commissioner of Indian Affairs who returned a polite but ambiguous reply, and nothing came of his suggestion at the time. But Mr. Ayer never ceased his efforts to find a practical solution of the problem, and his endeavors received the official endorsement and hearty cooperation of the Board. The matter was presented to Congress session after session; but Mr. Ayer had left the Board several years before Congress paid any particular attention to the admittedly evil situation caused by the lack of authority to enforce the ordinary laws of the land within Indian reserves. There is a fair prospect that before the Seventieth Congress (1928-29) ends a bill, which contains provisions designed to bring about what Commissioner Ayer wanted, will be enacted into a law.

The office files of the Board of Indian Commissioners in Washington contain many reports, letters, telegrams, and short notes signed "Edward E. Ayer." Their tone, their phraseology, their whole "make-up" disclose the fact that in the performance of his official duties Commissioner Ayer was individualistic. In setting forth his findings and making his recommendations he had little use for Government "red tape," high sounding phrases, and redundant paragraphs. What he had to say he said in a few words, succinctly, clearly, and frequently emphatically. The bulk of his many paged Menominee report is made up of appendices carrying the stenographer's report of questions and answers, statistics, and the like. His own observations and findings used but few of the printed pages. Most of his reports consisted of less than half a dozen typewritten sheets each.

Commissioner Ayer became known in the Indian country and in Washington as the firm friend of the United States Indian Field Service men and women: the superintendents of the Indian reservations, the clerks in Indian agency offices, the reservation physicians, and the principals, teachers, matrons, and laborers of the Government's Indian schools. He knew from personal observation of the hardships due to environment and isolation which the field service folk were compelled to endure. He knew about the low salaries, poor housing conditions, and the utter absence of ordinary comforts which made the living conditions of many reservations so unattractive that there were constant changes in the personnel.

His quick sympathy instantly responded to such situations, and he ceaselessly urged, even demanded, that the Indian Offices and Congress should take measures purposed to make the Indian Service employes happier, more contented, and better paid.

When they met Commissioner Ayer, the Government folk on reservations called him "Mr." or "Commissioner" Ayer, but among themselves he was generally designated "Uncle Ayer," a significant indication of their affectionate regard for the man who, as one superintendent said, "always went to the front for us."

The field officials of the Indian Service with whom Commissioner Ayer came in contact soon learned that he did not come into their jurisdictions as an investigator nor as an inspector, but as a friend who only wanted the opportunity to help them solve some of their problems. With most of them relations of mutual confidence were easily established, and they frankly discussed their affairs with him. One of the principal subjects of discussion was the frequent transfers from one jurisdiction to another of the superintendents, a practice which resulted in much inefficiency and dissatisfaction. Commissioner Ayer took it upon himself to get at the root of the matter. He prepared a questionnaire asking for the service history of every superintendent. He received 120 replies, practically a one hundred per cent return. The replies were reviewed by the office staff of the Board. It was found that only ten of the superintendents had never been transferred during their terms; the other 110 had been transferred from one to ten times each.

Commissioner Ayer sent this tabulation with his report thereupon to Chairman Vaux. His report on this important matter was short and to the point. It is here reproduced because it was so characteristic of his method of approach to the men "higher up."

MR. GEORGE VAUX, JR., *Chairman*
Board of Indian Commissioners
Philadelphia, Pennsylvania

Dear Sir:

I hand to you this report on the transferring of agents, which I wish you would please have transmitted to Secretary Lane in the usual manner.

During the time I have been on the Indian Commission I have been studying more or less the changing of Indian agents from post to post. It seems in some cases a man cannot be promoted unless he takes another place. Of course, I don't know under what administration the practice grew up of changing these men about so frequently and at such great distances, but whenever it was and whoever made the change, it was a very unbusinesslike proposition.

Our Indian Reservations reach from Florida to Maine, from Fort Yuma to the British Possessions, and from the Atlantic to the Pacific Ocean, taking in all sorts of climate, all sorts of methods of doing business, all sorts of lumbering, all sorts of agriculture, and a man may be an absolute expert in one of these places and be a fool in a district with which he is unfamiliar. In fact, he cannot be competent both in Louisiana and in Washington. Who would have any confidence in my business ability if I owned an automobile factory in Detroit, a sugar plantation in Louisiana, a cattle ranch in Arizona, a cotton plantation in Texas, and a lumber mill in the State of Washington, if every year or two I would take the man out of my sugar plantation and put him in charge of the cattle range in Arizona, and almost as bad methods as these are being made all of the time under this, to my mind, absurd rule, and I strongly recommend to the Secretary of the Interior and the Indian Department, that a change be made in this method of doing business.

Yours very truly,
EDWARD E. AYER

The report with its statistical analysis was sent to Secretary Franklin K. Lane of the Department of the Interior who replied as follows:

My Dear Mr. Ayer:

I have received from Mr. Vaux your letter in the matter of changing Indian agents from one reservation to another. The policy you suggest is exactly the policy we are following. Of course, if we find that an agent is particularly strong and broad visioned and has been successful in his work, and we need such a man at a larger reservation where the problems are difficult, we are very apt to transfer and promote him; but I do not understand at all that we merely shift our agents about from one place to another without there being some good and sufficient reason for doing so.

I thoroughly agree with your suggestions, and in placing our agents we are guided entirely by what is most beneficial to the Indians and not merely by the purpose of advancing the agents in salary.

Cordially yours,
FRANKLIN K. LANE

Commissioner Ayer was of the firm opinion that the best way to forward the progress of the Indian race was to help the Indian to help himself, and the quickest and surest way to do this was to get him a job and let him work himself into the status of a self-supporting citizen. In season and out of season he urged the Indian Office to seek gainful employment for Indians. He told Secretary Lane that he had successfully employed Navajo and Apache in his lumber mill at Flagstaff, and that the managing officials of the Santa Fe Railroad had told him that Indians, particularly the Navajo, Apache, and Mohave, made good section men in Arizona and California. In a report on the Indians of California and Arizona, dated August 11, 1915, he wrote:

In coming east over the Mohave Desert the first Indians are the Mohaves, a splendid tribe of probably the tallest and best Indians in America. Physically they are some of the most splendid people I ever saw in my life, and that has been the judgment of all people who have visited them from 1848 to the present time. There are only a few of them and they are self-sustaining practically. I met there Mr. J. W. Woods, who has been a contractor on the Santa Fe Road in cement work, etc. for twenty-five years. He has worked some of these Indians all of this time and is devoted to them as laborers. I asked him if they turned out as much work and as well as the Mexicans that were working on the railroad there. He said very nearly twice as much a day and that they were a tractable, reliable, splendid people. I asked him if any of them were employed as foremen. He said one of his head foremen was an Indian and he did not know what he would do without him.

Previous to making this report Commissioner Ayer had corresponded with Mr. Storey, Vice President of the Santa Fe Railroad, in regard to putting more Indians to work through Arizona and New Mexico. From then on Commissioner Ayer kept to the front his campaign to better the economic conditions of the Indians.

At a special meeting of the Board which was held at The Oaks, Lake Geneva, Wisconsin, the summer home of Commissioner Ayer, July 25-27, 1917, Commissioner Ayer presented a verbal report on the labor conditions in Arizona growing out of the rapid development of cotton raising in the Salt River Valley, irrigated by water from the Roosevelt Dam. The following month he embodied his views and recommendations in a short report which he sent to Secretary Lane. In the opinion of his colleagues this report was one of the most important, if not the most important, made by him. It presented a critical situation and offered a practical way out of a labor shortage through the employment of Arizona Indians as cotton pickers.

"What our Indians need most is to be taught to work," he asserted. "There are nearly 50,000 Indians in Arizona and a very small percentage of them do any useful work. It seems to me that this opportunity for a large body of the Indians of that section, at work which they can do, and with good pay, should be given prompt and favorable attention."

He urged that a competent man be detailed by the Indian Department to have charge of all Indians at work in the valley, to look after their interest and to see that they had proper tents, water, fuel, and other necessities. He further recommended that this employment agent should be kept there the year around, visiting the Arizona reservations, collecting Indians to work in the cotton fields and to arrange their transportation. More than that, he secured the personal interest of the leading business men of Phoenix in his scheme.

As a result an Indian Service agent was sent to Phoenix, and most of Commissioner Ayer's recommendations were put into practical effect. More than that, the whole question of Indian employment was taken up by the Indian Office. The World War interrupted the making of plans, but the present Commissioner of Indian Affairs, Mr. Charles H. Burke, is in hearty accord with the identical policies concerning the industrial advancement of the Indians which Commissioner Ayer so earnestly advocated in 1917.

The United States had entered the World War three months before this summer meeting of the Board was held at the Lake Geneva home of Commissioner Ayer. The occasion for the meeting was the consideration of the annual report. Aside from this the only formal action taken by the commissioners was the adoption of a resolution, presented by Commissioner Ayer, which read:

RESOLVED, That the Board of Indian Commissioners urge the Government to enlist one experimental regiment of Indian scouts for duty on the Mexican border.

This carried to the War Department an idea which had been formulating in Commissioner Ayer's mind for several years, the idea of placing Indians in the regular army as enlisted soldiers. In April 1916, he submitted a report urging the Secretary of the Interior to establish target practice as part of the training for the older boys in the larger Government boarding schools for Indians. This was his opening shot. He followed it by securing the approval by the Board of a recommendation for the organization of ten or fifteen regiments of Indian soldiers in the regular army to relieve the white soldiers who were on duty along the Mexican border. This idea of utilizing the military tendencies of the Indian aroused so much public interest that the editor of the *Chicago Herald* asked Commissioner Ayer to write an article on the subject, and he did so. It was printed in the *Chicago Herald* in February 1917, and presented Commissioner Ayer's views on this matter completely and concisely. It read as follows:

E. E. Ayer favors Indian Soldiers. Authority on ·Redmen Believes Several Regiments could be Enrolled—Lauds their Fitness—By Edward E. Ayer.

Having crossed the plains in an emigrant outfit in 1860, coming in contact with many tribes of Indians, some of them hostile; having served during the last half of 1861 in Southern California, and all of 1862, 1863, and up to June, 1864, fighting Indians in Arizona and New Mexico; and having seen more or less of them nearly every year since, collected a great library on the subject, and served on the Indian commission for several years, I have come to the following conclusions of what should have been done or started sixty years ago, and what would be easy to do now:

1. There always has been a first class foundation among the Indians to build upon—first, the Indian's great powers of endurance; second, he is proud of being trusted; third, he is truthful and brave. He becomes easily and greatly attached to one who treats him right. As to his endurance, whenever on scout duty in the old times in the West he often would run day after day distances that would stagger one. Ask General Wood and General Hugh Scott about it.

2. There is scarcely a record of an Indian not being true to any duty intrusted to him while he is under agreement or pay. Nearly all the Indian scouts who ran down Geronimo were from his tribe, and they were as true as steel while engaged.

The same men might go out on a raid after being released from their enlistment.

What Might Have Been

In my judgment, if our Government had commenced fifty or sixty years ago to enlist cavalry regiments of Indians, allowed them to bring their families in the neighborhood of the big posts, given them good horses, bridles, and saddles, with a good supply of German silver ornaments on them, and uniforms with considerable color; and had ten regiments of these troops, paying them the same wages as the white, these ten regiments would have kept our Western Indians under control, and at ten per cent of what it has already cost us. There has been a great improvement all along the line in the Indians' condition, commencing at the time they practically were confined on reservations. Take the Navajos, for instance. I was connected with the department which whipped them in 1863. They were moved down on the Pecos River at Bosque Redondo, about 500 miles from their reservation, about 10,000 of them. They were returned to their old ground and helped, and today there are 30,000 of them, and in sheep, cattle, blankets, etc., they are a very rich tribe. All the wild Apache tribes are now on reservations and doing well.

Students Need Task

The Government has established schools everywhere, where for several years many of the young men have been drilled in the manual of arms and marching and the girls trained in household duties, cooking, etc., I feel sure several regiments of very, very fine soldiers could be enrolled; and it would enormously relieve the situation on the reservations by giving the returned students something to do, lack of which has been one of the hardest questions in connection with the Indian question. This enlisting of Indians is no new question. During our civil war a good many companies of Indians were mixed with white soldiers. The Menominee tribe of Wisconsin alone gave several companies to their country, enough at least to keep up a Grand Army post exclusively of Indians on their reservation.

Urged Rifle Ranges

Last year as one of the Indian commissioners I recommended to Secretary of the Interior Franklin K. Lane, that each prominent Indian school should be provided with a rifle range, so that, if the Government ever wanted them as soldiers, they should know how to shoot.

I feel sure our Government now could get ten regiments of unique soldiers (especially for our Mexican border) in a very short time, and that number could be kept up for an indefinite period. Pay them the same wages. Have all non-commissioned officers Indians.

The schools have turned out hundreds perfectly capable of filling the positions. You would soon see that many could be promoted to lieutenants whose bravery and general character the white officers would be proud of.

Favors Two Commissions

I feel sure our Government now could get ten regiments of Commissioner on February 7, substantially on these lines, ending up by stating:

If you get authority to do this, I urge two commissions of three men each, made up out of the Indian service, taking such men as Mr. Thackery of the Pima Reservation, Mr. Peterson of the White Mountain, Mr. Odle of the Yuma, Mr. Conser of the Sherman School, and Dr. Breid of Lapwai. And you have a hundred just such splendid men to choose from for your two commissions. I feel sure that by visiting the different Indian reservations these men could get the required number of first-class men in a very short time"

Two months after this article appeared in the *Chicago Herald,* the United States had joined the Allies against Germany, and Congress concentrated its legislative functions on the Military Draft Bill and other war measures. On April 30, 1917, Representative Kahn of California, Chairman of the House Committee on Military Affairs and the leader in the fight for the Draft Bill, introduced a bill to authorize the organization of ten or more regiments of Indian cavalry to be designated "The North American Indian Cavalry," the regiments to be in command of regular army officers. In speaking for this bill, Mr. Kahn said these Indian troopers could be used on the Mexican border, thus releasing white troops for European battle fronts. On the same day Representative Charles Carter of Oklahoma, himself of Indian blood, introduced a similar bill, and a week later Senator Penrose of Pennsylvania introduced a measure for a regiment or regiments of Indians to be commanded by regular army officers.

The Military Draft bill became a law, and the question soon arose as to whether Indians who were "wards" of the Nation could be drafted. The courts ruled they could not. Commissioner Ayer then proposed that the Department of the Interior should undertake to raise a regiment of Indian volunteer soldiers. But before any official action could be taken on this recommendation it became known that Indians in large numbers, from all parts of the Indian country, were enlisting as volunteers. The idea of organizing them into racial units was abandoned. "These Indians beat us to it," commented Commissioner Ayer with a chuckle, "and I am glad of it, too. They will make grand soldiers, and I am proud of them."

At the time Commissioner Ayer submitted his first proposition for fifteen Indian regiments, calling for 15,000 Red Men, he was told there were not enough eligible Indians in the United States to fill that number of commands. After the close of the World War Commissioner Cato Sells of the Bureau of Indian Affairs officially reported that more than 15,000 Indians had enlisted for the war, and that several thousand more had slipped across the line to join the Canadian forces. When his attention was directed to this statement Commissioner Ayer said:

I estimated we had about twenty thousand first class fighting men in our Indian tribes. But I trimmed this estimate to fifteen thousand to be on the safe side. I was confident that if they were ever given the chance our Indians would stand by the Government, and that is just what they did. More than fifteen thousand joined the colors. Indians bought twenty-five million dollars of Liberty Bonds. Indians not only subscribed hundreds of thousands of dollars for the Red Cross, but hundreds of the Indian women and girls were active in Red Cross work. Anyone who knows Indians knows that patriotism is fundamental with them. Once it was tribal patriotism, but now it is for their country, the United States. Not only were Indians the first Americans, but they are first and last Americans as was proved by their record in the World War.

In March of 1918 Commissioner Ayer was in Arizona and noticed that the Indian children in the United States Indian Service schools were using bread made entirely of wheat flour. At the time the white people of the Nation were substituting rye, potatoes, corn, and rice for wheat, acting under instructions issued by the Food Administration. On March 10, Commissioner Ayer wrote the following letter to Secretary Lane:

Phoenix, Arizona
March 10, 1918

HON. SECRETARY FRANKLIN K. LANE
Washington, D. C.
Dear Sir:
Upon investigating the Indian schools at Sacaton and here at Phoenix, I find a curious and I think indefensible condition in regard to food—flour especially. About one thousand Indian pupils were fed on wheat flour solely, as far as bread is concerned. They use ten tons per month. The agents say they have the flour issued to them and have no money to purchase anything else, and that the Government furnishes nothing else for bread. You can see the saving would be five tons of flour a month from these two schools alone, if one-half flour were used with one-half of substitutes as you and I get, and as all the Indian schools are under the same law and rules, the saving would be immense in a year. The agents, of course, are helpless as they have no authority in the matter. But one-half of

the flour now issued to the Indians should be commandeered immediately and the same substitutes that the rest of us are using should be substituted.

I called attention of the Arizona Food Commission to conditions here in Arizona, but I am afraid these conditions are the same in all states and it has been going on all the time since the war started.

I am not reporting this as an Indian Commissioner but a patriotic American who fully believes that "Food will win the war."

Respectfully,
EDWARD E. AYER

Before this letter had time to reach Washington, Commissioner Ayer telegraphed Secretary Lane as follows:

Tucson, Arizona
March 12, 1918

HON. FRANKLIN K. LANE
Secretary of the Interior
    Washington, D. C.

There are 15,000 Indian school children receiving rations of flour. At the rate of issue at Sacaton and Phoenix they are receiving over five tons of wheat flour a day. Also issued to 30,000 dependent Indians ten tons making fifteen tons per day equal to 5,475 tons per annum. If one half of this had been other grains there would have been saved for our Allies sixty-nine carloads of forty tons each during past year and all this time our Government was frantically proclaiming "Save flour and win War." I have these figures from several absolutely reliable sources.

EDWARD E. AYER

Then ensued a rapid interchange of telegrams and letters; the officials of the Interior Department and the Indian Office took prompt action, cut red tape and the wheat thus saved was milled into flour and shipped to the Allies.

The World War held Commissioner Ayer on the Board of Indian Commissioners longer than he had expected. In the early part of 1917 he had indicated his desire to resign his

commission, saying that he was "getting old" and was sever-
ing his connections with other organizations. The annual
meeting for 1917 was in session the last of January, and
Commissioner Ayer was not present. As was the custom, the
Board members called upon the Secretary of the Interior, and
during the conversation he was informed that Commissioner
Ayer was thinking of withdrawing. Mr. Lane declared the
Board could not spare him. Thereupon the following message was telegraphed Commissioner Ayer:

EDWARD E. AYER
    Railway Exchange Bldg.
        Chicago, Illinois
    The Board of Indian Commissioners in joint session with
Secretary of Interior have officially determined your age to be
forty, that your services on the Board cannot be dispensed
with and that the Board looks forward with pleasurable anticipation to your presence and participation in the Board
meeting at Riverside, March tenth.

GEORGE VAUX
Chairman

The Fiftieth Annual Meeting of the Board was held in
Washington, January 28, 1919, and at this session Commissioner Ayer, notwithstanding the emphatic protests of his colleagues, sent his resignation to the President. Chairman Vaux
notified the Board of this action by reading to the members
the following letter:

January 29, 1919

DEAR MR. VAUX AND MEMBERS
    OF THE INDIAN COMMISSION:
    My final association with you and members of the Commis-
sion with whom I have been associated so intimately, and delightfully to me, since I have been on the Commission, I sever
today by passing in my resignation to Secretary Lane.
    Now gentlemen, if you think for a moment you are going
to get rid of me whenever I have the opportunity of intruding

myself upon any one of you, you are mistaken, and I hope that any time, anywhere, I can be of any service to any of you, you will command me.

Of course you all well know it is only my advanced age that has caused me to take this action, and while I have felt in only a slight degree the disadvantage of old age, still I know it is here, and I want to take better care of my health in the future than I could carrying on the work of investigations of the Indian reservations.

With the hope and prayer that each and every one of you, each member of your families and every individual that you care for, may have every blessing to which flesh is heir, I remain,

Your devoted friend,
EDWARD E. AYER

As soon as the reading of the letter was ended, Commissioner Daniel Smiley moved that "Mr. Edward E. Ayer of Chicago be and is hereby appointed librarian and curator of the Board of Indian Commissioners." The motion was seconded by all the other members and carried unanimously. Mr. Ayer was requested by Chairman Vaux to stand up and was formally notified of the new appointment. Continuing, Chairman Vaux told Mr. Ayer that his resignation as Commissioner had been received with sorrow and regret, and that the members wanted him to know that it was their earnest desire that he attend future meetings of the Board, because, although he had resigned his commissionership, they still regarded him as one of them. In reply Mr. Ayer said he had resigned only because he felt that his increasing years warranted him in giving up public work, and that one of the most pleasant associations of his life had been made possible by his membership with the Board of Indian Commissioners.

The adjournment of this Fiftieth annual meeting ended Mr. Ayer's official connection with the United States Board of Indian Commissioners. There was no such office as "librarian and curator." The Board's library consisted of a few hundred official reports, some law books, and Indian histories; the only Indian wares were a couple of Navajo rugs on the office floor. There was nothing for a librarian or curator to do; but the Board created the office and appointed Mr. Ayer an official for the sole purpose of keeping him in the Board's family. Thereafter Mr. Ayer received reports, bulletins, letters, and other matter from the Board's Secretary as though he were still a commissioner, and he attended several meetings.

It was at one of these meetings, the annual session of 1925, that Mr. Ayer started a movement which developed an important result. Trachoma is a contagious eye disease which is prevalent among American Indians. The Board of Indian Commissioners, in conjunction with the Department of the Interior and the Bureau of Indian Affairs, had been endeavoring to secure increased appropriations from Congress to be used in efforts to eradicate trachoma, but with little success. At this 1925 annual meeting trachoma was one of the principal subjects under consideration.

Mr. Ayer sat back listening attentively to the discussion for some time. Then he leaned forward and said,

"What is needed is about $250,000 to be placed in the hands of Secretary Work to be used in a trachoma campaign, and the organization to furnish the money is the Rockefeller Foundation. I am going to Chicago tomorrow, and if you gentlemen approve my proposition, I will see Martin Ryerson, who is director of the Rockefeller Foundation, and urge him to get this money for the Secretary."

The Board members authorized him to talk with Mr. Ryerson for the Board; other members said they, too, would see other directors of the Rockefeller Foundation. In a few days a telegram came from Mr. Ayer informing the Board's Secretary that Mr. Ryerson was much interested and would take the whole matter up with the directors of the Foundation. This was done. The International Health Board, which is the organization of the Rockefeller Foundation which conducts public health demonstrations and develops cooperative public health programs, sent agents to Washington to consult with the Indian Office.

The officials of the Health Board found that the Government did not have the required definite information concerning trachoma, and for a time the proposition languished. But the suggestion made by Mr. Ayer remained, and at length there developed out of it a complete survey of the whole Indian Service, including all activities of the Field Service. This survey was conducted by the Institute for Government Research, an endowed, non-Government organization in Washington, with funds contributed by the Rockefeller Foundation. The survey party went into all parts of the Indian Country, and its report, comprising nearly 900 pages, is the most important document of its kind ever printed. The International Health Board now is in possession of the precise facts it requires before entering upon any public health demonstration. It was Mr. Ayer's voluntary proposal, made at the 1925 annual meeting of the Board, that eventually brought about this survey, although at the time he made his suggestion neither he nor any other Board member had such an ambitious survey in mind.

Mr. Ayer died between two meetings of the Board of Indian Commissioners. The first session after his death was held at Lake Mohonk, New York, October 7, 1927. Chairman Vaux called the Board to order and then formally notified them of the death of "former Commissioner Edward E. Ayer." The members rose to their feet, and the Chairman appointed a committee to draft a suitable resolution which would stand in the Board's records as an appreciation of Mr. Ayer's work in the Board. The resolution, written by Dr.

Samuel A. Eliot, was prepared and adopted unanimously by a rising vote. It read as follows:

EDWARD E. AYER
A Resolution of the United States
Board of Indian Commissioners
October 7, 1927

The members of the United States Board of Indian Commissioners record their affectionate regard for their former associate and beloved friend, EDWARD E. AYER, who died in Pasadena, California, on May 3, 1927, at the age of eighty-five.

Happy memories of Mr. Ayer's long and honorable career mingle with sorrow for the loss of his genial companionship and judicious counsel. He possessed and applied an exceptional knowledge of Indian affairs drawn not only from his invaluable books and manuscripts gathered in his unique library but also from personal contacts with the Indian people in all parts of the land and extending over nearly three-quarters of a century.

A pioneer boyhood in Wisconsin, a young soldier's experiences in California and Arizona, a lumberman's work in the Southwest and, later, the habits of extensive travel and wide reading and acute observation united with the gifts of an inquiring mind and sympathetic heart, so that he became one of the foremost authorities in this country on Indian problems.

He was preeminently a practical idealist, keeping his feet firmly on the ground but ever having in view the true and lasting welfare of the Indian people. He always had the courage of his convictions and advocated justice for the Indians with vigorous and uncompromising speech and persuasive ardor. At the same time he told the Indians themselves that the way of their success must lie along the paths of good health, industrial education, obedience to the law, hard work, and good character.

His colleagues delighted in his comradeship and all good causes enjoyed his wise and generous support.

Thus ended the official relations of Edward E. Ayer with the United States Board of Indian Commissioners.

CHAPTER XIII

Public Service

MR. AYER was pre-eminently a Chicagoan. It was almost three-quarters of a century from the time that, as a boy, he first came to Chicago and heard the song of Adelina Patti and the magic playing of Ole Bull until the winter of 1926, when he saw it for the last time; but through these changing decades it had continually exerted a shaping influence on his growth and culture; and, on the other hand, his farsightedness and bounty in a hundred ways had through all these years contributed beauty, civic dignity, and intellectual stimulus to the city he loved supremely. At least three eminent Californians have made mention in the author's presence of the ardor of Mr. Ayer's devotion to Chicago—to his extreme pride, akin to that of a Greek for his Athens, in his own city as a center of American culture. "He shared with Charles L. Hutchinson and his fellows, some of whom are gone and some who remain at work, the ideals of a future for the Art Institute, the Field Museum, the Chicago Historical Society, the Chicago Symphony Orchestra, and especially the Newberry Library which his special contributions have lifted to unique importance." Indeed, if a full list of his activities in the interest of the higher life of Chicago were to be set down, it must needs go even farther than this and include his support of David Swing, his participation in the activities of the Commercial Club, his patronage of the Opera, his co-operation with Mr. Daniel Burnham, and his interest in the Greater Chicago Plan.

Mr. Ayer's connection with the Art Institute was too important to dismiss with a mere reference. What he did for it

alone is enough to place his name among the permanent benefactors of Chicago. His own comment on the origin and
growth of this Institution is of historic as well as personal
interest.

I have been a trustee of the Art Institute for thirty-five
years. At the time of the World's Fair the Institution was located in a building at the corner of Michigan Avenue and
Van Buren Street, that has since for many years been the home
of the Chicago Club. The Art Institute at that time did not
have enough material to occupy this moderate-sized building,
so rented only part of it. At the beginning of the World's Fair
this building was sold to the Chicago Club, and the city began
the erection of the building now occupied by the Institute and
required no rental. Part of this present building was the Lecture Room for the World's Fair in 1893.

The Art Institute has become one of the great educational
institutions in art. I am told that it has the largest single Art
school in America. The extent and value of its collections are
next to those of the Metropolitan Museum in New York, and
about a million people visit it each year. Its influence, therefore, has been immense in educating the people of the Middle
West; and through the training of young people with artistic
talent it has been instrumental to a great extent in refining
our understanding of art here in the Middle West.

During my connection with the Art Institute, I collected
about half of the five hundred pieces of antique lace acquired
by the Institution and about the same proportion of the great
stuff collections there.

Up to the breaking out of the World War, each year for
twenty-six consecutive years, it had been the habit of Mr. and
Mrs. Ayer to spend four months in foreign travel. It now became necessary for them to gratify their love of travel and
sight-seeing in their own land, so they turned enthusiastically
to the great West and Southwest, and particularly to inex-
haustible California. Year after year they made extended
and romantic tours in the Southwest and along the Pacific
Coast. They usually fixed upon Pasadena, the residence of

Mr. Ayer's daughter, Mrs. Frank S. Johnson, as their home center—their main point of arrival and departure. During these years Mr. Ayer revived his youthful fondness for California. Many leading Chicago people make their winter homes in Pasadena, so he was always surrounded by his old friends; and it goes without saying that wherever Mr. Ayer went he gathered new friends and admirers about him.

Out of all this it very naturally came about that Mr. Ayer was soon deeply enlisted in all good civic and cultural movements in California—just as in Chicago affairs, and just as he would have been in any community that might have been fortunate enough to capture him for three or four months of the year. The Californians were inclined to claim him as one of their own. They almost persuaded themselves that he was more enamored of Southern California than of Chicago and the Middle West. This, of course, never could have been; and, if he seemed to indulge them in their innocent vagary, it was for the purpose of encouraging them to expend more in the development of the fine arts and public education, and in the preservation and fuller enjoyment of their extraordinary natural resources. He noted with warm interest their almost unparalleled enthusiasm for growth, for art, for scientific progress, and for civic development. So during the last years of his life he gave freely of his enthusiasm and his means (and of course stimulated others to do likewise) to promote all worthy movements in California.

That the Southwest appreciates what he did for it is amply attested by the utterances from its leading men of culture. Mr. Charles F. Lummis wrote: "He is one of the most interesting characters in all our modern history of the Southwest; and I know of no man to whom the student Americanist owes more." Dr. Morse Stephens, of the University of California, at a banquet given in honor of a Berkeley scholar who was departing for Spain to work in the National Archives, said:

"I desire to give the first toast of the evening to a gentleman who is doing more for Spanish American History than any other man in America, Mr. Edward E. Ayer, of Chicago." Quoting words that he attributed to Marshall Field, Mr. Frank A. Miller of the Mission Inn, said to the writer: " 'Useful things made beautiful should be preserved.' It was Mr. Ayer," he continued, "who for fifteen years has been stirring me up to get an art gallery and museum here." At the time of this conversation Mr. Miller was exerting himself to do this; and on the night Mr. Ayer was taken fatally ill he was to have been Mr. Miller's guest at the Mission Inn to talk informally to an invited company about how to secure a museum and art gallery for Riverside.

Said Mr. Leslie E. Bliss, Librarian of the Henry E. Huntington Library and Art Gallery, "Next to Chicago, no section of the world seemed so dear to Mr. Ayer as California. The work of the Mt. Wilson Observatory and the California Institute of Technology always interested him deeply, both being headed by friends of long standing, George Ellery Hale and Robert Andrews Millikan; McGroarty's San Gabriel Mission Play was always attended many times each winter, and the playwright was a dear friend. The Los Angeles Museum in Exposition Park came in for many friendly visits, and he never ceased to marvel at their wonderful prehistoric collection of bones assembled from the pits of La Brea. And yet his love for the great Redwoods of the north, notably those of Mendocino and Humboldt Counties, probably exceeded his love for all other things Californian. . . . I hope that if another grove of these giants is set aside as a memorial park the name of Edward Everett Ayer will be given it. No one could better deserve this honor and no one would have been prouder of such a distinction could it have been given him in his lifetime."

This suggestion made by Mr. Bliss in the passage just

FOUR FAMOUS MEN

JOHN S. MCGROARTY—POET; ROBERT A. MILLIKAN—SCIENTIST;
EDWARD E. AYER—PHILANTHROPIST; REV. ROBERT FREEMAN

quoted calls attention to Mr. Ayer's most notable service to California—his efforts for the preservation of the Redwoods. He exerted himself precisely at the right time and, happily, with a requisite degree of ardor. Entered upon the records of the Save-the-Redwoods League is the following statement:

Mr. Edward E. Ayer was one of the pioneer workers in the Save-the-Redwoods movement. He became a member in October, 1919, and not long after that time became interested in establishing a Redwood memorial grove in honor of Hon. Franklin K. Lane, former Secretary of the Interior and the first president of the Save-the-Redwoods League. Mr. Ayer was largely instrumental in collecting money from friends and admirers of Mr. Lane, and in securing the original pledges which made the memorial possible. Besides his active aid in this regard, Mr. Ayer donated $2,500 toward the acquisition of the grove.

Of all trees the Redwoods are the tallest, most ancient, most majestic. They are the oldest living things known to man. If there is anything in the world that can match them in impressiveness and beauty, it is the language of feeling and imagination—such as these words of the poet Edwin Markham. "These great trees belong to the silences and the milenniums. Many of them have seen more than a hundred of our human generations rise, give out their little clamors and perish. They chide our pettishness, they rebuke our impiety. They seem, indeed, to be forms of immortality standing here among the transitory shapes of time."

Geologists say that "millions of years ago forests of giant Sequoias were widely distributed over the Northern Hemisphere." Today they have no living representatives upon earth except the Big Trees of the Sierras and the Redwoods that fringe the Northern California Coast. "In North America the climatic factors were such as to favor their persistence only in California. For untold thousands of years this race of trees has been growing here—the finest examples we have on earth today of the vegetation of the Miocene epoch."

In 1918, thanks to an article in the *Saturday Evening Post* on "The Last Stand of the Giants," California and the world woke up to the fact that the Redwoods were falling right and left before the onslaught of the lumberman, and that not an acre, not even a tree among these "green-robed senators" of countless time was in the possession of the state. One National Memorial Monument of 437 acres, Muir Woods, the gift of William Kent, had been established in 1908. At once leading citizens of California began to bestir themselves. The Save-the-Redwoods League was organized in 1918, with Franklin K. Lane, Secretary of the Interior, as president. Dr. John C. Merriam was Secretary and Treasurer; and many other nature lovers and prominent Californians enlisted in the movement "to preserve the Oldest Trees in the World." By the close of 1918, Big Basin Redwood Park, in Santa Cruz County, comprising 9,330 acres had been secured by the state. However, there was still surprising apathy on the part of Californians; the work of destruction among the giants was going right on, for as yet there had been aroused no widespread spirit of enthusiasm for their preservation.

For a number of years previous to 1919, Mr. and Mrs. Ayer had been making annual trips through the Redwood country. They had thus come to know all the roads and groves along the Coast, and had been studying as well as enjoying these magnificent forests, unequaled anywhere else in the world. They usually went through the Santa Cruz district, took in Muir Woods, then passed over the mountain to the Montgomery Woods about twelve miles farther on, and about a mile and a half off the road to Mendocino. From here they would continue north to Fort Bragg and Garberville, located on the west branch of the Eel River in Hum-

boldt County. Going from Eureka up the main branch of the
Eel River they passed through a very beautiful grove at Phil-
lipsville; and still proceeding north sixty or seventy miles to
Scotia, they found Redwoods nearly all the way.

As Mr. Ayer went back year after year, he found that
splendid public roads were being built into this region and
that sightseers were coming in by thousands; but he noticed
to his dismay that the timber was continually being cut and
slashed and that no reservations were being made along the
public highways. In May, 1919, he was more than ever
shocked as he gazed upon this spectacle of destruction, for, as
a practical timberman, he saw clearly how far the devastation
would go within a few years. With characteristic vigor he
went to work directly to do something about it. He persuaded
an editor in Eureka to publish a little article in his paper about
the situation, and when he reached San Francisco he called
on Mr. M. H. De Young, editor of the *San Francisco Chronicle,* a public-spirited and very influential man. Mr. De Young
was interested, but, at first, not greatly moved. He said:

"Oh, Mr. Ayer, those Redwoods have got to go into
lumber."

"As a lumberman, I know that better than anyone else,"
Mr. Ayer replied. "But what you Californians ought to know
is that the lumbermen themselves will be eager to preserve
some of these trees. If you would save five per cent of the
Redwoods now standing you would have several memorial
groves and parks. They can be saved on each side of your
main roads and seen and enjoyed by people as they drive
through there."

"Write me a letter about it."

"All right, I will, and will send you some photographs of
splendid vistas in the forest, and then others that will show
scenes of devastation going on unchecked. The best friends

you've got are the lumbermen who own this land, and they are more anxious to save the trees than you."

Mrs. Ayer took some very fine photographs that illustrated both the beauty of the forests and the processes of destruction that were going on up to the very edge of the highways. Not many weeks after the conversation between Mr. Ayer and Mr. De Young, the editor received a letter from Mr. Ayer in which he set forth his views in a practical and persuasive manner.

One year (he wrote), we went on to Crescent City, most of the way through Redwoods, to Grant's Pass, Oregon. A year ago last May, the road from Scotia to Phillipsville was one of the most beautiful drives in the world—at least that we had ever seen in automobiling over 250,000 miles and visiting over forty foreign countries and all of our own states. This year we found right upon this beautiful state road that they had been up three miles or more, and there were as many as ten tie camps and two saw mills, one north of Dyerville and one south. They were cutting these trees square up to the roots and cutting the road all to pieces drawing out the material. No battle field could look any worse.

Now, Mr. De Young, I am a lumberman myself, and have been for fifty-five years, and I thoroughly understand that ninety-five per cent of all these great Redwood forests in your state must eventually be worked into lumber, and nobody can object; but what is objectionable is that the state when building these magnificent roads did not reserve ten to twenty rods on each side of them. The lumbermen could not be expected to do it. The most they could be expected to do would be to make a fair price to the state for the lumber in the trees.

Mr. Ayer then proceeded to comment upon the great advantage to the state of its excellent macadam highways through the Redwoods. He pointed out that when these roads

ONE OF THE BIG TREES—*Sequoia Gigantia*—IN HUMBOLDT
COUNTY, CALIF.

were all completed they would attract thousands of tourists, and he earnestly recommended that a wonderful grove on the west side of the south branch of the Eel River four or five miles south of Dyerville be purchased for a park. He suggested that a strip a mile wide and at least two or three miles long be saved there. "I feel perfectly confident," he goes on to say, "that it is the finest little belt of timber in the world. Also the Montgomery Grove, twelve miles from Ukiah, should be saved. There are about five hundred acres in this grove, and I understand, from good authority at Ukiah that it could be purchased for about $65,000."

The substance of this letter was published in the *Chronicle*. The article was illustrated with photographs taken by Mrs. Ayer. They spoke a language as graphic as that of Mr. Ayer. There was an instant response throughout the state. The leaders of the Save-the-Redwoods League became more active than in the past and immediately began to follow up Mr. Ayer's suggestions with a definite program. Mr. Stephen T. Mather, Assistant Secretary of the Interior and Superintendent of National Parks and Monuments; Mr. Madison Grant, Secretary of the Zoological Society of New York; Mr. J. C. Sperry, and Mr. Kent went out and made a thorough investigation of the Redwood forests and formed clubs to assist in protecting them and to raise funds. They took the letter from the *Chronicle* with them and read it in the towns and villages they visited and great enthusiasm was aroused.

Mr. Ayer himself did not relax his efforts. He was an ardent friend and admirer of Secretary Franklin K. Lane, the first President of the Save-the-Redwoods League, and after Mr. Lane's death Mr. Ayer energetically set about the task of raising funds to buy the splendid stand of Redwoods at Kettintelbe (Phillipsville) for the purpose of having it set aside as the Franklin K. Lane Memorial Grove. He threw himself into this enterprise with great zest and was able to enlist the generous support of his Chicago friends as well as that of leading Californians. Mr. W. L. Brown, a pioneer Chicagoan who makes his home in Pasadena much of the time, a fast friend and great admirer of Mr. Ayer, gives this account of the manner in which Mr. Ayer approached his associates for benefactions of this sort.

"He was up in the Redwoods when all of a sudden he woke up to the fact that these trees were being destroyed too fast. He had been to see Crocker and the editor of the *San Francisco Chronicle* and his wide circle of friends. He got down here to Pasadena and blew into my home one day. He said:

" 'Come into your den, get out your checkbook, and give me a thousand dollars,'

" 'Now, Mr. Ed. Ayer, this has gone far enough,' I said.

" 'You go and draw that check,' was his only reply.

" 'It doesn't appeal to me very much,' I protested. 'Let the Californians do it.'

" 'They won't do it and we've got to,' he retorted.

"So I drew the check, and he went after others in the same way."

Thus it was that California was enabled to preserve one of its very noblest tracts of Redwood and that the great American, Franklin K. Lane, was honored with an appropriate monument: "A monument," to use Mr. Ayer's own words, "such as no king on earth could boast." The dedication of this memorial took place August 24, 1924. This extract from a page of the printed Dedication Program describes the monument and gives fitting recognition to the men and women who transmuted a generous dream into a splendid and enduring reality.

THE LARGEST REDWOOD TREE (SEMPERVIRENS) IN THE BULL CREEK FOREST; MENDOCINO
COUNTY, CALIF.

Mrs. E. E. Ayer

The Franklin K. Lane Memorial Grove is a magnificent stand of Redwoods directly on the State Highway at Kettintelbe (Phillipsville), 228 miles north of San Francisco. It contains 195 acres. Adjoining the grove is a public camp ground established by the donors of the fund.

The funds for the purchase of the Memorial were contributed by friends and associates of Franklin K. Lane, under the leadership of Mr. Edward E. Ayer of Chicago, a Councilor of the Save-the-Redwoods League, and former Indian Commissioner under Franklin K. Lane. Among those who contributed to this fund are Mr. and Mrs. Edward E. Ayer, Hon. Stephen T. Mather, Mr. and Mrs. Edward L. Doheny, Mr. and Mrs. Julius Rosenwald, Dr. Norman Bridge, Mr. Frank Miller, Mr. William L. Brown, Mr. Richard T. Crane, Mr. and Mrs. Edward Butler, Mr. and Mrs. Martin A. Ryerson, Mrs. Harriet S. Carscallen, Mr. Samuel Mather, and Mr. William G. Mather.

TO

FRANKLIN K. LANE

1864-1921

WELL-BELOVED SON OF CALIFORNIA.

"CREATIVE STATESMAN IN A DEMOCRACY."

THIS PIECE OF THE FOREST PRIMEVAL

IS FOREVER DEDICATED IN AFFECTION

AND REVERENCE

At the time that the Franklin K. Lane Memorial Grove was secured, provision was made for enough open land adjoining the tract to establish a model camp for the travelers who might come to see and enjoy the Grove. It is the desire of the officers of the League to show by example how the dignity and beauty of these Redwood Groves may be preserved by wise management. By restricting campers to grounds immediately adjacent to the Grove, but not a part of it, danger of destruction by fire is minimized, and tramping of vegetation avoided. Telegraph and telephone wires have been removed to a considerable distance from the highway, so as to leave the view of the Memorial Grove unobstructed; the dust nuisance has been allayed by the oiling of the road; and, by the replanting of native flowers and ferns and the piping in of water to keep them alive and growing throughout the summer, the region to a great extent has been brought back to its original state of wild beauty.

The Save-the-Redwoods League deserves the praise and thanks of all men for what it has done and for what it is planning to do in the future. The original stand of Redwoods in California was 1,406,000 acres. Up to January 1, 1928, 530,000 acres of this had been cut over. There is still standing of the virgin Redwood 876,000 acres. This is being cut at the rate of 10,000 acres a year, so the remaining stand can hardly last a hundred years. Of 876,000 acres still standing, the public has preserved only a little more than 14,000 acres, or just about one and one half per cent. In all, about a million dollars worth of primeval Redwood forest has come into the possession of the public. The Avenue of the Giants extending fifteen miles along the Redwood Highway has been preserved "in state parks which future generations of Americans may enjoy, thrilled by the beauty and the majesty of these mighty forests." But the League has still other great accomplishments in view. A ten-year program has been adopted that looks toward the purchase of a number of main Redwood areas at a cost of several million dollars. It is gratifying to all nature lovers that out of the League's organized effort to save the Redwoods has grown a vast and comprehensive plan for a public park system throughout California "under which it is confidently hoped that the finest of the state's attractions, her forests, her ocean shore, her mountains and her deserts, her spots of historic and scientific interest, will be preserved from commercial exploitation and private appropriation, in representative examples of those scenic and recreational areas which make up the charm of California."

CHAPTER XIV

Leisure and Recreation

IT is not easy to say where work ceased and play began for
Mr. Ayer. He found enjoyment in everything, and his
social qualities are to be counted among his finest business
assets. Speaking of him, someone said: "He had as many
thoughts of value sitting on the deck of a boat on the Nile, as
in his own office." In the early, eager days when he was building up his business as a railway-tie contractor, he, perhaps, devoted himself too incessantly to work and travel; but as he advanced in years, to an extraordinary degree, he was able to
throw off care and find relaxation and recreation in all sorts
of ways.

He was always fond of a gun, and during some of his life
he took pleasure in fishing. In the early strenuous days when
he began to realize that he was working too hard, he would
spend several weeks each year shooting. He was an excellent
shot, and was a welcome addition to any hunting party. He
shot birds almost exclusively. Often he went duck-hunting in
the Green Bay country, and then for a long time he enjoyed
shooting expeditions in the South. He was never a big game
hunter, and he said he never shot a wild turkey in his life.
On two or three occasions, however, he went deer hunting in
Michigan.

Many years ago a congenial company of Chicago gentlemen used to go each spring and autumn to Pelee Island, situated in Canadian waters in Lake Erie, north of Sandusky,
Ohio. This club is no longer in existence; but before the automobile came into use and previous to the time when golf became a universal enticement to lure men to the enjoyment of

the open fields and the blue skies, this fishing club was popular
and afforded much-needed refreshment to over-worked Chicago business men. The company was limited to twenty-five
and was a social as well as a sporting organization. At the
club house on Pelee Island each man had his own room, which
he furnished to suit himself. For a number of years Mr.
Ayer was a member of this club, and he found much pleasure
in the outings each season—as much, perhaps, for the opportunity it gave him for leisurely games and conversation with
men whose company he liked as for the active sport and contact with wild nature. Other prominent members were
Charles L. Hutchinson, Marshall Field, George M. Pullman, Martin A. Ryerson, Anson Stager, Benjamin Campbell,
and the brothers A. A. and O. S. A. Sprague. It was permissi-
ble for the members to take guests with them, and sometimes
General Phil Sheridan and General John M. Schofield were
of the party. The members would first go to Sandusky, where
they would charter a large steamer to carry them to Pelee
Island. This boat would be retained for two weeks. They
would draw their fishing boats onto the deck of the steamer
and be transported thus to any point where they desired to fish.
Black bass was the prey they sought, and only black bass
counted in the day's reckoning.

After Mr. Ayer began to tour Europe each year he gave
up shooting almost entirely. He played golf a good deal at
Lake Geneva, but travel—especially automobiling—became
the chief outdoor recreation of his later years. This activity
afforded him endless diversion; and he traveled hundreds of
thousands of miles by automobile into all sorts of interesting
and out-of-the-way places. Said his friend Edward B. Butler:

He was an adventurer and a pioneer. There was no place
on earth that he would not attempt to go. If necessary he and
Mrs. Ayer would rough it in their automobile. They carried
canvas to put down on the Sahara Desert, and in places ran

their car, when needed, on strips of canvas. If there is any place or anything worth seeing, that could be reached on foot, on the back of a horse, a mule, or a camel, or that could be found in the course of driving a Hotchkiss, a Locomobile, or a Pierce-Arrow an aggregate distance of something like 300,000 miles, then Ed. Ayer has seen it.

At one time Mr. Ayer took up farming as a recreation. He bought pieces of woodland back of his home on the shore of Lake Geneva and secured two or three adjoining farms that were worn out so that they would no longer produce wheat. He then set about developing and fertilizing these fields. He said,

I had about seven hundred acres of plowland. I had a great deal of enjoyment fixing up these farms. I got in touch with the Department of Agriculture at the State University in Madison, and followed the advice of the scientists in fertilizing and all that sort of thing. I got the stones out of these old farms, put in tiles to drain them, fenced them with fine fences, built some splendid barns and milk-houses, and, in fact, put in the best improvements everywhere. I bought about a hundred Holstein cattle, secured the finest pigs, and each fall I fattened about one hundred steers. At last I had these farms in first class shape. For a good many years all the land in that part of Wisconsin and Illinois had been out of wheat raising, but I fertilized with the view of bringing it back to a productive condition. Finally I planted a few acres of wheat as an experiment and got a yield of forty-eight bushels to the acre. The following year I planted one hundred acres, and the year after that two hundred acres more; and I never got less than forty-three bushels to the acre; whereas, the general average per acre of the wheat crops of the United States during these years was not over fourteen bushels.

I had to get my fertilizing material at the railroad station at Walworth, on the St. Paul road about two miles and a half from my farm. The inhabitants of this village were nearly all farmers who, having made money on their farms, had moved into town and bought little homes there. Of course I had known them all ever since I was born. They would sit around the little park in Walworth and watch my team drawing phosphate, rock, lime, etc. from the station and would laugh and say, "Look at Ed. Ayer, hauling rock to put on those old farms." It seemed curious to them. The third year I raised wheat almost as high as I was, and was cutting it with a tractor. The fence posts around the field were about ten feet apart, and between every two of these posts, sometimes for two or three hundred feet, there would be one of those farmers looking at that wheat. Of course the outcome of my experiment was a service to the neighborhood and the people.

Several of my city friends would ask me if it paid. One time before the automobile came into use Byron Smith, of the Northern Trust Company, and his family were my guests at Lake Geneva. I had my friend out in a four-in-hand, showing him the different drives and views and the improvements on my farm. Finally he asked,

"Ed., does it pay?"

I said, "Byron, I make money on it."

"How much?" he asked.

"Last year I made about 20 per cent on this farm and I will do about the same this year."

"Well," he said, "how did you do it?"

My reply was, "Byron, haven't you had a good ride, aren't the woods lovely, and isn't it fine to ride through here? Haven't you had a good afternoon?"

"Perfectly splendid," he replied.

"Tonight," I said, "I will credit up the farm 5 per cent."

His answer was, "Oh!"

On other occasions when I was asked about my farms and about my success as a farmer, I would say,

"You needn't laugh, my farm raises a good many bushels of wheat and it has paid 10 per cent ever since I started it."

"For heaven's sake, Ayer, how do you do it?" my friends would ask.

My answer was, "Well, every expense of every name or nature—the purchase of machinery, or of any blooded stock, any outlay for labor, or new buildings, or additional land, and everything whatsoever, I charge to Mrs. Ayer's living expenses. Don't you see—everything I get off of the farm is net."

Mr. Ayer was a good clubman. He had membership in the Chicago, Caxton, and Commercial Clubs of Chicago, and in the Lake Geneva Country Club. After he had won a secure place in business, he spent many afternoon hours of leisure at the Chicago Club playing cards and conversing with other prominent men of affairs in Chicago. It was here that he most frequently met his railroad friends and other business associates.

At the Chicago Club for a generation or more a group of men sat down together at what is known as the Railroad Table. Eminence in the railroad profession, or in activities directly connected with railroading, was the qualification for admission to this interesting circle. Nearly all the leading Chicago railway officials of the past forty years have at one time or another lunched at this famous table. Here Edward P. Ripley, James T. Harahan, Paul Morton, George B. Harris, W. B. Storey, E. G. Wells, Hale Holden, and many others of like prominence used to sit and talk together. Mr. Edward E. Ayer and his partner, Mr. John B. Lord, were frequently of this company. There was much and good conversation— sometimes solid and serious, very often witty, sparkling, and interspersed with anecdote.

These men were all alike absorbed in the tremendous problems constantly arising in the railroad business, and of course, had much in common to talk about and to solve. But at the same time they were competitors, so that each one was on the alert for the best interests of his own road or business, and naturally there was now and then much good-natured banter and raillery among them. The discussions had to do for the most part with matters of common importance to the railroad profession. Far-sighted policies and perplexing problems were broached here, and from the friction of great minds and the free interchange of ideas much of practical value was evolved. No point affecting the management and development of the railroads of America was too insignificant to discuss, nor was any so great that it was excluded. Standardization of freight cars, the electrifying of railroads, the smooth, easy starting and stopping of passenger trains, the making of "pools" and freight-rates, and cut-throat competition for the passenger trade—these questions and many others of both greater and less importance came up for comment and consideration.

Mr. Ayer found much enjoyment at this table through a long series of years. He was a general favorite; he knew every one; he was a veteran in the railway business; he was a keen observer and was full of original ideas. From his extended foreign travel he could offer valuable comparisons and contrasts between railroad methods at home and abroad: and he always contributed a spirit of merriment and vivacity to the company. His associates were interested in his travels and in his ardor as a collector, and more than once they aided him in securing some desired relic or other acquisition of value. In the Field Museum there is an Egyptian mummy, known as "the railroad mummy." It was purchased by Mr. Ayer with money raised by his associates at this table and handed to him as he was about to set out on one of his extended tours to Egypt.

In 1889, by his election to membership in the Commercial Club, Mr. Ayer was brought into active and intimate association with Chicago's outstanding civic leaders. No honor that ever came to him was more gratifying that this. A unique and powerful organization, the Commercial Club for a full half century has had a shaping influence upon the life of Chicago, yet, because it has operated with quiet dignity and has never heralded its deeds, few citizens seem conscious either of its existence or its achievements. It was organized December 27, 1877, and on February 11, 1907, it effected a union with the Merchants Club of Chicago, an organization with like aim, made up of much younger men. Both clubs were organized "for the purpose of advancing, by social intercourse and a free interchange of views and of co-operative effort, the public welfare and the commercial interests of the City of Chicago." Membership in this club has come to be looked upon as "a sufficient charter of nobility"; and since its personnel is recruited solely from citizens who have won distinction by service to the city, perhaps no other civic honor is so much prized by men of affairs.

The active membership of the Commercial Club is limited to one hundred men. Sometimes a period of two years will pass without an èlection. No active member is chosen who is above the age of fifty-five. An active member must accept any reasonable assignment of work made by the executive committee, though he may at the age of sixty-five years, upon written request to the executive committee, become an associate member. Each nominee must secure the unanimous approval of the executive committee before his name is submitted for election, and admission is by practically unanimous vote. No other social engagement may take precedence of a regular meeting of the Club, and members failing to attend regular meetings without a reason therefor that is satisfactory to the executive committee must pay a fine. Repeated absence if not satisfactorily explained results in the forfeiture of membership.

Among the men who served as president of the Commercial Club previous to 1907, were Levi Z. Leiter, John W. Doane, Franklin Mac Veagh, Lyman J. Gage, Adolphus C. Bartlett, Charles L. Hutchinson, Marvin Hughitt, Alexander C. McClurg, William T. Baker, Cyrus H. McCormick, Martin A. Ryerson, and Edward B. Butler. Other eminent names that appear in the list of membership during the first thirty years are George M. Pullman, Marshall Field, James L. Houghteling, Philip D. Armour, Harlow N. Higinbotham, Melville E. Stone, Edward P. Ripley, Daniel H. Burnham, James H. Eckels, Charles H. Wacker, Victor F. Lawson,

John J. Mitchell, and Robert T. Lincoln. These and many more, whose fame shone with equal luster and who deserve a permanent place in Chicago's Hall of Fame, are to be found on the roster of this truly remarkable organization. These and men of equal merit who came later were Mr. Ayer's intimate associates and fellow workers through a period of almost forty years. Surely, to be admitted to such a fellowship and to have a part in such a record of civic service as this club achieved is equivalent to the bestowal of any civic wreath of antiquity.

A list of representative topics discussed by the Club at various times will serve to indicate its scope, its interests, and the spirit of fellowship that it engendered. Almost every great interest that affects the life of the people has been dealt with at one time or another. By studying the following list of topics in connection with the date at which a given subject was discussed, one familiar with the growth of Chicago can almost form a chart of its progress: "Our Sewerage," "Does Punishment Follow Crime in This Community?" "Unemployed Laborers," "Has Chicago Reached a Period in Its Growth when Special Attention Should Be Paid to the Fostering of Art, Literature, and Science?" "The Saloon in Politics," "Railroads," "Manual Training: How to Get It," "A World's Fair Memorial," "Civic Reform," "The Presentation of the Chicago Plan."

A spirit of good fellowship pervaded all the meetings and many occasions were stately affairs of national or even international importance. General Grant was tendered a dinner by the Club on his return from his tour around the world; a complimentary and farewell dinner was given to Lieutenant General Phil Sheridan; various Presidents of the United States were honored with sumptuous banquets; a formal dinner was given for the Right Honorable Lord Chief Justice of England; and Marshall Joffre, of France was entertained in a similar manner. On one occasion Honorable Grover Cleveland and Reverend Frank W. Gunsaulus discussed "American Good Citizenship" before the Club; Governor Woodrow Wilson, when President-elect of the United States, spoke on "The Business Future of the Country"; and in April, 1907, the Right Honorable James Bryce, British Ambassador, addressed the Club on "The City and the State."

The urbanity and social charm that characterized the meetings of the Commercial Club is wafted to us across the years in the historical notes and personal reminiscences of various members. On April 10, 1909, the Club met as the guests of Mr. John J. Glessner, at his home, 1800 Prairie Avenue. Mr. Glessner was then a Nestor in the organization. He was moreover, endowed with a certain Boswellian gift which enabled him to etch lifelike literary portraits of leading men among the founders, and to interpret the genius and charm of the organization. This he did in a little book entitled *Should Auld Acquaintance Be Forgot* that he printed privately in 1924, and sent to his fellow club members as a Christmas greeting. He quotes this couplet from Lowell,

"So you'll excuse me if I'm sometimes fain
To tie the Past's warm night-cap o'er my brain,"

and says in apologetic strain, "I find that often I have used the expressions of smiling eyes, genial, open countenance, friendly manners, and the like. These repetitions transgress good literary form, I know, but I wouldn't take them back; they are true where written, and might justly have been written oftener. These attributes indicate humor, and humor is a saving grace to keep men from sinning against conventions."

Mr. Glessner praises the two earliest secretaries, George Clinton Clarke and John Janes, and points out how "they insisted upon dignified formalities in dress and conversation and behavior, and so cultivated gentle manners. In those days they spent much time before the monthly dinners, aided by a special committee for each occasion, in so seating the members at table as to please each most." Mr. Glessner's book is a distinct contribution to Chicago's history, witty, full of cheerful and familiar chat, crowded with anecdotes about Chicago's great men of the last quarter of the nineteenth century; and, throughout, it gives a revealing insight into the social and commercial activities of the Club and Chicago as he knew them in his prime.

The greatest single achievement of the Commercial Club was the preparation and presentation of the Plan of Chicago to the city. The Plan of Chicago was the dream of Daniel H. Burnham, the great architect who conceived and brought to perfection the White City that Chicago erected on the Lake Front for the accommodation of the Columbian Exposition. The Fair City by the Lake was a dream that vanished; but out of it there grew in the brain of the architect the vision of an enduring city of Chicago, equally beautiful, that should be a glory to the whole Lake Front and should adapt itself to every practical and aesthetic need of modern urban civilization.

The young men of the Merchants Club were fired with enthusiasm at Burnham's idea of making Chicago the most splendid city in the world: a place, so far as possible, made perfect for "men and women to work in and for children to grow up in." They saw that here was a dream that might come true. Ardently and generously they cooperated with Mr. Burnham. Much had been done by 1907, and when the Merchants Club was absorbed in the Commercial Club the chief object of the combined organization became the realization of the Burnham Plan. Members of the Club subscribed large sums of money to carry on the work. The committee met every week and some members almost daily. The advice and services of some of the leading artists and engineers of

the world were secured. In order that there might be room
to work conveniently and to display the plans and drawings
as they developed, rooms were built on the roof of the Railway Exchange Building especially adapted for the work. On
July 4, 1909, the Commercial Club presented the completed
Plan, in book form, to the city, with the request that a committee be appointed to study the Plan and carry it out. Four
months later such a committee was appointed, and during the
following ten years, at a cost of upward of a hundred million dollars, the Plan was to a great extent realized.

Mr. Ayer had a genius for friendship. His wide experience,
his sense of humor, his conversational gifts, and his affability
and human kindness made him a desired guest wherever he
might be. His frequent and prolonged visits to Europe afforded him many opportunities of meeting distinguished men
abroad in social intercourse. In London he dined with Robert
T. Lincoln when he was Ambassador to England, and while
on a visit to Rome he was the dinner guest of Thomas Nelson
Page, our Ambassador to Italy. In America, too, the Ayers
often met world famous people on an intimate footing at dinner parties and receptions.

Among Mr. Ayer's very warm friends was his Chicago
neighbor, Lyman J. Gage. When Mr. Gage left Chicago to
serve in the cabinet of President McKinley he said to Mr.
Ayer, "You must be sure to make us a visit of not less than
a week while we are in Washington." In due time this request
was followed by a formal invitation, and the Ayers found
themselves guests for some days in the home of a cabinet
member at the height of the social season in Washington. It
was all very pleasant and exciting to these people of the mid-
west. The dignity, gayety, and splendor of a presidential reception recalled to their minds tales they had read of the fêtes
of royalty in lands over the sea. The crowning event of their
stay in Washington, however, was the enjoyment of a dinner

given by Secretary John Hay and his wife to President and Mrs. McKinley.

Said Mrs. Gage to her guests one afternoon as they came in from a sight-seeing walk, "You are the luckiest people in the world. An invitation has come from Mrs. John Hay to attend a dinner she is giving to President and Mrs. McKinley tonight. You are to take the places of two people who have dropped out at the last moment. And, besides dining at a Cabinet dinner given to the President, you are to meet the biggest lion of the day—Admiral George Dewey is to be present."

Mrs. Ayer was surprised and perhaps, too, a little dismayed when, upon arriving at the Hay mansion, she was informed by Mrs. Gage that Admiral Dewey was to take her out to dinner. Mr. Ayer accompanied Mrs. Dewey. The company walked out to dinner according to rank, so as a matter of course the Ayers had distinguished places at the table. Mr. Ayer sat opposite the President, whose frail wife was seated at his right, the object of constant and devoted attention from her chivalrous husband. The talk was largely of the Philippines and of problems in connection with the Indians—subjects that Mr. Ayer was able to talk about in an interesting and informing manner even in the presence of the President of the United States and his Cabinet.

CHAPTER XV

Home Life

IT was at his Lake Geneva home, The Oaks, that Edward Ayer spent many of the happiest hours of his life. Here he found perfect relaxation from the strenuous activities described in the foregoing chapters. All too late the author came into Mr. Ayer's circle of acquaintance to set down from observation and knowledge the scenes and activities of his home life that intimate friends delight to record. It is the writer's good fortune, though, to receive from those who best knew Mr. Ayer in the heyday of his happiness and hospitality descriptions of his home, his habits, and fireside companions.

In boyhood, with his playmates, Edward Ayer had haunted the shores of this lovely Lake Geneva (whose Indian name was Kishwaukatoc), swimming and fishing in its waters and, in the fields and forests around, learning that deep love of Nature that remained with him throughout life. No insignificant body of water, it lies framed in green hills, "a turquoise in an emerald setting." It is placid under a serene sky, but it can rage and boil into great foam-capped waves when the winds are boisterous. On the shores of this lake, in the far past, the Indians of the Bigfoot tribe (the Pottawatamies) built their wigwams, and across its waters they paddled their canoes. It was natural, when manhood came, and success in business, that Mr. Ayer should build his summer home on the spot dear to his boyhood memory. And what place could have been more fitting for this man who labored always for the good of his "American brothers," loved their myths and legends, and collected every book and manuscript bearing upon their history that could be found, in order that he might place them in a great library accessible through all time to scholars and lovers of the Red man!

So Mr. Ayer, early in his business career, bought a tract of some twelve acres, sloping to the border of the lake, and built a simple cottage. He had begun housekeeping in Harvard, the town his father founded, and here he made his permanent home up to the time he moved to Chicago. At the little Harvard home, some fourteen months after their marriage, there was born to Mr. and Mrs. Ayer the little daughter Elizabeth, who brought much joy into their lives. All the girlhood summers of this only child were passed at the Lake Geneva home, and it was here that she grew into lovely womanhood, developing many of the traits of her wonderful father: generosity of soul, the spirit of helpfulness, the desire to bring happiness to others, and an ardor for beauty wherever found, whether in Nature or in Art.

To this summer cottage by the lake Mr. Ayer brought many of his collected treasures—especially those easiest to live with, and such as could be spared from the collections for his beloved Museum. To these—that he might have them close at hand and enjoy them with his many guests—he gave places in the big living-room of the cottage. Edward Ayer had a sense for the spacious and he built this room in his cottage to gratify this taste, so there was an abundance of places for the personal treasures, as they accumulated year by year. He reveled in the beauty of some of these articles, and rejoiced equally in the fascinating ugliness of others. Mr. Ayer's week-end guests found rare entertainment in the stories of adventure connected with the acquisition of his storehouse of wonders, for every article called up some interesting tale or explanation.

Upon entering this main room from the front door, newcomers were astonished and much impressed with its size—its length, and lofty ceiling rising to a height of fourteen feet—and its beauty—the walls paneled with Georgia pine, the color which, with the passing of the years, had deepened into a rich yellow. The modest exterior of the cottage had given no sign of all this. At the far end of this hall, or living-room, was a large fireplace with high, wrought, antique fire-dogs holding big logs cut from the woods of the estate. When the chill winds of autumn were on, these logs blazed a welcome to those coming in. The mantelpiece was draped with fine old Mexican rebozos in rich coloring of dull reds and blues bought by the collector on one of his many trips into the southern Republic. Under the mantelpiece were crossed two double-handed old German swords. On the hearth, at the left of the fireplace, for years unbroken though fragile, stood an enormous Mexican *olla*. This great terra cotta jar often excited the curiosity of visitors.

When asked what it was, and where it came from, the host would reply, "It is what they call an *olla*. It is porous, and they use it to keep water cool. I found it in the Indian market of the City of Mexico, where one sees the descendants of the Aztecs in fascinating colors in their dress and undress. The market was filthy and the odors unbearable; but the color, the crowds, and the scenes—these are beyond description! I paid two dollars for this jar in the market, but it cost me twelve dollars to get it home."

On the east side of the long room were placed two very finely carved cabinets of black oak—one of Italian workman-ship, the other, and finer one, from Holland. Their beauty was accentuated against the yellow walls of the room. A tall old English clock (also black oak) stood nearby. One might suppose from the fierce aspect of the war god of barbaric times—sculptured in high relief on the door—who glared at the visitor, that this clock stood guard over the treasures in the hall. Mr. Ayer would open the long door, and pointing to the disk of the pendulum, on which was painted a round bucolic face, merrily winking an eye at the gazer, would say laughingly,

"He has been out all night, and evidently needs this war god to guard him."

This clock had been found in an old shop in Chester, England. It dated back to 1714. Judging from its richness of carving, it must have stood in some stately English hall and chimed the hours away with sonorous musical tones like those given forth by the clock in the Parliament House in London.

Beyond the archway that opened into a writing room, with glimpses of Oriental arms of richly inlaid work adorning the walls, was a heavily carved ancient English black oak hall settle, with sculptured coat-of-arms almost covering the back. The seat could be opened, and stored inside were some rare, and fine Mexican rebozos; some rugs from far Kairouan, the sacred city of the Mohammedans in Tunisia; and some blankets made by our own American Indians, almost as fine as the best. It was a joy to the collector to pull these out, and to spread them around on the floor in heaps, in order to show his guests their fineness of weave, curious designs and softness of touch to the fingers. It was pleasant to see his face light up as he told of the way he bargained to secure some dull crimson beauty. It may be noted here, however, that it was not the host—the fervent collector—who engaged in the task of smoothing, folding, and returning these woven treasures to their receptacle. That employment always fell to the hands of another member of the family, and was faithfully and reverently performed.

The glory of the room was a very large, dark Spanish oak chest that stood under the great eastern window through which the morning sun shed its splendor. This chest Mr. Ayer found in Madrid, and many anxious hours he bargained for it before he was able to secure it. The carvings on it are in high relief, and are of great historic interest—the designs having been copied from the reliefs on the retablo behind the altar in the royal chapel at Grenada, where the bodies of Ferdinand and Isabella were placed. Mr. Ayer often remarked, after the New Mission Playhouse in San Gabriel, California was erected:

"This chest should be given to the Mission Playhouse. It is of great value, but that is the proper home for it."

His wish was respected. After his death the chest was sent to Mr. John S. McGroarty—his devoted friend, and the pervading spirit of the Mission Playhouse. It has been placed in the foyer of the Playhouse, on a low dais, with a suitable inscription to the memory of Edward Everett Ayer, so that now, and forever, visitors who go to see the Mission Play may view this very interesting chest.

Among the curios, on the west side of the room, was a Spanish cabinet which Mr. Ayer considered one of his most valuable treasures. It was a Vargueño (so called from the name of a village in Spain). The much gilt, the bands of vermilion, the twisted ivory columns, the inlaid pieces of shell and ivory, showed Moorish workmanship; but from the small, gilded statues of the Madonna placed in the recesses of the many little drawers, it was apparent that this was done under Spanish influence.

Mr. Ayer piqued the curiosity of his guests by telling them that the cabinet contained secret drawers; and when they gave up the task of finding them as hopeless, he took delight in showing how plain the secret was. The heavy, crude, carved wood of the cover, the strong iron clasps, and the big lock and key, gave evidence that this cabinet had been used to hold treasures of great value.

Down the long hall wherever the visitor looked, through open door, or diamond-paned window, he could catch glimpses of blue lake, green foliage, or softly colored hills. Everywhere, too, his glance would take in antique treasures from every country and clime: in the garden, on the piazza, and the lawn—a very storehouse, or museum of wonders, this; yet, most wonderful of all, the guest could not fail to feel above everything else the warmth and enjoyment of a home-like atmosphere. It was obvious that all this variety and wealth of collected treasure had been brought together with loving care—not to be displayed in glass cases as in a museum, but to be lived with, and to be shared with friends. One friend, a painter not unknown to fame, who made the passion for antiques a cult, and came sometimes to revel among these assembled "spoils" of remote lands and times, bewailed the fact that there were some "American rocking chairs" in this room. In his own severely artistic city home he would have no chairs but carved ones, with high backs, and seats of Spanish or Italian leather—all from castles in Spain, or cathedrals in Italy—beautiful to look at, but agonizing to sit upon. At the Lake Geneva home a member of the family with a plebian instinct for comfort, had quietly introduced from time to time these "few rocking chairs" of dark wood and simple design, padded with soft silken cushions of a color in tone with the yellow walls, curtains, and portières. In the evening, when the day "in the open" was over, pleasantly weary, one could sit at ease and feast one's eyes with loving glances at the treasures spread about; could drop one's book and fall to dreaming about the centuries long past, and the far-away countries here represented; could here worship forms of genuine beauty, instead of the many grotesque and ugly things of today that people often collect for their homes.

In the long lifetime of Mr. and Mrs. Ayer this hospitable hall had been the scene of many festivities. Most notable among these feast days and anniversaries was the celebration of their Golden Wedding on September 7, 1915. Mr. Charles Hutchinson, a dearly loved friend and a man of rare taste, took charge of the adorning of the great living-room and

MRS. EDWARD E. AYER

porches for this important event. For three days, with loving
attention to every detail, he devoted himself to the creation
of an ideal golden wedding setting. From the high mantel at
the far end of the room he hung a bishop's cope of great richness and beauty. On the floor at each side of this he placed
high, carved and gilded Italian candlesticks surmounted with
great wax candles, and brought such other treasures near as
would add to the effect. Against this background, he then
placed side by side two carved Italian chairs for the "Golden
Couple" seated there to receive the many friends who had
gathered for the occasion. Above the mantel a copy of Luca
della Robbia's Madonna and child seemed to smile a blessing
down upon them. The great jars here and there about the big
room held many flowers, golden yellow in color. Through the
open doors could be seen the wide piazza rails adorned with
the autumn golden rod. On the porch sat the famous harpist,
Enrico Tramonti, with his own golden harp, and three of his
pupils, also with harps, who added their music to the charm of
the Golden Wedding. It is worthy of mention here that in
Edward Ayer's family his father and mother; his sisters,
Mrs. Annie Burbank, Mrs. Julia Minier, and Mrs. Eva Law;
all lived to pass their fiftieth wedding anniversary.

The dining room of this famous country home was as
unique as the living-room, but of an entirely different type.
Blue and white was the prevailing color impression the guest
received upon entering this room. The effect was made by the
blue and white curtains in Japanese designs, and the big
Chinese and old Spanish rugs, also in blue and white. The high
blue and white chimney-piece, toward which a visitor was
immediately drawn, always elicited some exclamations of
wonder. It was not strange that it attracted attention. Under
this high, black mantel, were set old white and blue Delft tiles
five feet above the hearth below, which was also paved with
them.

"These tiles," Mr. Ayer would explain, "were originally in a Dutch house two hundred years old which was taken from Amsterdam, and brought over to Chicago to be set up at the World's Fair. The wainscoting consisted of these valuable Delft tiles. When the Dutch house was dismantled at the close of the exposition, I was lucky enough to secure enough of them for this chimney-piece and hearth."

On each tile was a pictorial subject in blue and white, taken from the Bible, showing in letters and figures the chapter and verse that supplied the inscription for each scene. The host derived much pleasure from testing the Scriptural knowledge of his guests—who usually were not ready in replying—by asking them from what book and verse the pictured stories came. On the high mantelpiece was an array of vases and jars of fine old blue Delft, and below on long hooks depended some Delft and German beer mugs and tankards in greys and blues giving a decorative touch. On the hearth at each side of the fireplace stood silver candlesticks from a church in Belgium, with huge white candles in them. At night, on occasions of special festivity, these were lighted. On the walls above the windows, which were in part of diamond panes, were narrow shelves on which were displayed jugs and stone vases from Austria, and tankards and guild cups from Germany. Here, too, were pewter cups and various curious pots and pitchers, also of pewter, from Nuremburg and Rothenburg.

The eye of the visitor was always attracted to certain dusky old portraits hung high on the walls of this room.

"Are they portraits of your family?" some guest would ask.

To this Mr. Ayer would respond with his hearty laugh. "Oh, they are a mixed lot that we bought at various antique shops in France and Italy—whose proprietors must have thought us crazy. Mrs. Ayer wanted this American dining room to have a flavor of an Old English one. She declares

SOUTH END OF THE HALL (OR "LIVING ROOM") AS ARRANGED FOR THE GOLDEN WEDDING
SEPTEMBER SEVENTH, 1915

that all the glum, dark-browed ones are my ancestors and that
the gay, cheerful ones are hers."

It would be a pleasant exercise to let one's mind run back
over the long years and recall the many charming and distinguished guests who sat at Edward Ayer's hospitable table
in this Lake Geneva home. There would emerge the grave,
kindly face and the historic figure of General Leonard
Wood, sitting with quiet yet commanding distinction at the
right hand of his hostess. In the summer time Lyman J. Gage
used often to come. He and Mr. Ayer differed decidedly in
their opinions concerning some of the Government policies,
and this sometimes resulted in high-wrought arguments that
led some more placid guests to fear that the friendship of
these two might "go upon the rocks" and be shattered. But
the debate over, they were the most cordial of friends, each
one satisfied that he had got the better of the argument, and
that for the present, at least, the Government was safe. Often
in the early days of his fame Professor James Breasted came
as a house guest. One member of the family when she was told
that the great Egyptologist was expected for the week-end
exclaimed,

"Alas, how tiresome he will be! He won't talk of anything
but mummies and scarabs."

But the young and interesting professor, with a fund of
stories delightfully told, proved the life of the week-end
party; and not a mummy did he mention, or even a scarab.

On one occasion the cherished friend, Charles Hutchinson,
being invited to The Oaks for dinner, brought with him as his
guest James Bryce, then British Ambassador to the United
States. Mr. Bryce and Edward Ayer became friends at once.
At the dinner table there was a brilliant "passage at arms"
between these two on the subject of free trade in England.
Said the host,

"I wish, Mr. Bryce, you would give me your country for

half an hour," and, thereupon he told what he would do with it: "I would abolish the tariff on tea, but would protect many other articles."

Mr. Bryce listened smilingly to the end of Mr. Ayer's eloquent settlement of the tariff in England, and then throwing up his hands exclaimed,

"Dear! Dear! You have ruined my poor country! You have ruined my poor country! Give it back to me!"

Among Mr. Ayer's friends were many who studied the worlds in space as well as those who delved in "the sands of time." Across the lake to the north, in plain view from the veranda of the Ayer home, is the Yerkes Observatory, and the Director of this Institution during the early years, Dr. George Ellery Hale, frequently was a welcome guest at The Oaks. Dr. Edwin Frost, also a Director at a later period, came with his wealth of astronomical lore and his saint-like spirit of patience and submission under affliction, and proved a friend, a guide, and a source of inspiration to his neighbors. Professor Edward Barnard, who had dared to photograph the sun and the nebulae in space, a gentle astronomer, never quite at home upon the earth, came to dine and to talk of other worlds in space to the delight of his host and hostess.

A delightful guest, from the University of Chicago, was the genial geologist, Dr. Rollin D. Salisbury. His study of rocks and geological epochs had not made him hard and unresponsive as they are. His conversation fairly sparkled when he foregathered with other brilliant men about the Ayer board. Another beloved friend and visitor was Edward Ripley, the great railroad president. He discussed with his host the perplexing railroad problems that sometimes arose, and he was glad to accept the advice that Mr. Ayer was able to offer for the untangling of these problems. There came, also, to sit at the Ayer table for a Sunday dinner, or a week-end, President Judson, of the University of Chicago, a delightful

CHARLES L. HUTCHINSON
1854–1924
PHILANTHROPIST, PRESIDENT OF THE ART INSTITUTE
OF CHICAGO 41 YEARS

man, of genial presence, wide knowledge, and a delicious
sense of humor, revealed in the good stories that he told to the
enjoyment of himself as well as the company who listened to
him. Another man who was received at the Lake Geneva
home with reverence and pride was Dr. William H. Holmes.
He combined in himself the artist, the geologist, and the anthropologist. He seemed a superman. There was nothing in
art or science that he could not do or comprehend. He is
Director of the New National Museum in Washington at
present. More than eighty years of age, and no longer able to
"go afield" as in the days gone by, he is still a "delver into the
past," and a creator of beauty in the present, with his lovely
water colors, painted from studies made in "the open" in the
years gone by.

When one thinks of Edward Ayer's intimates, two nearest
his heart are sure to come to mind: Charles Hutchinson, for
forty years President of the Chicago Art Institute, and Martin Ryerson ("Martin the Just," as Edward Ayer called
him) for thirty years President of the Board of Trustees of
the University of Chicago. Charles Hutchinson was one
whose heart overflowed with love and sympathy for all suffering humanity. He had, too, a wealth of affection for all beautiful things. The very flowers he arranged so lovingly in jars
and vases seemed to know he understood them and always
responded to his touch. His going away left a void in Edward
Ayer's life, as long as he remained, a void never quite filled by
any other friend. Martin Ryerson is a man of such sound
judgment and excellent sense that his decisions, no matter on
what subject invoked, always settle a disputed point to the
satisfaction of all parties. He is an alert and persevering student and critic of pictures—one of the finest in the United
States, and though his forte is the primitives, his interest and
taste extend to both ancient and modern art. His city home is
a museum of pictures, in which both the past and present

are well represented. These two friends and their charming wives were always invited to special feasts and were at liberty to bring any of their visiting guests.

Daniel Burnham must not be forgotten! None of his many devoted friends loved him more than did Edward Ayer, who never tired of praising his work as an architect, and his untiring labors for the World's Fair in Chicago. He was always received with enthusiasm when he came to the home by the lake, and the "fatted calf" was killed for him; or, more accurately, upon the arrival of Mr. Burnham a plump pig was often sacrificed on the altar of friendship. The pig, roasted to a crisp brown, was much relished by this distinguished guest; and as crisp and delicious as the pig itself were the choice stories—humorous to a degree—that Mr. Burnham contributed on such occasions.

From the piazza, looking to the north, the view was very beautiful. The lawn sloped gently some three hundred feet to the edge of the blue lake across which flew sail boats on breezy days, their white sails picturesque against the green hills opposite. Over there, straight across, set in forests of oak and maple, was to be seen the shining dome of the Observatory (which, on different hours of the day, took every change of color and tint that a mountain does). One could not look at it without a thrill at the thought of the highly trained minds there, studying other worlds far beyond. The piazza was a place of infinite coolness and comfort. Hammocks and easy chairs piled with soft cushions invited one to rest. Here were gay rugs, long and wide, from various countries; some had been used to decorate the tents of Arab sheiks, others were rebozos from Mexico, and still others of Navajo manufacture—barbaricly fascinating in color but coarse in texture.

Some distance down the veranda was a huge Japanese gong suspended from a teakwood frame, carved in blue lines and

MARTIN A. RYERSON
FOR THIRTY YEARS PRESIDENT OF THE BOARD OF TRUSTEES
OF THE UNIVERSITY OF CHICAGO

colored to represent water. Said Mr. Ayer, "I secured this not without difficulty from the guardsman of an old Japanese temple at Kamakura. At night when near a temple one would be thrilled to hear the deep booming of one of these gongs, like a warning of some terrible tragedy to come. This one had always been carried at the head of the Army, and no doubt it roused the little Jap soldiers to fight with fierce energy."

It was one of Mr. Ayer's pleasures, when dinner was ready, to take up the drum stick with round, stuffed leather head and strike this large bronze gong with such force that it gave out deep sonorous tones to the delight of the listeners. Still days its notes could be heard at the Observatory across the lake. On the lawn, close to the veranda, is an antique that no one can pass without comment. It is a perfectly moulded terra cotta jar about four feet high and of like diameter. It came from a villa of Boscoreale, where it had been buried beneath the ashes of the same eruption that destroyed Pompeii. Mr. and Mrs. Ayer were present and saw the workmen slowly uncover this enormous wine or oil jar that had not seen the sun's rays since that far-off day, when, evidently, having been cleaned and turned over to drain in the back court of the aristocratic villa, it was slowly covered with ashes and lava.

There was a certain stout, ample chair, well-cushioned, at the outermost angle of the front piazza, that was Mr. Ayer's chosen seat, as evening after evening he would sit to see the summer sun go down across the lake. This sunset, reflected in the lake, he declared, had no equal in the world. He had a favorite chair in the living-room, also, in which he liked to ensconce himself on a chill evening. It was in the library corner near the fireplace. Above and behind him, on a wide shelf, smiled the statue of the Etruscan woman (called by the workmen on the place "The smilin' lady") which he had brought from Italy. Graceful allusion is made to the genial host sitting there, and to the bust, in a familiar letter from a lady who was always a welcome guest at The Oaks. She writes: "I want to thank you for the smile—guess—the smile on the face of that Etruscan woman—the bust on the shelf in your reading corner by the fire—out at Lake Geneva—just think of the wonder and charm of it—the head wrought in stone, but the face full of beauty and sensitive and vital, with the mystery and the reserve of it still there. The Etruscans were an ancient people, but that face speaks the language of today." This "smilin' lady" has been presented to the Field Museum.

The principal feast of the year at the lakeside home was that of the Fourth of July; as the Birthday Dinner, November 16, was the chief event in the Chicago home. Having been a soldier as well as a son of parents pre-eminent for patriotism, Mr. Ayer made much of the Fourth. It was celebrated with elaborate rites, not only as a national holiday but, also, as a festal occasion for family and friends. On the morning of the Fourth he would be around a little earlier than usual to make sure that the flags were all flying from flagpole and piazza. The effect of the gay national draperies was most thrilling— particularly as seen from the lake by excursionists.

The Fourth of July dinner was an event, never to be forgotten by one who had had the good fortune to participate in it. That it was a gustatory triumph goes without saying, for a roast pig was always provided, the son in this respect observing the custom of his fathers; but the aesthetic sense was also regaled; since to the art of the housewife in the very attractive decking out of the table was added the highly effective arrangement of flowers at the hand of the gardener for many years at the Lake Geneva estate, an Englishman whose sense of color combinations in flowers was wondered at and admired by every guest. Then, to crown and heighten all, there was the service of blue glass. Mr. Ayer, among his

EDWARD E. AYER'S FAVORITE CORNER AND CHAIR IN THE LIVING
ROOM OF THE LAKE GENEVA HOME

many predilections had a passion for glass. He had made a notable collection of the rare old ruby glass or Rubinen of Austria. The art of producing the vivid transparent red of this glass seems to have been lost. Mr. Ayer had picked up many pieces, one by one, and had installed them in a cabinet in the city house, with the thought of giving them to a museum eventually. He had a rare collection of Murano and Venetian glass, also, but these were too fragile to permit of his enjoying them on his table for daily use. However, as he found that glass-making was becoming an art in America, he turned his attention to modern glass to decorate his table. It was a delight to see Mr. Ayer, at his happiest, carving at the dinner on feast days, for carving was not a lost art in his family. Speaking of these festal occasions, a friend who came often to The Oaks said, "In his home Mr. Ayer was at his best. He was the kindliest of men and the most responsive of hosts. It was not merely a gracious manner—it was of the very essence of his hospitality. Since you were at his fireside, you were of the family assembled about it. This no doubt was the attitude of the generation of Wisconsin pioneers among whom he was born and bred."

There was never any lack of amusement and recreation at the Lake Geneva home. In the early days the young people who came as the daughter's guests added to the life and gayety of the older people. Mr. Ayer then owned a steam yacht, the second fastest on the lake. It was named *Tula* after a daughter of Montezuma. She is described in Lew Wallace's *The Fair God* which the family had read during their travels in Mexico. The *Tula* could carry sixty people, and the services of an engineer and a pilot were required to run it, though the master himself usually preferred to be at the wheel. To the young people the moonlight rides on a warm summer evening seemed most romantic and entrancing, but the men enjoyed better the regattas on breezy days, when they would lay bets

on their favorite sailboats, as in the *Tula* they excitedly followed the races through the nine mile course from Lake
Geneva village down the lake.

In the days before the automobiles came Edward Ayer had
horses, and good ones, of course. He owned a four-in-hand
and tandem team which he drove with great skill. In his cavalry days he had been both a crack rider and a crack shot.
Often when out with his guests he would exhibit his horse-
manship by throwing his hat on the ground and then riding
by and snatching it up at full gallop. Sometimes, though, he
would attempt this feat before one he wished most to please,
and, to her amusement and other lookers on, would get a spill,
while his horse would continue on its wild career.

After the Civil War he came into possession of a horse
called Buckskin because of its color. This animal had belonged
to a friend named Delaney who was also a cavalryman during
the Civil War. Delaney and his horse were captured in one
of Moseby's raids, but both were exchanged after a short
time. At the end of the war Delaney sent Buckskin to his
friend Ayer, feeling sure that the fiery high-spirited horse
would be cared for to the end of his honorable career. And this
was true. The horse lived in comfort all the rest of his long
life. Once in a while some member of the family would drive
him down to the parade ground where the Northwestern Military and Naval Academy now has its home. Even in his old
age the sound of the bugle would so stir in Buckskin the war-
like spirit of the past that he would throw up his head and
tail and go galloping off around the grounds, to the great
alarm of any guest who might be riding or driving him in the
natural belief that his great age made him a perfectly safe
animal. So he kept up his youthful vigor to the end of his
days; and at the last he was buried with military honors on the
grounds at Lake Geneva.

As time went on Mr. Ayer added to his estate about three

hundred acres of woodland. He laid out roads and paths through this forest, driving his buggy through pleasant ways, thick with bushes and lush in brake and ferns, while his men followed with axes and stakes to mark his course. He took delight on warm summer days in driving his guests through these shady forest roads. In the autumn the oaks and maples were a glory to see, and even in Edward Ayer's old age, after the automobile had come into use, he found nothing that afforded him greater pleasure than a drive through these beautiful woods. He would loiter to observe a particular effect of shade, the flight of a bird through an open space in the woodland, or to alight and pick for his guests the asters and goldenrod that added their autumn splendor to the woods.

The summer days came and went, and the daughter, now grown to womanhood, met and married a distinguished and beloved physician, Dr. Frank Seward Johnson of Chicago. He was the son of Dr. Hosmer Allen Johnson, whose work in the Civil War made him famous. The marriage took place at Lake Geneva. Two grandsons were born to Edward Ayer—Hosmer Ayer Johnson and Edward Ayer Johnson, named for their grandfathers, respectively. The boys passed their summers at the Lake Geneva home, enjoying the usual boyhood sports of sailing, rowing, swimming, and riding. Hosmer, the elder, entered Harvard University and took both his B. A. and M. A. degrees there. Edward graduated at the Northwestern Military and Naval Academy at Lake Geneva. When the World War broke out both of these young men eagerly volunteered for overseas service, to the great satisfaction of their patriotic grandfather. Not long after his return from the war, Hosmer Johnson was married to Adelaide Stickney, daughter of Dr. Edwin Stickney, of Arlington, Massachusetts. Later Edward married Roberta Watson, of Coronado, California. A son who died in infancy, and two daughters were born to Hosmer and Adelaide Johnson; and three sons to Edward and Roberta. So Edward Everett Ayer entered into old age rejoicing in the possession of five great grandchildren.

Sometime before his sons were married, Dr. Johnson, on account of ill-health, was obliged to give up his practice in Chicago and seek the more genial climate of California. He and Mrs. Johnson resided in Los Angeles for a while, but later went to Pasadena and there made their home up to the time of Dr. Johnson's death, which occurred in April, 1922. After her husband's death Mrs. Johnson decided to spend the rest of her life in Pasadena. She joined the Presbyterian Church of that city, presided over by the eloquent minister, Dr. Robert Freeman. In her loneliness and sorrow she took up as her particular part of the church work the visiting of the sick; and in so doing, has won an honored place in the community and has found contentment and consolation for herself.

There was no little sentiment connected with the building of Mr. Ayer's city house. He had the granite boulders gathered from the fields and waysides where he had roamed in his boyhood and built into a somewhat stately edifice at the corner of State and Banks Streets. The same sentiment and originality are revealed in the interior of this house, particularly in Mr. Ayer's special library in which the woodwork is all of Redwood lumber from California, the state in which he began his army career. It is to be noticed, too, that in this library room the mantelpieces are built of fragments of red petrified wood, secured in Arizona, not far from the Santa Fe railroad for which he had furnished the ties. In his travels in Mexico Mr. Ayer had selected slabs of Mexican onyx of clouded green and white effects and of clouded milk-white which were used in the drawing-room and dining room mantels.

From time to time at the Chicago home many interesting

ELIZABETH AYER JOHNSON

and celebrated men were entertained. Across the way from the Ayers came to live soon after their home was built Franklin Head, the well-known writer, author of many books, his best-known work, perhaps, being *The Insomnia of Shakespeare*. Mr. Head and Mr. Ayer, both men of genial humor, and endowed in common with the knack of story-telling, became fast friends and much enjoyed each other's society. Most of the literary celebrities who passed through Chicago were drawn to the hospitable home of Mr. Head. Mr. John Fiske was often the guest of the local author. On one occasion when Mr. Ayer learned that Mr. Fiske was coming, he greatly desired to give a dinner in his honor and invite some friends to meet him. He had heard that this famous scholar and writer was known as an epicure, also; so Mrs. Ayer spared no pains to make the dinner an excellent one.

"Now, we shall have a most wonderful evening," she said to her husband. "Mr. Fiske is said to talk as brilliantly as he writes, so we shall have a 'feast of reason and a flow of soul.' "

At the designated hour the guests arrived. But alas! the dinner was *too* good; so wholly to Mr. Fiske's taste that he applied himself to it and spoke scarcely a word during the course of the feast, the discourse being left almost wholly to Edward Ayer's eloquent friend, Norman Ream, assisted a *little* now and then by the host.

By chance there came once to dine at this Chicago home the Italian historian Guglielmo Ferrero. President Judson was there to meet him, but so grave and dignified was the foreign scholar that the gayety of the company was somewhat subdued.

A dear friend of Mr. Ayer's was Edward B. Butler, a genial, whole-souled "man of infinite wit and jest." As the years rolled by he was often at the Birthday feast. His early years were devoted to the acquisition of an ample fortune; but in middle life he found leisure to take up the study of painting and, as a result, became an artist of no mean fame. Art and works of philanthropy occupied his days during the Indian summer of his life until, suddenly, came "the inevitable hour."

There was another genial and well-known philanthropist— Julius Rosenwald—who loved Edward Ayer as Edward Ayer loved him. On one of the Birthday celebrations, rather late in the evening the doorbell rang, and who should appear but Julius Rosenwald. He came in and, approaching his friend, threw his arm about him and exclaimed,

"Edward, I love you, and I want to give you a birthday gift! Here is a check for $25,000 which I want you to spend for what you think best for the Field Museum."

Can words express Edward Ayer's happiness over such a gift, from such a man!

Professor David Swing, the poet preacher, can by no means be forgotten. In his plain, strong face shone the eloquence of his beautiful soul. Driven from his church for being a fearless seeker after truth, he founded Central Church, most of his former parishioners going with him. Mr. Ayer greatly admired him and often sat under his ministry. The "Fessor," as Edward Ayer called him, often came for an intimate Sunday supper with him downstairs in the collector's favorite resort, "the Indian Room." This room was not a "den," though many a lion came there to chat, and relax, with Mr. Ayer. It was called "the Indian room" because it was richly adorned with Indian blankets, and on the floor besides Indian blankets, there were long rugs from the tents of Arab sheiks; also unusual Indian baskets and pottery with mystic designs. All these articles at a later time were donated to the Field Museum.

In this "Indian Room downstairs," always so called, which had been the original repository of the volumes that went to make up the "Ayer Collection" in the Newberry Library, Ed-

THE CHICAGO HOME AS IT APPEARED AFTER THE SNOWSTORM OF
JANUARY, 1918

ward Ayer used to love to sit of an evening with his wife near him, while he pored over catalogues from foreign book sellers, who offered rare volumes for sale. Haply he might come across the two *Jesuit Relations* that had hitherto eluded his diligent search! Failing catalogues, there were histories and biographies to be read, and in these, too, he delighted. More and more he loved this quiet, restful room, especially on a winter night, when the logs cut from the Lake Geneva woodlands burned cheerfully in the fireplace under the mantelpiece set with slabs of petrified wood, reminders of his adventurous exploits in Arizona. One day, with regret, he stepped across the threshold of this room and went to take one of his many journeys to the west. He never came back again to go down the stairs to the pleasant, restful "Indian room."

CHAPTER XVI

Personality and Character

How shall we sum up the qualities of this unique American? His name will live and grow in the memory of men for the achievements that have been set forth in these chapters; and, since this is true, succeeding generations as they enter into the enjoyment of his gifts and feel the influence of his personality will want to know what manner of man he was. He was, in the first place, a great business man closely associated with many of the foremost commercial captains of his day and recognized as an equal among them. Yet his mind was not occupied chiefly with business affairs. It was said by his friends that he gave much thought but little attention to business. His organizing ability and his skill in the selection of subordinates made it possible for him to withdraw from the petty and harrowing details of trade early in his career.

Mr. Ayer belongs with that remarkable group of American business men—J. P. Morgan, Andrew Carnegie, Henry E. Huntington, and others of like caliber and taste—who, while exerting a masterful control over the material things of this world and inspiring and directing the wills of countless other men in vast constructive enterprises, were able at the same time to rise above the lure of money and the slavery of business routine into the realm of ideas, of beauty, of culture. Mr. Frank A. Miller, of Riverside, speaking of Mr. Ayer, said, "Some of us think we have to drive men to do things, and grab if we get what we want, but Mr. Ayer was not that way. The love of beauty and the pursuit of culture does not minimize success in business. It is what makes men big and discerning and lifts them up." Mr. Ayer, perhaps earlier than these others, saw that true growth and enjoyment was to be found in the disinterested pursuit of the True, the Beautiful, and the Good. He knew how to make money and he understood the usefulness of money, but he saw clearly that there are higher values than those that are purely monetary.

The author pictures Mr. Ayer as he knew him, at the age of eighty-five, in the spring of 1927, only ten days before his death. He was about five feet and seven inches in height. His figure was sturdy, his chest deep, his shoulders broad and strong, his face ruddy and healthfully bronzed. He was all alive—quick and prompt in his movements. As he went here and there about the room in search of a favorite volume, manuscript, or notebook, his eyes blazed with excited interest or grew dim in tender reminiscence as he told about some friend or alluded to some treasure acquired by good chance or happy foresight. It was a tonic to be in his company; genial and gracious, he expanded in the warm glow of his own generous heart. He talked about portolan charts, Waldeck drawings, Mexican codices, Indian dialects, Pompeiian marbles, and the "dusty antiquities" of Egypt, Greece, and China as familiarly as the ordinary business or college man converses about radio, Bernard Shaw, Babe Ruth, the Boulder Dam, Copper stock or the Ford machine.

The first and last thing that impressed me in my conversation with Mr. Ayer was a sense of amazement that so much of the richness, joy, and wisdom of life could be packed into the experience of one man. To him had been granted length of days, and health, and worthy work well done, travel and adventure, patriotic service, aesthetic pleasure and intellectual enlightenment, friendship and affection, and crowning all of this—and most wonderful of all—a rare gift of appreciation for all these good things that had come to him; so that there in his old age he was finding his highest joy in a simple and humble feeling of gratefulness that God and the Universe and his fellow beings had been so good to him. He liked best to talk about his family and his true and tried friends—what they had done for him and what he in the course of his abounding good fortune had had the privilege of doing for them. As one talked with him, or read his reminiscences, one was continually struck with these two things: his fresh and unfailing enjoyment of all the wonders and beauties of this world, and his grateful and repeated tributes to the friends whom he had met along the many highways he had traveled. On every page, on every day of the year, in every land he was having "a fine time," and all the people whom he met or talked about were "noble, dear, and kind."

No one could converse with Mr. Ayer on his favorite topics without noticing the sympathetic and melodious quality of his voice. One friend at least has caught and interpreted the rare music of his discourse, now forever silenced. On the night before Mr. Ayer set out for California on the last of his many journeys across the Plains, Mr. J. Christian Bay drew him out concerning his early experiences as a collector. Mr. Bay gives this account of the impressions he carried away with him from this interview.

The events of that evening would be fresh in my memory even if they did not now stand out as the last occasion when I listened to the live voice of one of Chicago's greatest and most unselfish men. Mr. Ayer literally lectured as he might have done before an audience. He spoke easily and coherently of his experiences, and set out in orderly sequence the events on which I needed as much light as possible. Jotting down a précis of his talk, I was astounded at Mr. Ayer's ready speech, alert memory and precise attention to details, remarkable in a man past his eighty-fifth birthday; but what impressed me unforgettably was the man's unconscious and unstudied disregard of his own initiative, enthusiasm and success as a collector. He gave praise to Marshall Field as Chicago's greatest benefactor through museum education and recounted numerous examples of the rare foresight and devotion of the Trustees of the Field Museum, mentioning specific acts which qualified such men as Mr. Stanley Field, Mr. James Simpson, and others, for their service, and enumerated many events in museum history and library history in Chicago—all leading up to the final result and corollary to all these events: that he, Edward Everett Ayer, indeed was a singularly fortunate man, in that his associates in the administration of the Field Museum, the Art Institute and the Newberry Library had permitted him to do what he desired and had met his preference with kindness and confidence.

And while on this subject, let me add that Mr. Ayer's voice had a quality long to be remembered. Pity that our powers of describing such intangible human features are poor and incomplete—but his tone, as I dwell upon it now, had a sound of youth and eagerness in it, with a curious rising note, as if the speaker came fresh from some great wonder in nature, or had witnessed a gladsome event, or heard a strong voice within himself. It now has gone out of this world, but craves this feeble attempt at a reminiscential record, because I heard it but twice in all my life: in the speech of Mr. Ayer and in that of the old giant Frederick Hjorth, of Ledgeville, one of the founders of Wisconsin. Those who are fortunate enough to call it to mind, never can forget it.

A quality of Mr. Ayer's personality that endeared him to his associates was his enthusiasm. Everything interested him. His admiration for the marvel and beauty of the Universe never left him. It was as fresh in age as in youth. No matter where he was, that, he felt sure, was the best place on earth to be; whatever was his was the finest and best that could be. His friends declare that, if he started out on an automobile trip for some distant point and was delayed for a day or a week at some out-of-the-way place by an accident to his car, he would say to them the first time he saw them, "Do you know I have had the greatest piece of luck you ever heard of. My car broke down at ——, and while I was waiting for new parts, I discovered two most remarkable cathedrals that I had never heard of before. I never had such a good time in my life. Don't fail to stop over and see those cathedrals." He was able to extract the best from everything.

Along with his enthusiasm went a spirit of optimism that was irrepressible. Nothing could long overcloud his sunny disposition. He radiated good cheer. He was able to rise above physical pain and the discomforts of old age; and when deprived of one enjoyment he was quick to find some equally delightful one to replace it. He pitched his camp in high places, beyond foul weather, malarial insects, and the dust of the rabble. Says one of his most intimate friends, "The disappointments which affected him were always those connected with public projects he had at heart when they did not progress to his satisfaction. I do not remember ever having seen him worried over business affairs, these at least during the latter part of his life, seemed entirely subordinated to his public interests."

Mr. Ayer was a man of tremendous force and tireless activity. Nearly all of his business associates lay stress upon his energy and initiative. Said Mr. W. B. Storey, "Activity seemed absolutely essential to him; and this seems to have been responsible for his success in business, for his success as a collector, for his ability to keep well, and for his great interest in life." "I was not only long, and closely associated with Mr. Ayer in business," said Mr. John J. Mitchell, "but we had farms near each other. We were both fond of horses, too. But Ayer had much wider interests and broader business connections than did I. He possessed great energy; he was never idle; he was interested in everything. He was bursting with interest and enthusiasm. He was always doing something so that both mind and body were kept busy."

The variety and rounded completeness of Mr. Ayer's occupations and avocations were what called out the admiration and comment of his friend Mr. A. C. Bartlett. "I am thinking of your life, which through sane living has been prolonged beyond man's allotted years; one in which energy has found an outlet for its activities in the study of the history and development of the races which preceded our own in this country, to the end that valuable knowledge has been added to the human store; one in which a business man has not devoted all his time and strength to the accumulation of money, but just enough of each to insure exceeding comfort to his family, and ability to minister to the wants of the poor and afflicted, and to forward any good cause that appealed to him."

Mr. Ayer was a man of vision. He was able to look into the future and to forecast lines of national and industrial development. With this gift of shrewdness and foresight and business tenacity, he was no less prompt to improve than he was quick to perceive a business advantage; and when he gripped a situation he was not disposed to relax his hold. Along with all these qualities of American enterprise went downright and absolute honesty. His associates had unbounded confidence in his integrity, and that confidence was never betrayed. He sought no unjust advantage over others; nor was there resort to the cruel predatory practices that so discredited big business a generation ago. He wanted his fair share and knew how to get it, but he was glad to contribute to the success of others and to "pass prosperity around." To be sure, he did sometimes take delight in outwitting a grasping competitor, but never by unfair means. And these same qualities of alertness, foresight, and instant pursuit of a desired object or a perceived advantage, characterized his work as a collector and a public servant as well as his business dealings. As a philanthropist, too, he displayed like wisdom and vision. Other large givers scattered their money in various directions or bestowed it upon causes that had no permanent foundation, but he centered his benefactions upon two or three worthy and enduring institutions: the Ayer Collection, the Field Museum, and the Art Institute, and so fixed his benefits and his name securely in living and growing monuments of civilization.

Less than six months before his death, in reply to a letter addressed to him by Dr. Daniel L. Marsh, President of Boston University, Mr. Ayer gave a summary of what he considered basic requirements for the sound training of young people. The qualities he enumerates and the methods he emphasizes were those he himself exemplified. The questions and his answers are as follows:

1. What do you consider to be the essentials of sound character?
Honesty, industry, patriotism, reasonable generosity and sympathy.
2. How can these be best developed in young people?
By their parents, who should be patterns for them to follow.
3. If you were head of a large university (we have 11,744 students), what ideals of character would you seek to impress upon the students?
The above.
4. Do you consider moral and religious training a necessary basis for the best development of character?
I certainly do.
5. Should this training be given at home, in church, or at the school?
This training should be given at home, in church, at school, and everywhere.

Mr. Ayer had a most tenacious memory for dates and figures, and the minute details of whatever interested him in everyday life. He was fond of tabulating and summarizing, and his habit of keeping a record of the number of miles he had traveled by automobile, the number of cathedrals and art galleries he had visited, the sum total of his trips across the Plains, or his voyages across the ocean, or the aggregate times he had heard this or that actor or singer was a source of wonder and entertainment to his friends. "He went fourteen times to see *Old Ironsides*," declared one of his most intimate Chicago friends. "He would take a party, entertain them at a fine dinner, inviting people each time who had never been before; and so he would go any number of times with undiminished delight. He went to hear Galli Curci ninety times, I believe. When he takes a fancy to a play, or a singer, or anything else, he not only believes in it but wants to prove it so that you will agree with him. Every fellow he likes is the very best fellow in the world."

Mr. Ayer possessed many ingratiating qualities. He was rich in that most human, most indispensable gift, humor. In boyhood it showed itself in the form of mischief; and throughout life it found expression in shrewd witticisms, spontaneous merriment, and the habit of hyperbole. His power of extravagant statement for humorous effect was little short of genius. It was in the true American vein and tradition. Artemus Ward, Bill Nye, and Mark Twain would have found in him a boon companion; and, had his taste and training led him into the field of creative writing, a worthy rival. He was fond of banter, and was as much pleased when he was the object of good-natured raillery as when he was its instigator.

It was the human quality in this remarkable man that so endeared him to all who came to know him. He was not one who wore his heart upon his sleeve, yet his warmth of affection would often express itself openly toward his cherished friends. Mr. Martin A. Ryerson, one of the nearest and truest of his friends—a man whom he continually delighted to honor—writes thus concerning him:

He was a lovable character, blameless in private life, honest and efficient in business, public-spirited to an eminent degree. He was a loyal and devoted friend, and unusually demonstrative for a man, never hesitating to express in the warmest

terms his affection for those he was fond of, and always seeing them in the most favorable light. Though he was fifteen
years my senior, as the years went by we were drawn together more and more, and latterly, both at Chicago and at
Lake Geneva, he was frequently at my home. Only absence
of one of us or his illness kept him from coming, in Chicago,
every Sunday morning.

Mr. Ayer's generosity knew no limit. His liberality was as
wide as the world and as unheralded as the light. He was in-
genious in discovering ways to give happiness to others. The
author found it an absorbing occupation to turn over packets
of his papers, including a correspondence that reached a good
way into the past. Now a little girl writes to thank him for the
gift of a lovely doll, and then comes a communication from
His Majesty, Don Manuel of Portugal, gratefully acknowledging the receipt of photostats specially made for him from
a rare book in the Ayer Library. Next is a letter from the
President and Board of Trustees of Williams College, thank-
ing him for the transfer of the Ephraim Williams will, of
1748, from the Ayer Collection to Williams College; and,
not less worthy of mention, a rector in the town of Harvard,
where Mr. Ayer spent his youth, writes to congratulate him
for his secret charities to obscure people there whom he has
had "under his care and protection." Then there comes to
light this letter from a Kansas City business man:

It was my pleasure to have spent a few days near your
beautiful home and I availed myself of the generosity you accord the public, of visiting your beautiful ground. As I did not
have the pleasure of meeting you, and probably never shall, I
take this method of expressing my thanks for the use of your
garden. Of all the places along the lake I admired yours the
most, and spent many happy hours in your beautiful garden
and woods. I appreciate the thoughtful care expressed in pro-
viding for the public those marvelous paths and drives. It is
not often that we find business men who are willing to do these
things for others.

It was these "little unremembered acts of kindness and of love" that made up the warp and woof of his life, and it is both interesting and gratifying to note how, a thousand times, bread thus cast upon the waters returned to him.

In the light of the concrete examples of Mr. Ayer's habitual kindness cited above, it is easy to understand how friends of long standing could write as do the two now to be quoted: Dr. F. W. Hodge, of the Museum of the American Indian, New York City, and the distinguished Mr. John Steven McGroarty, creator of *The Mission Play*. Here is Mr. Hodges' tribute:

> I regard him as the most remarkable man I ever knew, and in every way the most helpful. His love of those who tried to do things to advance the cause of learning, his inspiring enthusiasm in the many tasks he undertook and carried to successful fruition, and the fine example he set to all whose religion is the Golden Rule, made him beloved by every mortal.

And these are the words of the eloquent Californian, Mr. McGroarty:

> When I am asked, as I often am, what manner of man the late Edward E. Ayer was, I always say first that he was a kind man. He was, indeed, the kindliest man I have ever known— evenly, habitually, tirelessly, kind. It was his nature to be so. God made him that way—kind to everybody and to every animate or inanimate thing. Kind to trees, kind to all that he saw or touched. He was a great man, but not all great men are kind. And because he was kind he was beloved by all who ever knew him. Not only was he the kindliest man I have ever known, but he was also the best loved man it has ever been my lot to meet.

"You of all the men I know, have learned how to get the most out of life," wrote Mr. Stanley Field to Mr. Ayer in a letter acknowledging the gift of Prescott's *History of the Conquest of Mexico*. All who knew Mr. Ayer would accept this statement as true. He seemed to have embraced life as a whole, to have entered joyously into every fruitful experience, and to have retained up to the last day of his life the attitude of expectancy, wonder, and admiration. He became a part of all that he touched. His educational handicaps were great, but he was pre-eminently educable, highly receptive, reverent and humble in the presence of new truth. He yielded himself to the specialists and experts in each new field that he entered, and in modesty of spirit, led by them into the realms of art, and archaeology, and ethnology, and architecture, and ornithology, he became broad and wise and cultured. Few men of his day are better qualified to interpret the essential values of life than Mr. Frank A. Miller, the great, good, and lovable man who dispenses hospitality and radiates culture as Master of the Mission Inn at Riverside, California. He and Mr. Ayer were kindred spirits, and this appreciation from his pen seems an adequate interpretation of Mr. Ayer as he really was:

I would sum up Mr. Ayer's nature as I came in contact with it as expressive of eternal youth, enthusiasm and joy of living. Whenever he would drop in at Mission Inn I would crave a visit with him alone in my office, knowing that I would receive mental and spiritual refreshment from seeing and talking to him. He seemed to have the power to make of every experience a thing of rich interest and enthralling adventure. This was not because he was a romancer so much as it was that his keen judgment penetrated to the heart of things and gave the proper proportionate values to this life of ours whose real actuality is all on the side of mind and spirit. He was a true poet, whether he was dealing with railroad ties or with the newer processes of wider education as so splendidly carried out in the work of the Field Museum. His remarkable memory stored everything, but he never recounted any of the past except in a fascinating way.

I am sure that no two lives could have been happier together than that of Mr. and Mrs. Ayer in their long and perfect companionship.

Mr. Ayer died at Pasadena, California, May 3, 1927. It seems very appropriate that the sun of his earthly life should have sunk there in the glowing West. It was late evening for him, and his ear was not unprepared for the mellow curfew note. He had lived very long, had brought every great enterprise to which he had laid his hand to a fitting close, and his mind was at peace with the world. Time drew her curtains gently about him. During the winter and the spring he had been surrounded by the people and the influences that he loved most. Many of his closest Chicago friends were also in Pasadena for the winter, and he had seen much of them. California never had been lovelier in its indescribable wealth of floral beauty. He had again enjoyed the Mission Inn, *The Mission Play,* and all the bright charm of Pasadena—social, civic, and cultural. He had renewed with increasing intimacy his associations with Mr. Henry E. Huntington, his fellow collector, and had been shown marks of appreciation both by Mr. Huntington and the staff of the Huntington Library. Moreover, he had received letter after letter of appreciation from scholars, scientists and literary men for his own remarkable work as a collector. And, finally, wife and daughter, his most cherished loved ones, were with him at the end.

He had prepared himself a simple yet stately mausoleum in the little cemetery at Harvard, Illinois, not far from the shaft which he himself had erected to the memory of his father and mother; and here, on June tenth, he was laid to rest, his casket for the last service draped with the flag, one sent from the Loyal Legion—a tribute to Edward Everett Ayer as having been a soldier. In addition to his immediate family, many relatives had come to do him honor, and there were present numerous Chicago friends and business associates —not a few of them leading men of affairs in the life of Chicago during the last half century. There had assembled, also, a large company of old friends from Harvard and the adjoining countryside; among them several who had known Mr. Ayer in his boyhood seventy-five years before and shared with him the joys and hardships of a pioneer life. As a mark of respect to the parents whom Mr. Ayer had so much loved and honored—the founders of Harvard—the cortege paused several minutes at the massive granite monument of Elbridge Gerry Ayer and Mary Dean Ayer. The day was one of glorious brightness and serenity. Across the bluest of blue skies floated occasionally a soft white cloud. The solemn quiet was broken now and then by the friendly call of birds. Beauty, not decay, seemed to rule here; spirit, not matter; life, not death. Here Nature in chastened yet exultant mood, arrayed in loveliest guise, seemed to have prepared herself to welcome back into her embrace the child she had cherished of old—the man, who with reverence and delight had ever held "communion with all her visible forms."

INDEX

Agnese, Baptista, 171-172.

Alameda, California, first camp of Company E., First California Cavalry, 37.

Algiers, travels in, 149-154; 248-249.

Aguas Calientes, Mexico, 96; 124-126; 132.

Arivaca, Arizona, 47; 119; 120.

Arizona, 38; 44; 50; 56.

Art Institute, Chicago, 76; the Robert pictures, 137-138; 200; 202; legislature of Illinois authorizes tax for support, 207; 235; Mr. Ayer trustee for, 236; extent and value of collections, 236; largest Art school in America, 236; 283.

Automobiling, a pioneer tour of Europe, 139-141; in Algeria and Tunisia, 149; Sahara Desert, 248.

Atlantic and Pacific Railroad, 93-95.

Ayer and Lord Tie Company, 67; 69; established, 114; contract with Illinois Central Railroad, 114; expansion, 115.

Ayer, Anna Maria, 3; 265.

Ayer, Edward Everett, ancestry, 1-9; birth, 3; boyhood, 10-21; schooling, 12-14; education, 133; Adelina Patti, 17-18; en route to California, 22-31; begins career in Wesley Diggins' woodyard, 32; life in San Francisco, 32-35; works in planing mill, 35; enlists at outbreak of Civil War, 36; first man mustered on Pacific Coast, 36; Corporal in Company E, First California Cavalry, 37; Camp Carlton, 38; San Bernardino, 38; camp life, 39-43; from California to Arizona, 44; escort

duty, 45; by request of Colonel Lalley guards Cerro Colorado mine, 46; Prescott's History of the Conquest of Mexico, 45; expedition to Libertad, Mexico, 50; detachment rejoins company at Mesilla, 52; sergeant in The Carlton Escort, 54; escort duty and dispatch riding, 54; Second Lieutenant in The First New Mexico Infantry, 55; member of court-martial with General Kit Carson, 56; period of enlistment expires, 56; forwards resignation, 56; letter of release, 56; homeward bound, 56-59; fight with the Indians, 57-58; at home, 59-60; given interest in father's store, 60; larger activities, 61; supplies Chicago and Northwestern Railroad with cordwood, 61; Lot Smith, his future manager, 61-64; courtship of Miss Emma Burbank, 64-65; marriage, 66; beginning of career as railroad builder, 66; contract with Chicago and Northwestern Railroad, 69; secures financial backing of George Sturges, 70; refuses to speculate, 70-73; résumé of activities between 1865-1875, 73; moves to Chicago, 74; becomes one of world's great art collectors, 75; incentives and purposes, 76-78; collecting Indian relics and handiwork, 78-81; Indian Library, 81-82; beginning of Egyptian collection, 81; presents collections to Field Museum, 81; his private library, 82-83; collects matchless source material on America, 83; other collections, 83; 192-210; collections dealing with the Philippine and Hawaiian Islands, 83-87; acquires notable library on

293

CPSIA information can be obtained at www.ICGtesting.com
Printed in the USA
LVOW10s0709180214

374150LV00029B/528/P